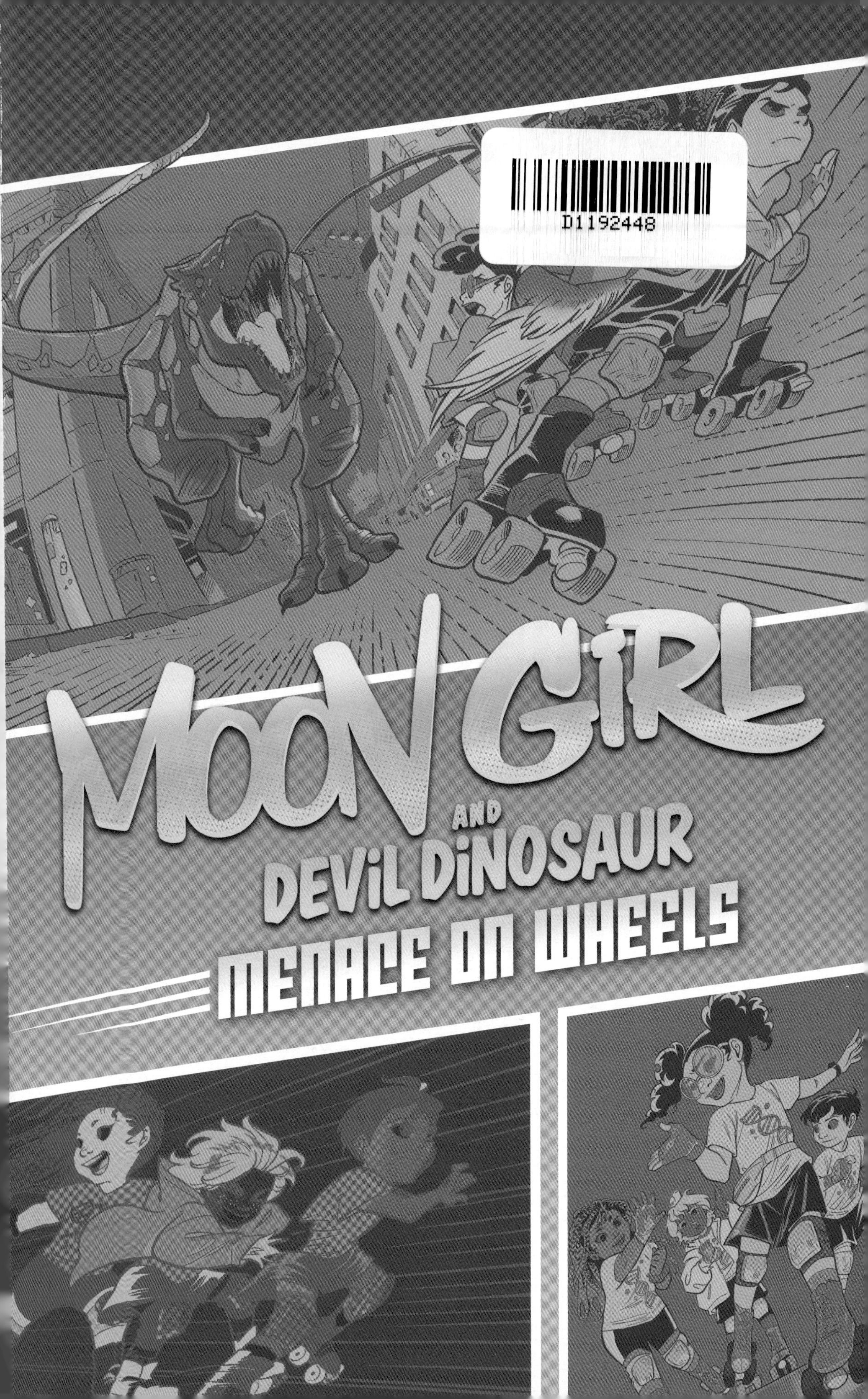
MOON GIRL
AND
DEVIL DINOSAUR
MENACE ON WHEELS

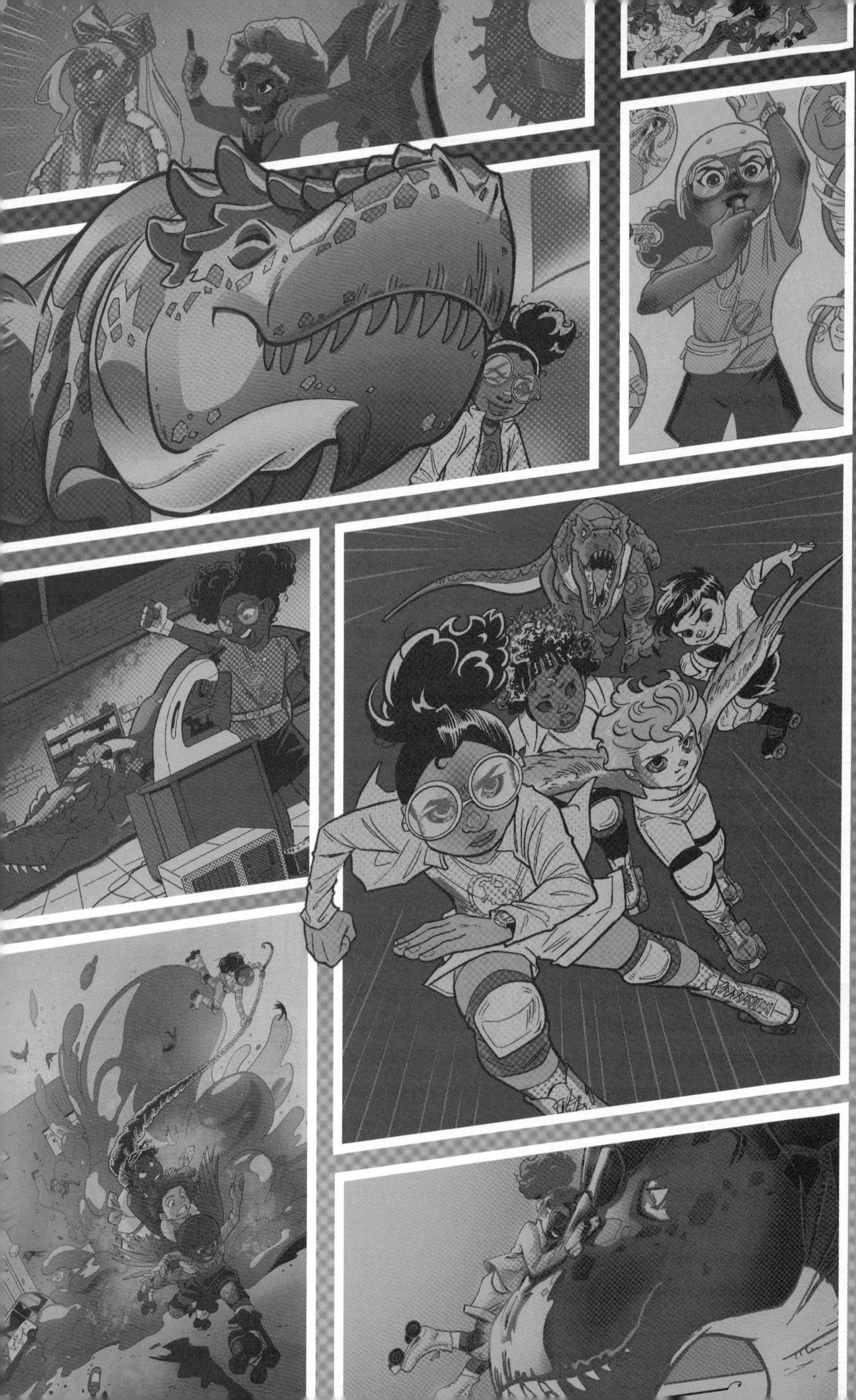

MOON GIRL AND DEVIL DINOSAUR

MENACE ON WHEELS

JORDAN IFUEKO
WRITER

ALBA GLEZ
PENCILER

JOSÉ MARZAN JR.
WITH **LORENZO RUGGIERO** [#3]
INKERS

KJ DÍAZ
COLORIST

VC's **TRAVIS LANHAM**
LETTERER

KEN LASHLEY & **RAIN BEREDO**
COVER ART

CAITLIN O'CONNELL
ASSOCIATE EDITOR

LAUREN BISOM
EDITOR

DEVIL DINOSAUR CREATED BY **JACK KIRBY**

COLLECTION EDITOR: **DANIEL KIRCHHOFFER**
ASSISTANT MANAGING EDITOR: **MAIA LOY**
ASSOCIATE MANAGER, TALENT RELATIONS: **LISA MONTALBANO**
DIRECTOR, PRODUCTION & SPECIAL PROJECTS: **JENNIFER GRÜNWALD**
VP PRODUCTION & SPECIAL PROJECTS: **JEFF YOUNGQUIST**

BOOK DESIGNER: **STACIE ZUCKER**
MANAGER & SENIOR DESIGNER: **ADAM DEL RE**
LEAD DESIGNER: **JAY BOWEN**
SVP PRINT, SALES & MARKETING: **DAVID GABRIEL**
EDITOR IN CHIEF: **C.B. CEBULSKI**

MOON GIRL AND DEVIL DINOSAUR: MENACE ON WHEELS. Contains material originally published in magazine form as MOON GIRL AND DEVIL DINOSAUR (2022) #1-5. First printing 2023. ISBN 978-1-302-93125-4. Published by MARVEL WORLDWIDE, INC., a subsidiary of MARVEL ENTERTAINMENT, LLC. OFFICE OF PUBLICATION: 1290 Avenue of the Americas, New York, NY 10104.

Printed in the U.S.A. KEVIN FEIGE, Chief Creative Officer; DAN BUCKLEY, President, Marvel Entertainment; DAVID BOGART, Associate Publisher & SVP of Talent Affairs; TOM BREVOORT, VP, Executive Editor; NICK LOWE, Executive Editor, VP of Content, Digital Publishing; DAVID GABRIEL, VP of Print & Digital Publishing; SVEN LARSEN, VP of Licensed Publishing; MARK ANNUNZIATO, VP of Planning & Forecasting; JEFF YOUNGQUIST, VP of Production & Special Projects; ALEX MORALES, Director of Publishing Operations; DAN EDINGTON, Director of Editorial Operations; RICKEY PURDIN, Director of Talent Relations; JENNIFER GRÜNWALD, Director of Production & Special Projects; SUSAN CRESPI, Production Manager; STAN LEE, Chairman Emeritus. For information regarding advertising in Marvel Comics or on Marvel.com, please contact Vit DeBellis, Custom Solutions & Integrated Advertising Manager, at vdebellis@marvel.com. For Marvel subscription inquiries, please call 888-511-5480. **Manufactured between 5/5/2023 and 6/6/2023 by SEAWAY PRINTING, GREEN BAY, WI, USA.**

10 9 8 7 6 5 4 3 2 1

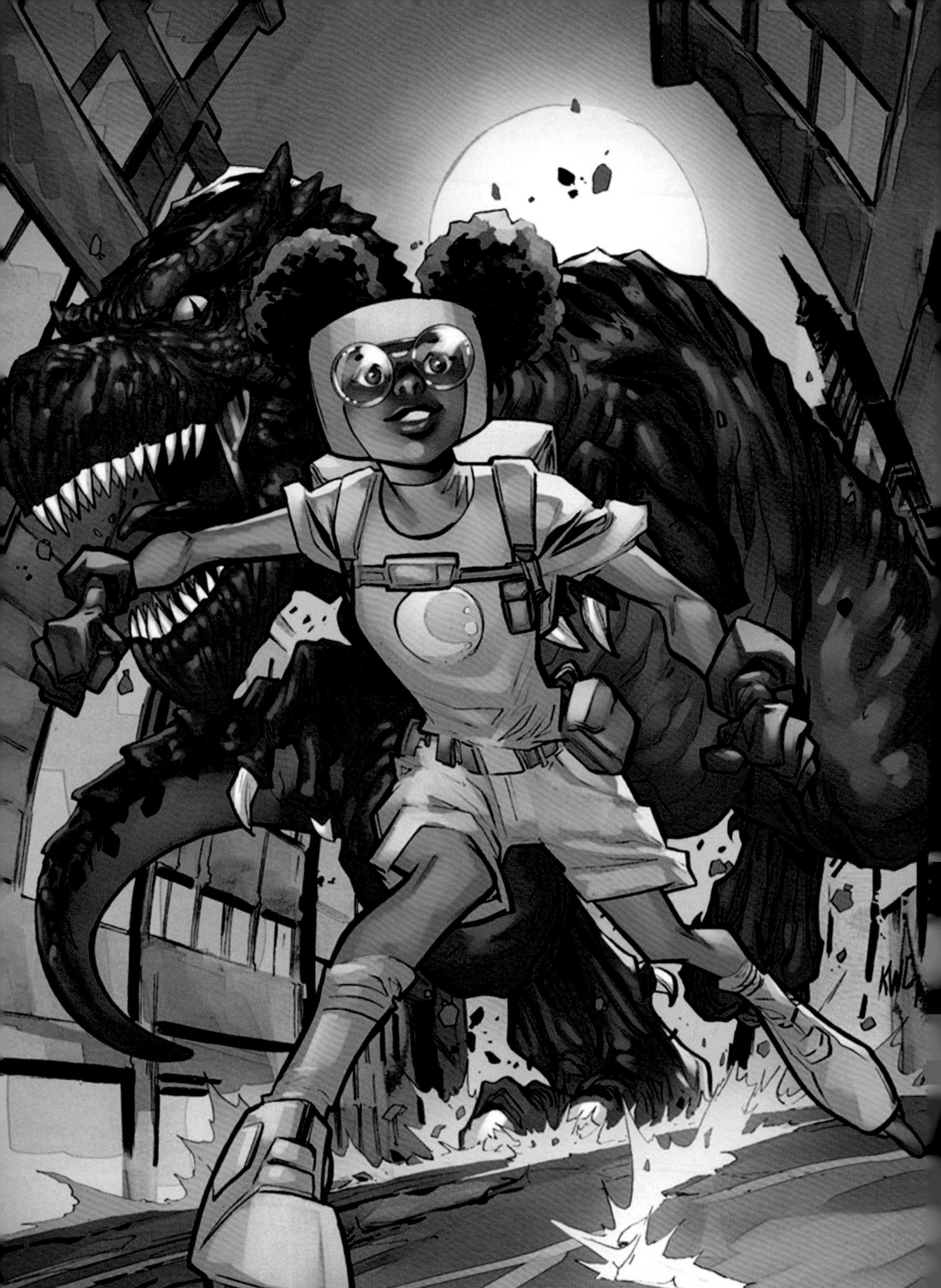

1

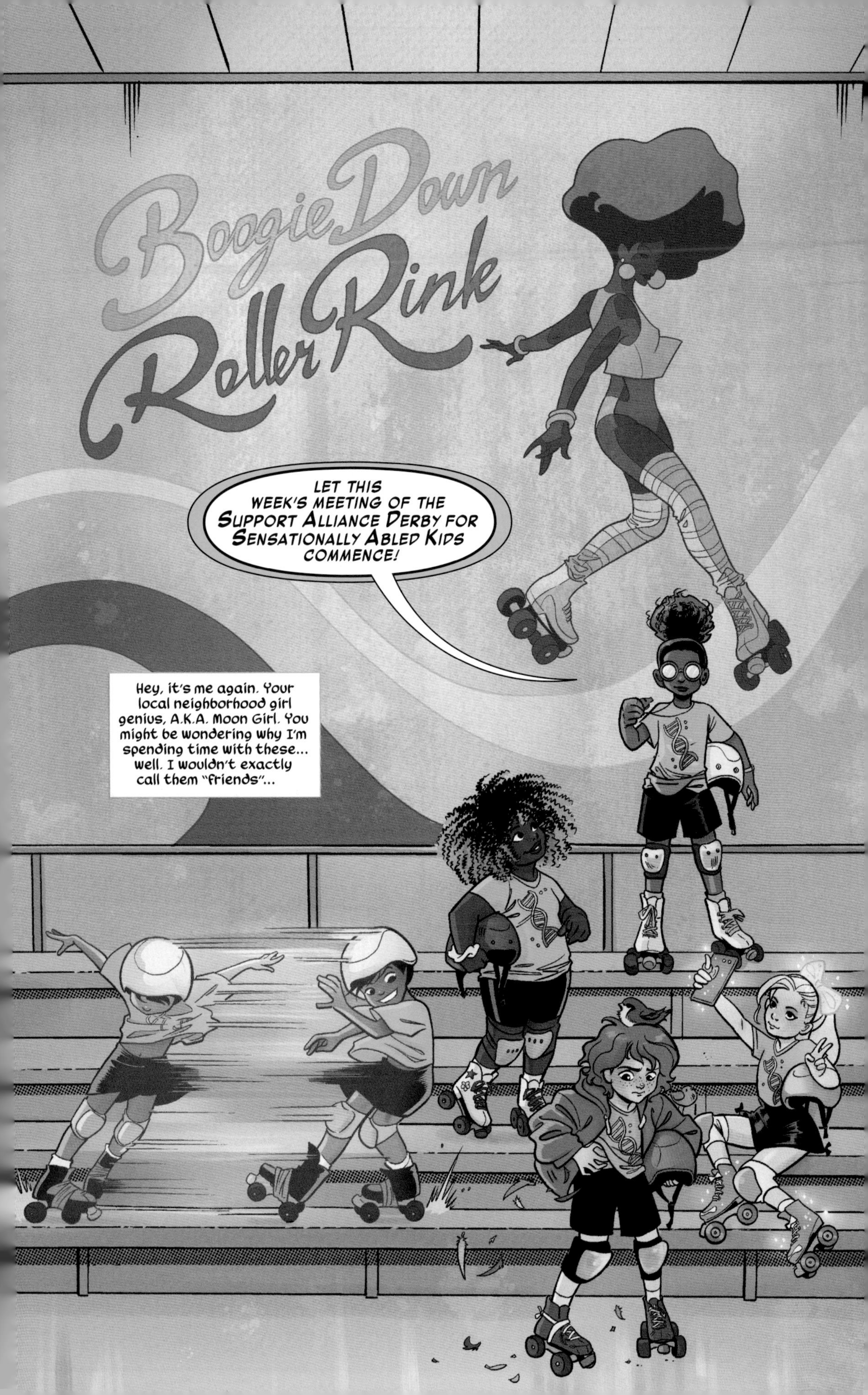
Boogie Down Roller Rink
LET THIS WEEK'S MEETING OF THE SUPPORT ALLIANCE DERBY FOR SENSATIONALLY ABLED KIDS COMMENCE!
Hey, it's me again. Your local neighborhood girl genius, A.K.A. Moon Girl. You might be wondering why I'm spending time with these... well, I wouldn't exactly call them "friends"...

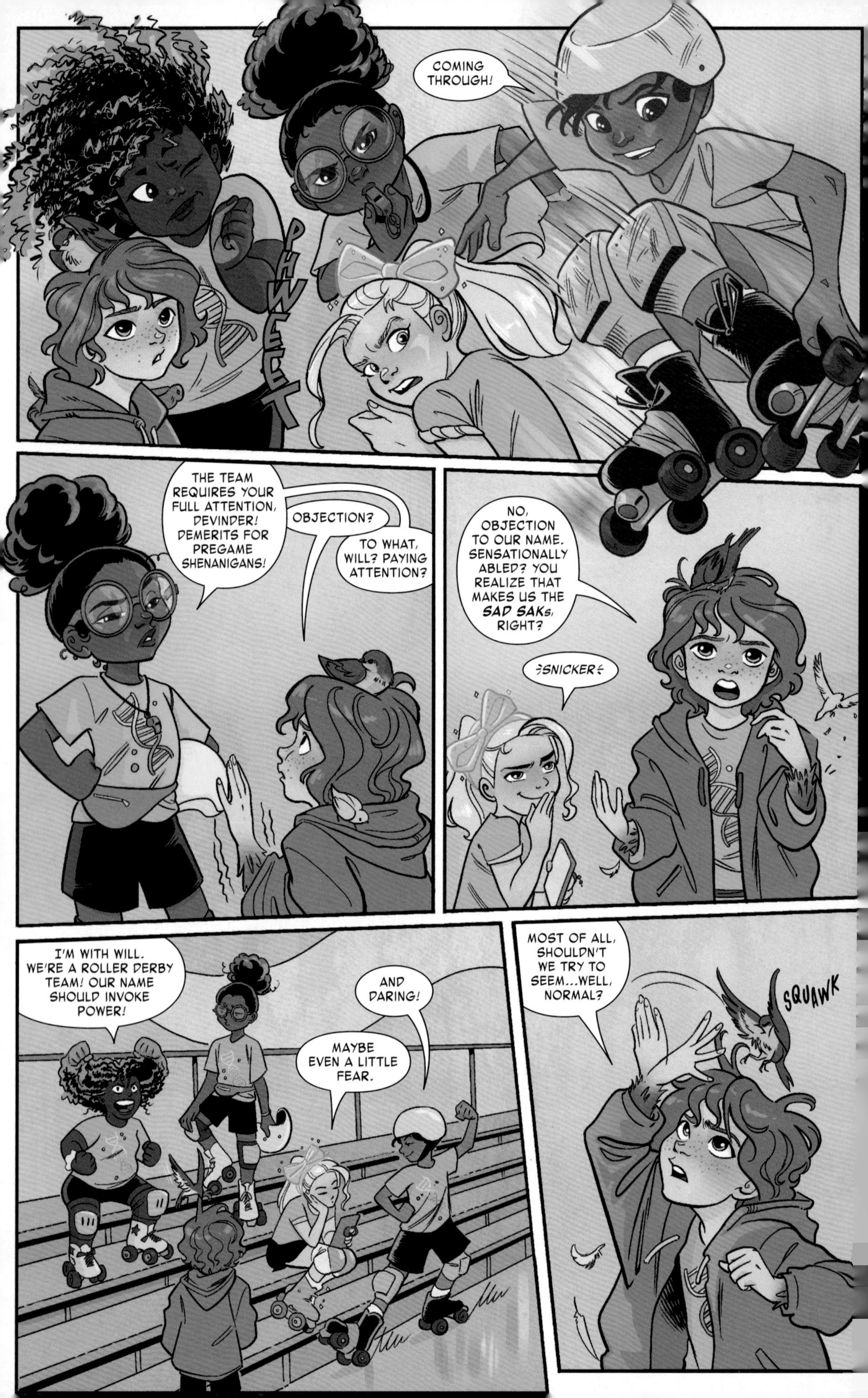
COMING THROUGH!
PHWEEEET
THE TEAM REQUIRES YOUR FULL ATTENTION, DEVINDER! DEMERITS FOR PREGAME SHENANIGANS!
OBJECTION?
TO WHAT, WILL? PAYING ATTENTION?
NO, OBJECTION TO OUR NAME. SENSATIONALLY ABLED? YOU REALIZE THAT MAKES US THE SAD SAKs, RIGHT?
SNICKER
I'M WITH WILL. WE'RE A ROLLER DERBY TEAM! OUR NAME SHOULD INVOKE POWER!
AND DARING!
MAYBE EVEN A LITTLE FEAR.
MOST OF ALL, SHOULDN'T WE TRY TO SEEM...WELL, NORMAL?
SQUAWK

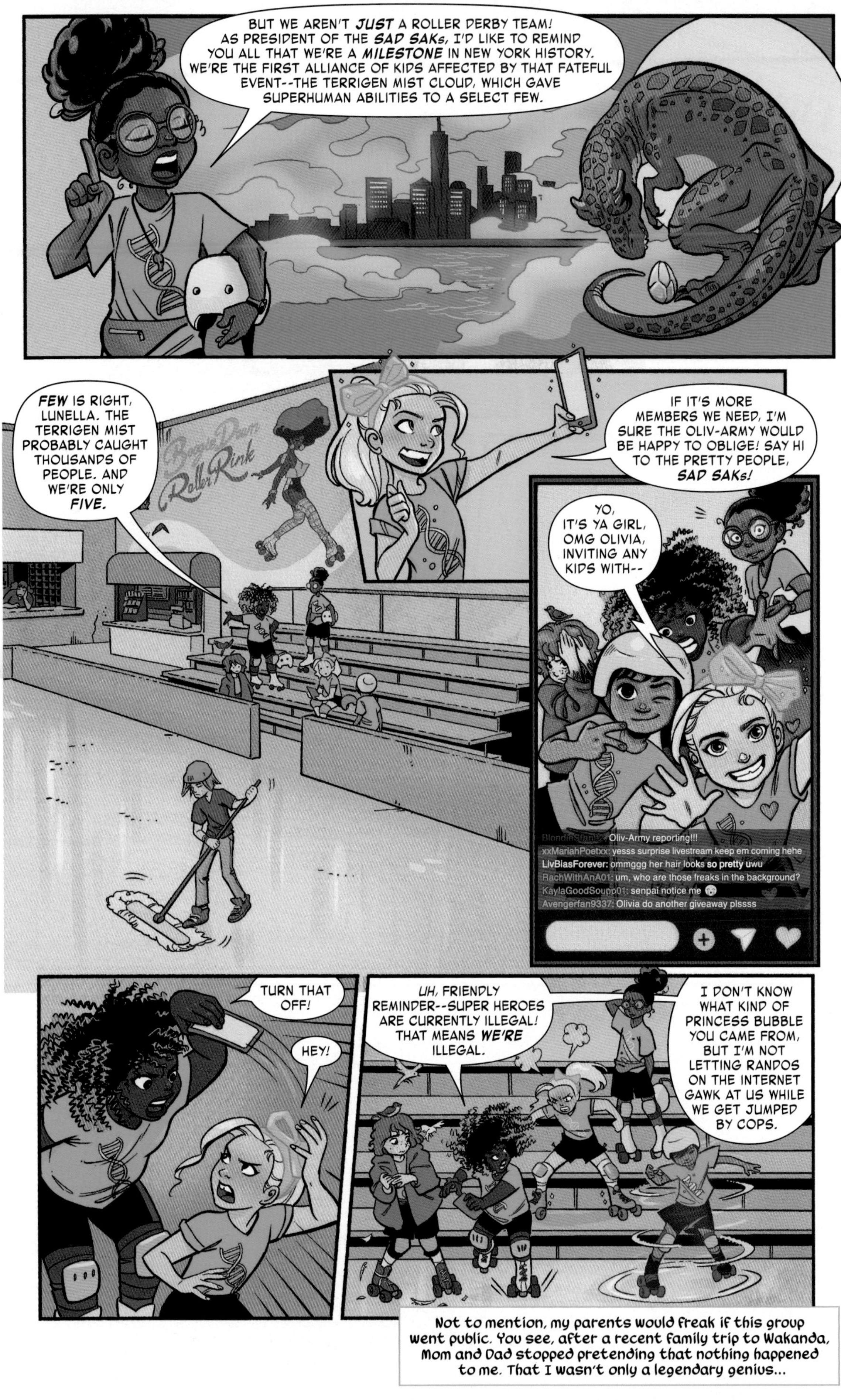

BUT WE AREN'T *JUST* A ROLLER DERBY TEAM! AS PRESIDENT OF THE *SAD SAKs*, I'D LIKE TO REMIND YOU ALL THAT WE'RE A *MILESTONE* IN NEW YORK HISTORY. WE'RE THE FIRST ALLIANCE OF KIDS AFFECTED BY THAT FATEFUL EVENT--THE TERRIGEN MIST CLOUD, WHICH GAVE SUPERHUMAN ABILITIES TO A SELECT FEW.
FEW IS RIGHT, LUNELLA. THE TERRIGEN MIST PROBABLY CAUGHT THOUSANDS OF PEOPLE. AND WE'RE ONLY *FIVE.*
Roller Rink
IF IT'S MORE MEMBERS WE NEED, I'M SURE THE OLIV-ARMY WOULD BE HAPPY TO OBLIGE! SAY HI TO THE PRETTY PEOPLE, *SAD SAKs!*
YO, IT'S YA GIRL, OMG OLIVIA, INVITING ANY KIDS WITH--
Oliv-Army reporting!!!
xxMariahPoetxx: yesss surprise livestream keep em coming hehe
LivBiasForever: ommggg her hair looks so pretty uwu
RachWithAnA01: um, who are those freaks in the background?
KaylaGoodSoupp01: senpai notice me
Avengerfan9337: Olivia do another giveaway plssss
TURN THAT OFF!
HEY!
UH, FRIENDLY REMINDER--SUPER HEROES ARE CURRENTLY ILLEGAL! THAT MEANS *WE'RE* ILLEGAL.
I DON'T KNOW WHAT KIND OF PRINCESS BUBBLE YOU CAME FROM, BUT I'M NOT LETTING RANDOS ON THE INTERNET GAWK AT US WHILE WE GET JUMPED BY COPS.
Not to mention, my parents would freak if this group went public. You see, after a recent family trip to Wakanda, Mom and Dad stopped pretending that nothing happened to me. That I wasn't only a legendary genius...

The Daily Bugle

SWARM ATTACKS!

...I was also Moon Girl. The kid they'd seen on the news, fighting monsters and the occasional alien.

I tried to make them feel better.

OKAY, SO THE OTHER MONSTERS WERE SCARY, BUT THIS MONSTER IS ON *MY* SIDE, MOM! DEVIL DINO IS MY FRIEND. WE SHARE *MINDS.*

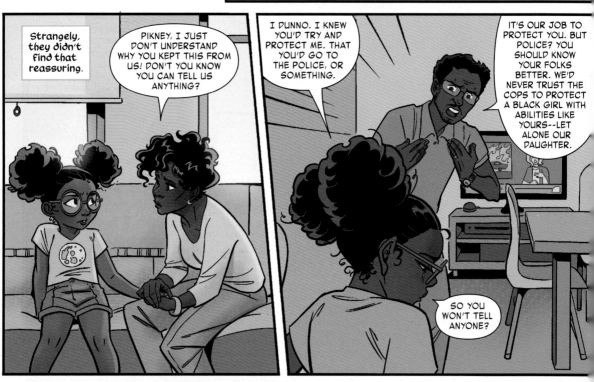

Strangely, they didn't find that reassuring.

PIKNEY, I JUST DON'T UNDERSTAND WHY YOU KEPT THIS FROM US! DON'T YOU KNOW YOU CAN TELL US ANYTHING?

I DUNNO. I KNEW YOU'D TRY AND PROTECT ME. THAT YOU'D GO TO THE POLICE, OR SOMETHING.

IT'S OUR JOB TO PROTECT YOU. BUT POLICE? YOU SHOULD KNOW YOUR FOLKS BETTER. WE'D NEVER TRUST THE COPS TO PROTECT A BLACK GIRL WITH ABILITIES LIKE YOURS--LET ALONE OUR DAUGHTER.

SO YOU WON'T TELL ANYONE?

WE WON'T. BUT *NO MORE* MOON GIRL ADVENTURES.

MOM!

ABSOLUTELY NONE. WE WON'T LET YOU PUT YOURSELF IN DANGER, ESPECIALLY WHILE THEY'RE CRACKING DOWN ON SUPER-POWERS. AND LOOK AT THE NEWS! IT'S CRAZIER THAN EVER OUT THERE!

RUMORS OF KREE OPERATIVES MASQUERADING AS HUMAN CITIZENS HAVE SOME BRACING FOR YET ANOTHER ALIEN INVASION...

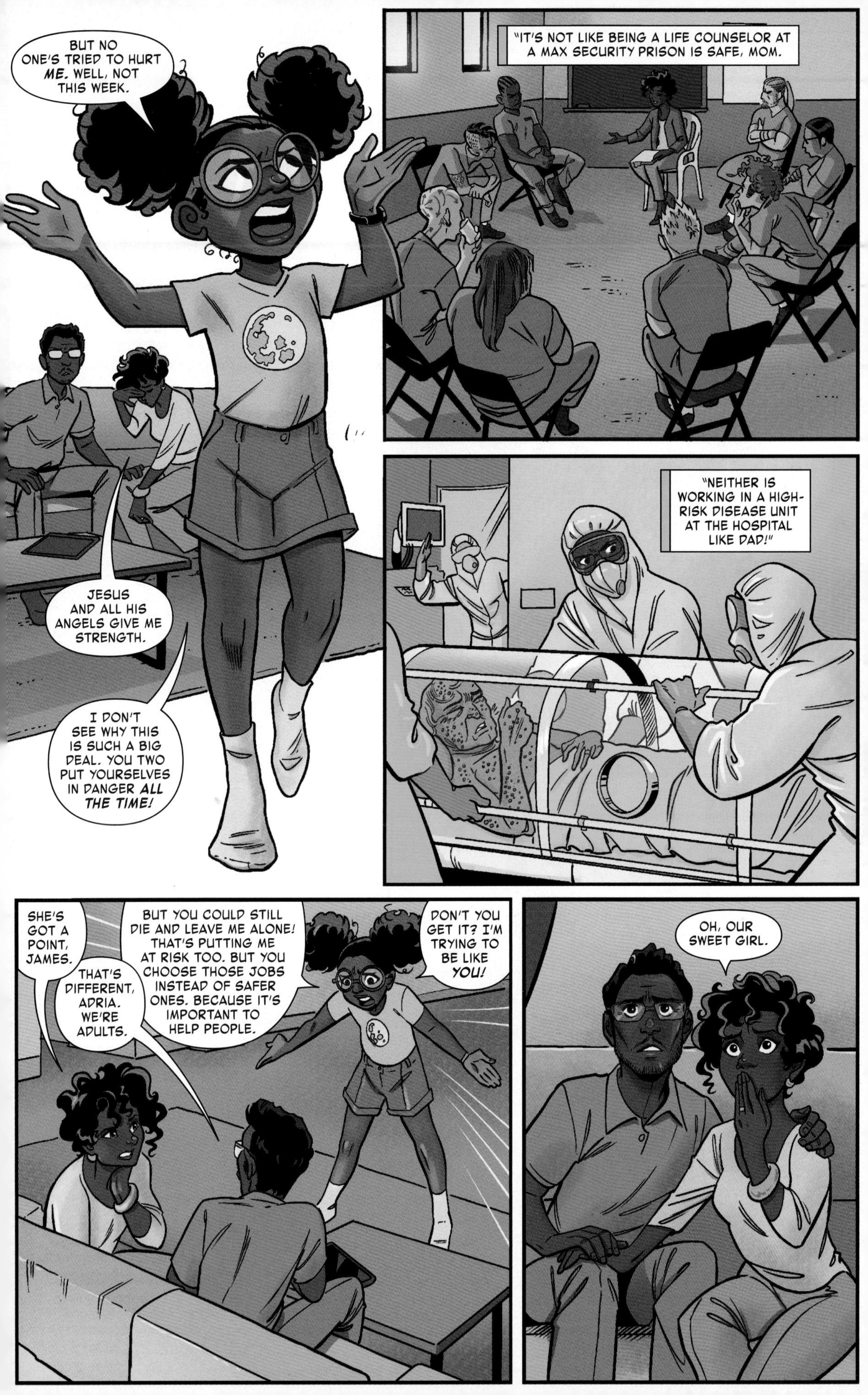
BUT NO ONE'S TRIED TO HURT *ME.* WELL, NOT THIS WEEK.
"IT'S NOT LIKE BEING A LIFE COUNSELOR AT A MAX SECURITY PRISON IS SAFE, MOM.
"NEITHER IS WORKING IN A HIGH-RISK DISEASE UNIT AT THE HOSPITAL LIKE DAD!"
JESUS AND ALL HIS ANGELS GIVE ME STRENGTH.
I DON'T SEE WHY THIS IS SUCH A BIG DEAL. YOU TWO PUT YOURSELVES IN DANGER *ALL THE TIME!*
SHE'S GOT A POINT, JAMES.
THAT'S DIFFERENT, ADRIA. WE'RE ADULTS.
BUT YOU COULD STILL DIE AND LEAVE ME ALONE! THAT'S PUTTING ME AT RISK TOO. BUT YOU CHOOSE THOSE JOBS INSTEAD OF SAFER ONES. BECAUSE IT'S IMPORTANT TO HELP PEOPLE.
DON'T YOU GET IT? I'M TRYING TO BE LIKE *YOU!*
OH, OUR SWEET GIRL.

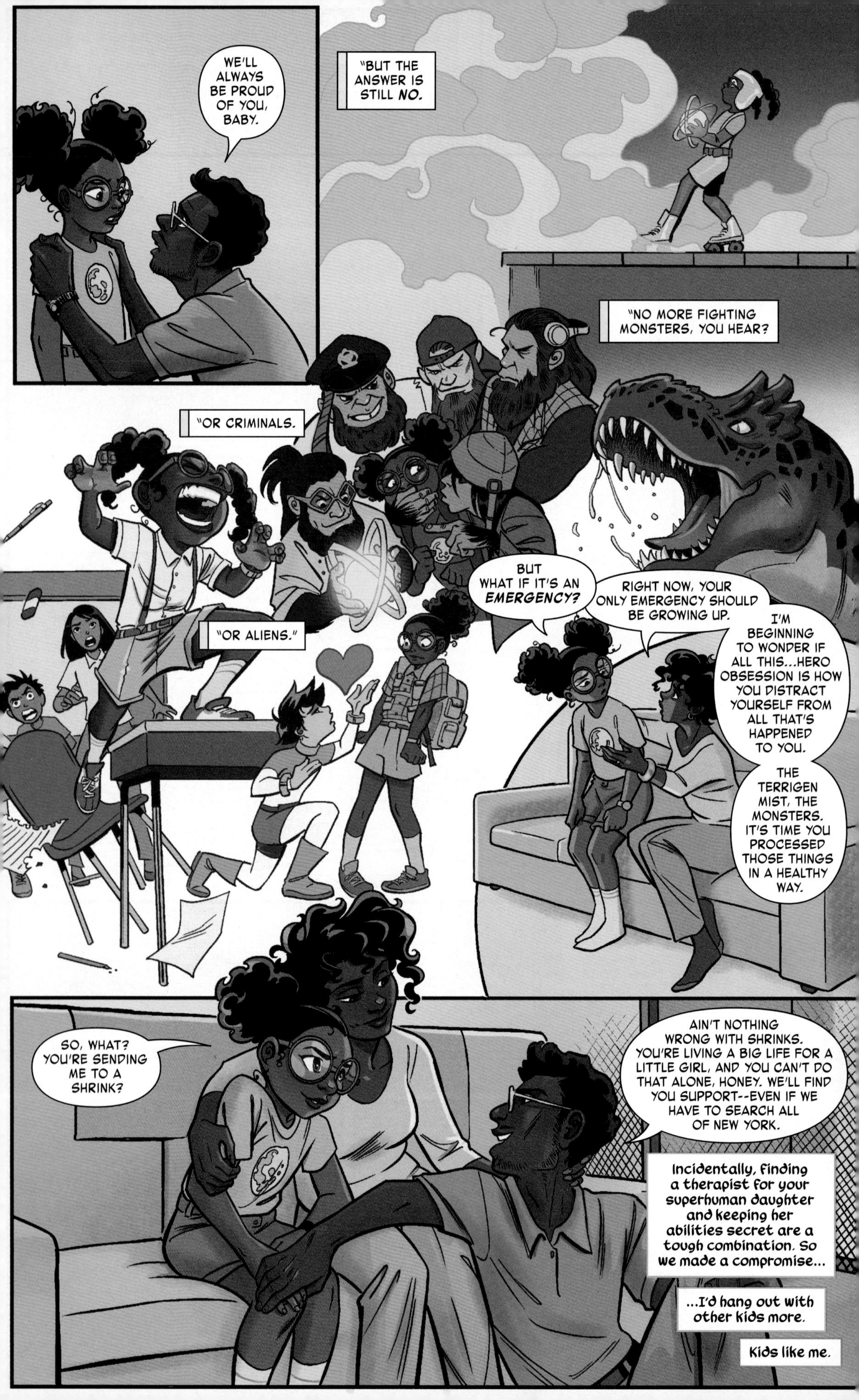
WE'LL ALWAYS BE PROUD OF YOU, BABY.
"BUT THE ANSWER IS STILL NO.
"NO MORE FIGHTING MONSTERS, YOU HEAR?
"OR CRIMINALS.
"OR ALIENS."
BUT WHAT IF IT'S AN EMERGENCY?
RIGHT NOW, YOUR ONLY EMERGENCY SHOULD BE GROWING UP.
I'M BEGINNING TO WONDER IF ALL THIS...HERO OBSESSION IS HOW YOU DISTRACT YOURSELF FROM ALL THAT'S HAPPENED TO YOU.
THE TERRIGEN MIST, THE MONSTERS. IT'S TIME YOU PROCESSED THOSE THINGS IN A HEALTHY WAY.
SO, WHAT? YOU'RE SENDING ME TO A SHRINK?
AIN'T NOTHING WRONG WITH SHRINKS. YOU'RE LIVING A BIG LIFE FOR A LITTLE GIRL, AND YOU CAN'T DO THAT ALONE, HONEY. WE'LL FIND YOU SUPPORT--EVEN IF WE HAVE TO SEARCH ALL OF NEW YORK.
Incidentally, finding a therapist for your superhuman daughter and keeping her abilities secret are a tough combination. So we made a compromise...
...I'd hang out with other kids more.
Kids like me.

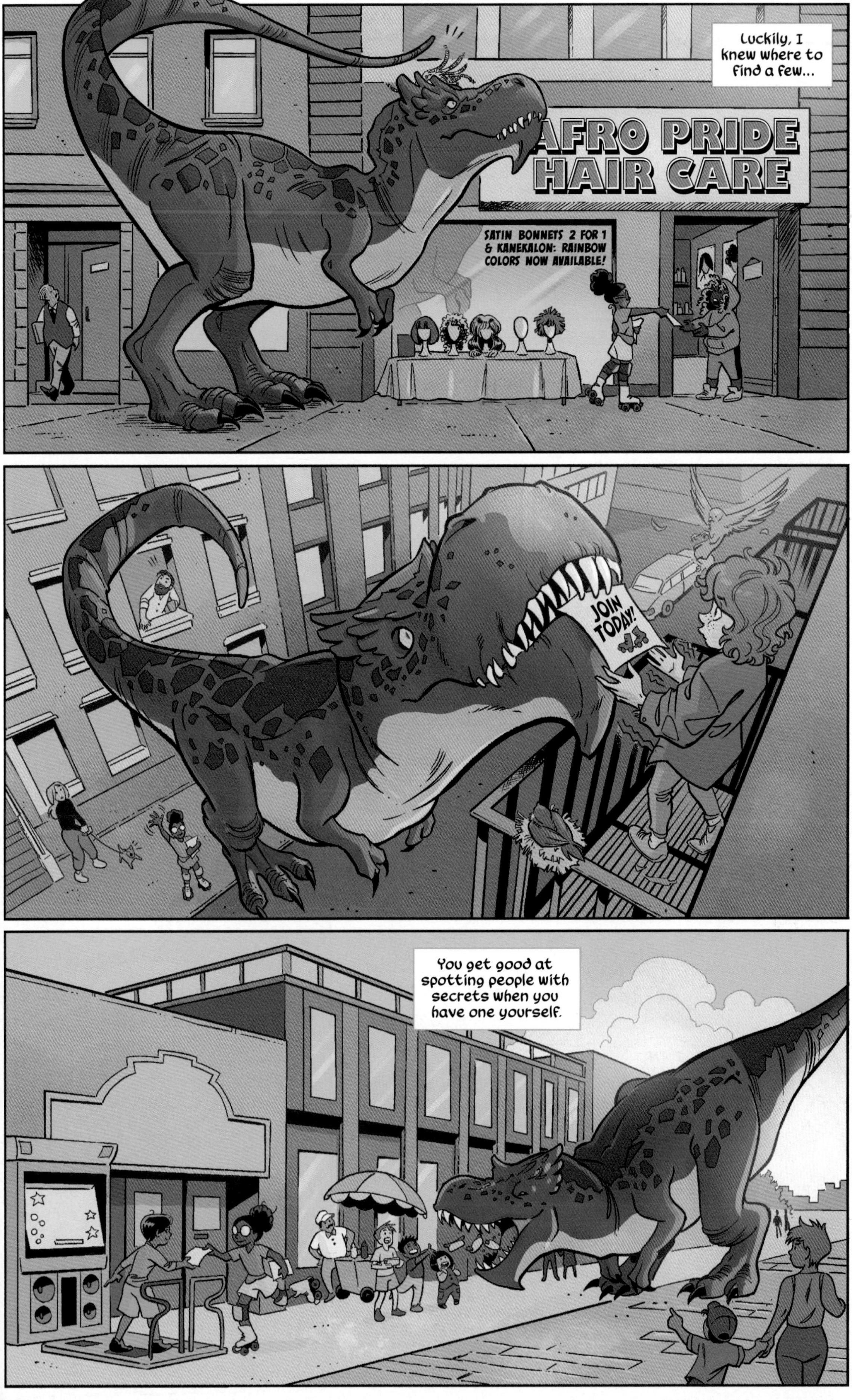
Luckily, I knew where to find a few...
AFRO PRIDE HAIR CARE
SATIN BONNETS 2 FOR 1 & KANEKALON: RAINBOW COLORS NOW AVAILABLE!
JOIN TODAY!
You get good at spotting people with secrets when you have one yourself.

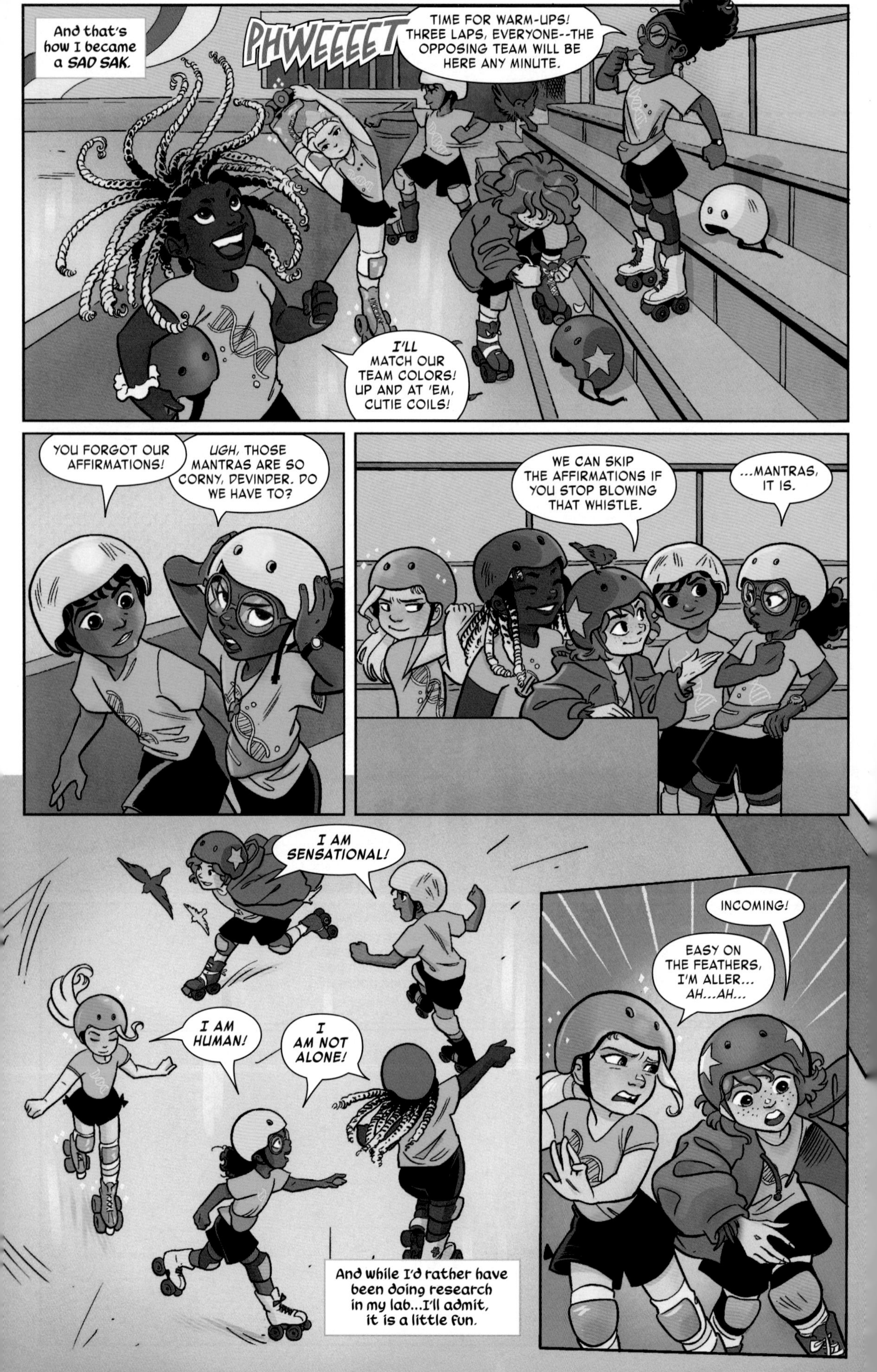

And that's how I became a *SAD SAK.*
PHWEEEEET
TIME FOR WARM-UPS! THREE LAPS, EVERYONE--THE OPPOSING TEAM WILL BE HERE ANY MINUTE.
I'LL MATCH OUR TEAM COLORS! UP AND AT 'EM, CUTIE COILS!
YOU FORGOT OUR AFFIRMATIONS!
UGH, THOSE MANTRAS ARE SO CORNY, DEVINDER. DO WE HAVE TO?
WE CAN SKIP THE AFFIRMATIONS IF YOU STOP BLOWING THAT WHISTLE.
...MANTRAS, IT IS.
I AM SENSATIONAL!
I AM HUMAN!
I AM NOT ALONE!
And while I'd rather have been doing research in my lab...I'll admit, it is a little fun.
INCOMING!
EASY ON THE FEATHERS, I'M ALLER... *AH...AH...*

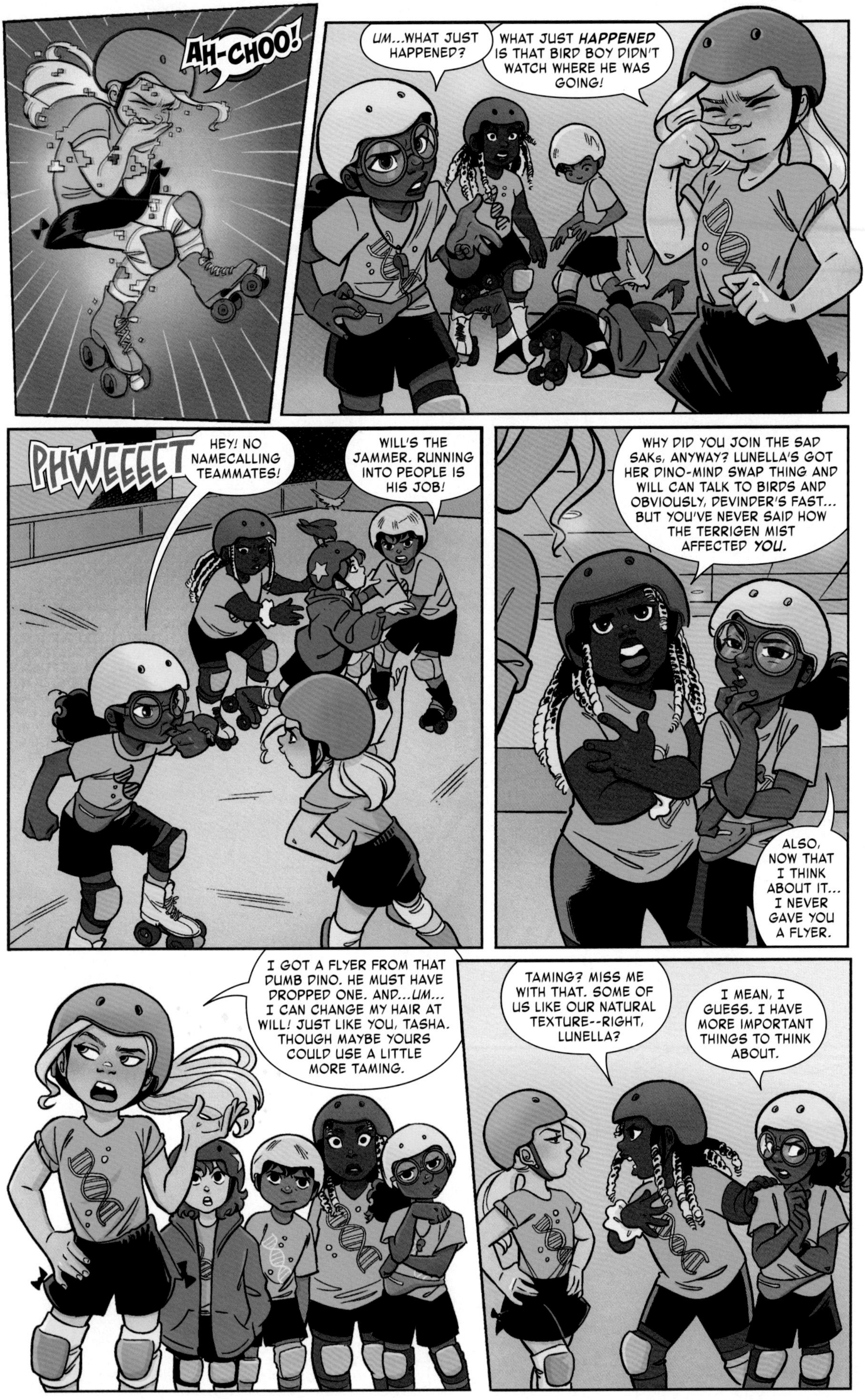
AH-CHOO!
UM...WHAT JUST HAPPENED?
WHAT JUST HAPPENED IS THAT BIRD BOY DIDN'T WATCH WHERE HE WAS GOING!
PHWEEEEET
HEY! NO NAMECALLING TEAMMATES!
WILL'S THE JAMMER. RUNNING INTO PEOPLE IS HIS JOB!
WHY DID YOU JOIN THE SAD SAKs, ANYWAY? LUNELLA'S GOT HER DINO-MIND SWAP THING AND WILL CAN TALK TO BIRDS AND OBVIOUSLY, DEVINDER'S FAST... BUT YOU'VE NEVER SAID HOW THE TERRIGEN MIST AFFECTED YOU.
ALSO, NOW THAT I THINK ABOUT IT... I NEVER GAVE YOU A FLYER.
I GOT A FLYER FROM THAT DUMB DINO. HE MUST HAVE DROPPED ONE. AND...UM... I CAN CHANGE MY HAIR AT WILL! JUST LIKE YOU, TASHA. THOUGH MAYBE YOURS COULD USE A LITTLE MORE TAMING.
TAMING? MISS ME WITH THAT. SOME OF US LIKE OUR NATURAL TEXTURE--RIGHT, LUNELLA?
I MEAN, I GUESS. I HAVE MORE IMPORTANT THINGS TO THINK ABOUT.

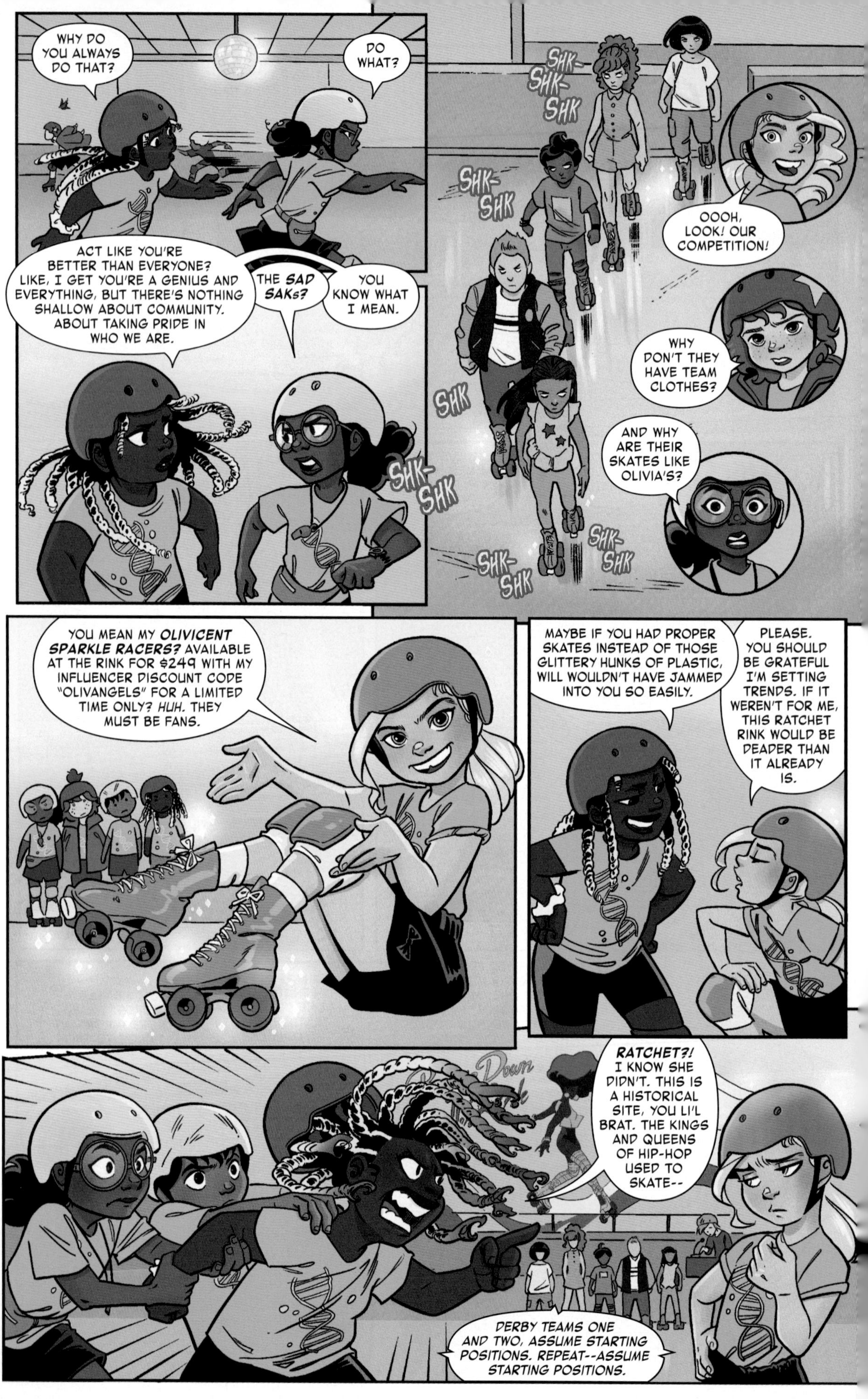

WHY DO YOU ALWAYS DO THAT?
DO WHAT?
ACT LIKE YOU'RE BETTER THAN EVERYONE? LIKE, I GET YOU'RE A GENIUS AND EVERYTHING, BUT THERE'S NOTHING SHALLOW ABOUT COMMUNITY. ABOUT TAKING PRIDE IN WHO WE ARE.
THE SAD SAKs?
YOU KNOW WHAT I MEAN.
SHK-SHK-SHK
SHK-SHK
SHK
SHK-SHK
SHK-SHK
SHK-SHK
OOOH, LOOK! OUR COMPETITION!
WHY DON'T THEY HAVE TEAM CLOTHES?
AND WHY ARE THEIR SKATES LIKE OLIVIA'S?
YOU MEAN MY OLIVICENT SPARKLE RACERS? AVAILABLE AT THE RINK FOR $249 WITH MY INFLUENCER DISCOUNT CODE "OLIVANGELS" FOR A LIMITED TIME ONLY? HUH. THEY MUST BE FANS.
MAYBE IF YOU HAD PROPER SKATES INSTEAD OF THOSE GLITTERY HUNKS OF PLASTIC, WILL WOULDN'T HAVE JAMMED INTO YOU SO EASILY.
PLEASE. YOU SHOULD BE GRATEFUL I'M SETTING TRENDS. IF IT WEREN'T FOR ME, THIS RATCHET RINK WOULD BE DEADER THAN IT ALREADY IS.
RATCHET?! I KNOW SHE DIDN'T. THIS IS A HISTORICAL SITE, YOU LI'L BRAT. THE KINGS AND QUEENS OF HIP-HOP USED TO SKATE--
DERBY TEAMS ONE AND TWO, ASSUME STARTING POSITIONS. REPEAT--ASSUME STARTING POSITIONS.

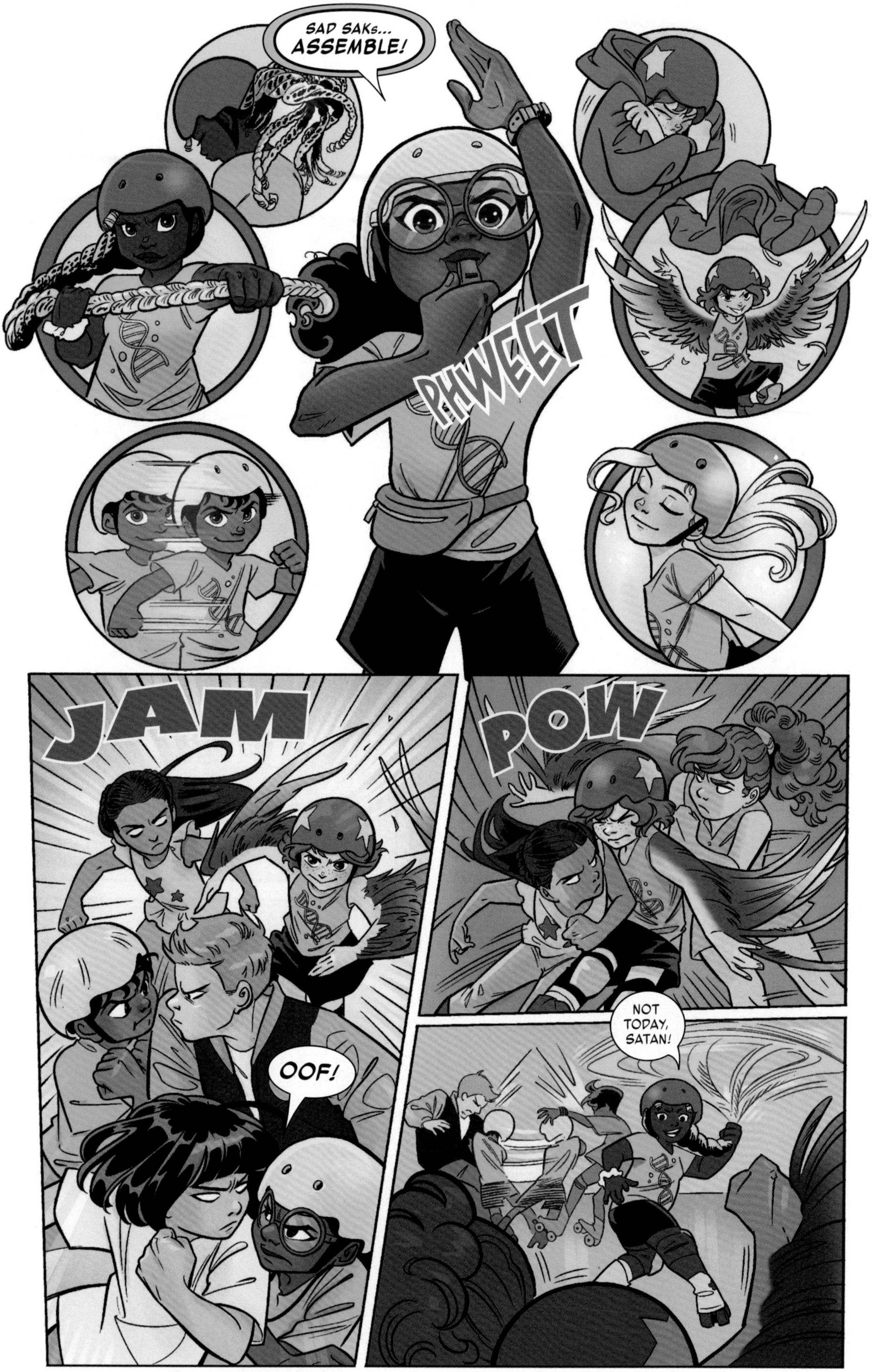
SAD SAKs... ASSEMBLE!
PHWEET
JAM
OOF!
POW
NOT TODAY, SATAN!

SMAK

WHIRRR

AAAAND THAT'S TIME! BREAK!

ZHOOP

OLIVIA, LOOK OUT!

WE SHOULD HAVE CALLED FOUL! THEY COULD HAVE CRUSHED OLIVIA AGAINST THE WALL!

WELL, ROLLER DERBY IS A CONTACT SPORT.

SHK-SHK

SHK-SHK-SHK

HEY, DON'T THEY KNOW THE DERBY RULES? ONLY FIVE MEMBERS PER TEAM IN THE RINK!

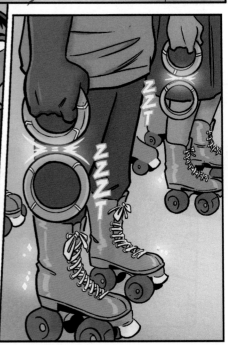

ZZT

ZZT

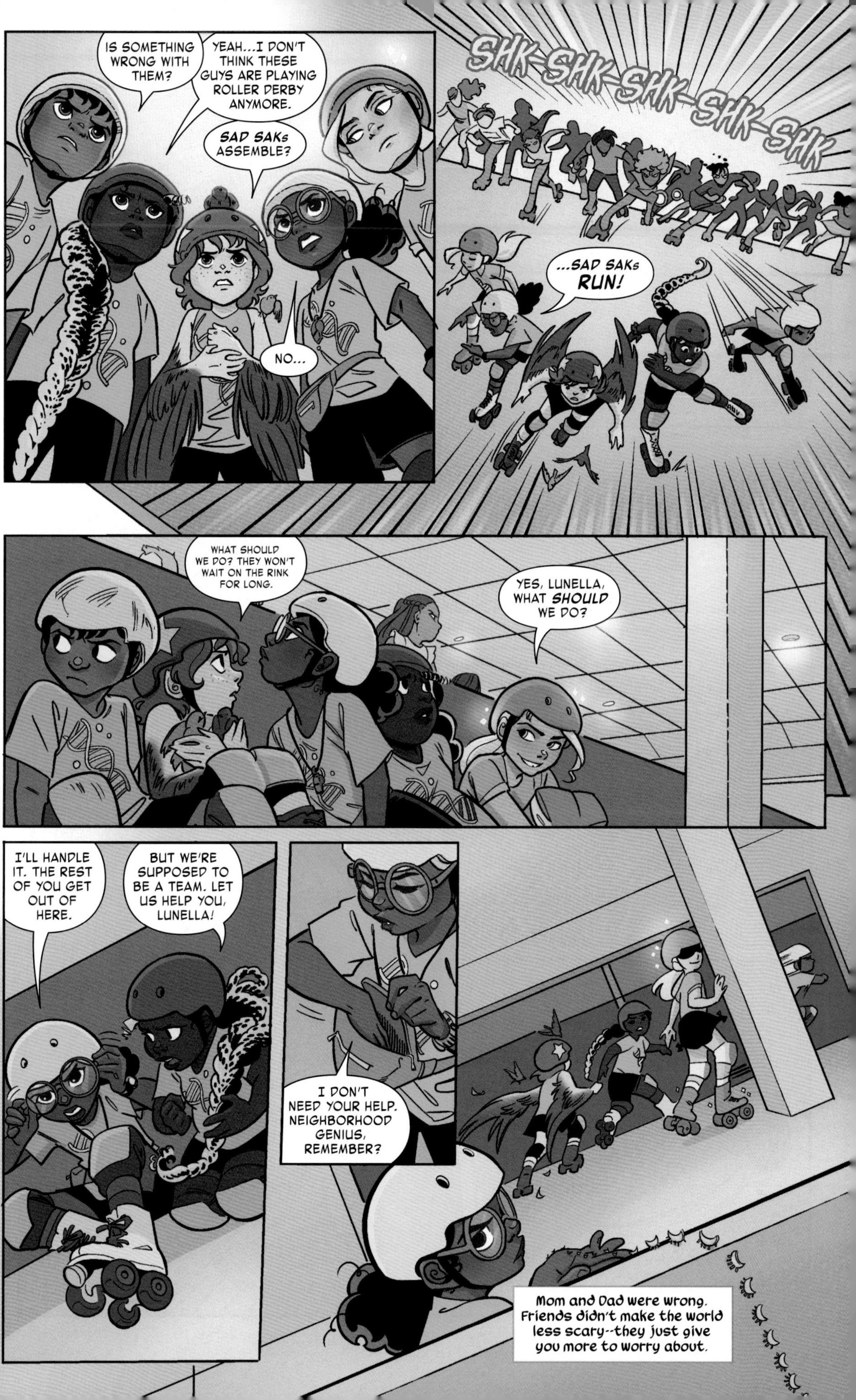
IS SOMETHING WRONG WITH THEM?
YEAH...I DON'T THINK THESE GUYS ARE PLAYING ROLLER DERBY ANYMORE.
SAD SAKs ASSEMBLE?
NO...
SHK-SHK-SHK-SHK-SHK
...SAD SAKs RUN!
WHAT SHOULD WE DO? THEY WON'T WAIT ON THE RINK FOR LONG.
YES, LUNELLA, WHAT SHOULD WE DO?
I'LL HANDLE IT. THE REST OF YOU GET OUT OF HERE.
BUT WE'RE SUPPOSED TO BE A TEAM. LET US HELP YOU, LUNELLA!
I DON'T NEED YOUR HELP. NEIGHBORHOOD GENIUS, REMEMBER?
Mom and Dad were wrong. Friends didn't make the world less scary--they just give you more to worry about.

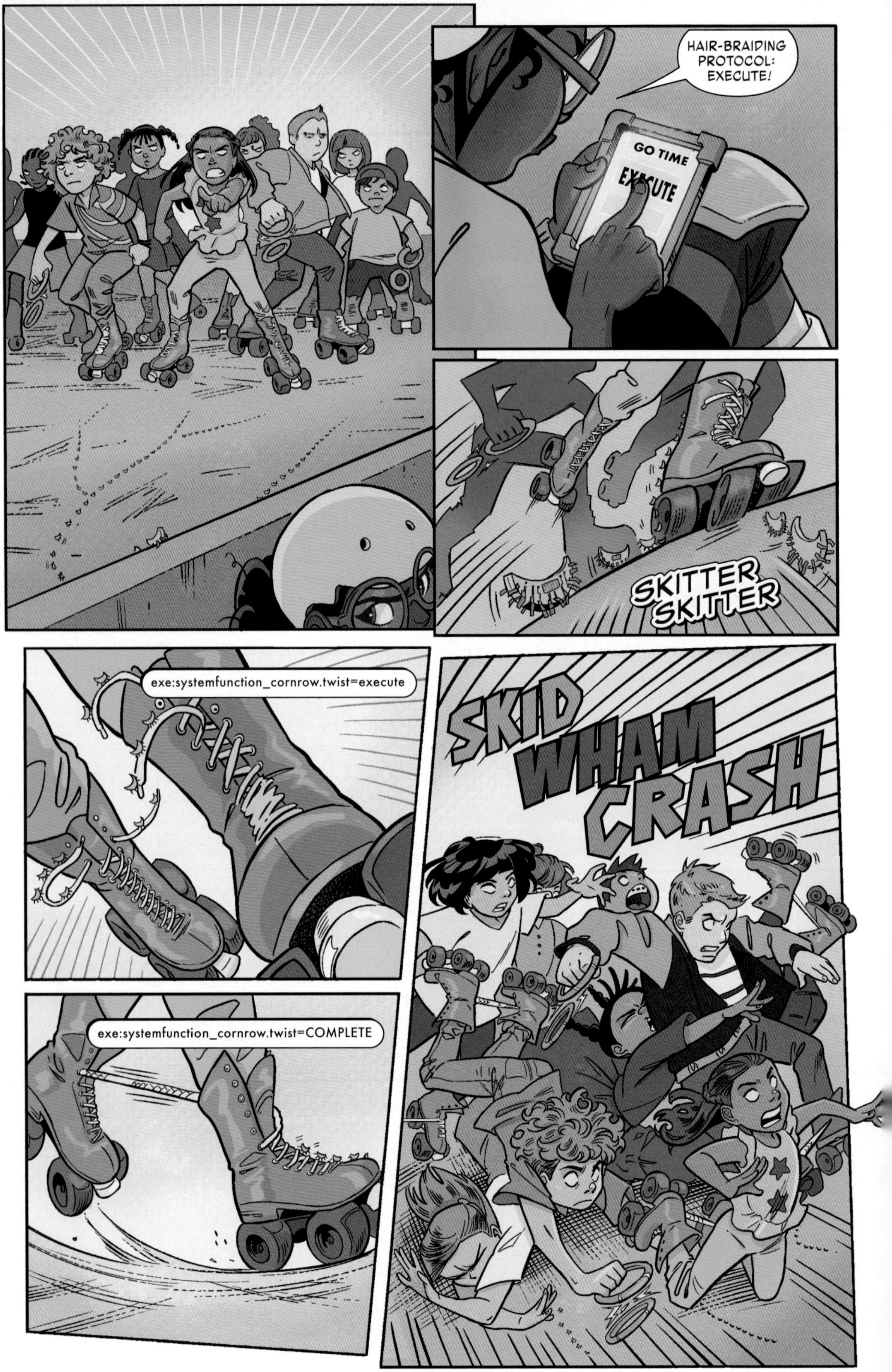
HAIR-BRAIDING PROTOCOL: EXECUTE!
GO TIME
EXECUTE
SKITTER SKITTER
exe:systemfunction_cornrow.twist=execute
exe:systemfunction_cornrow.twist=COMPLETE
SKID
WHAM
CRASH

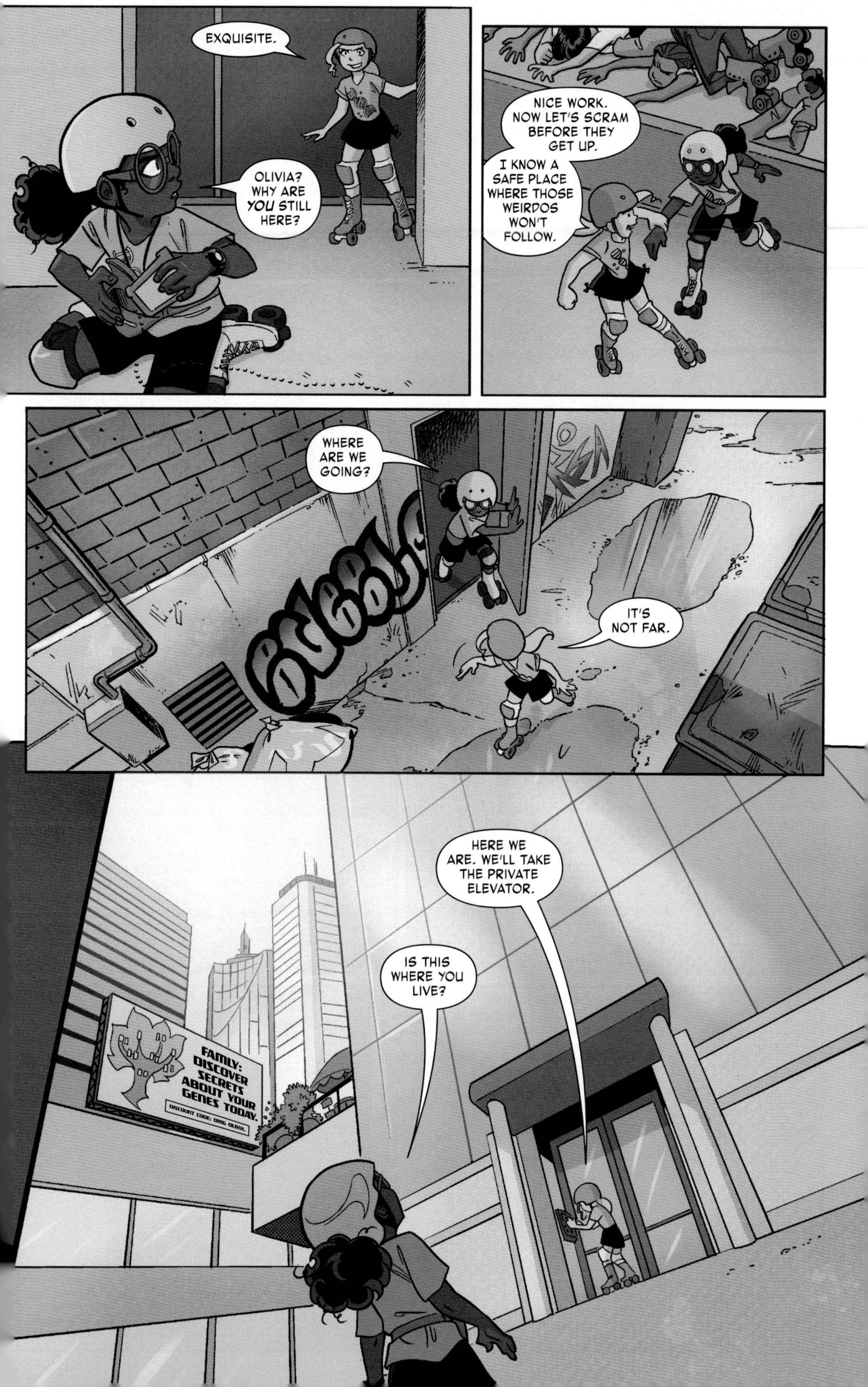
EXQUISITE.
OLIVIA? WHY ARE *YOU* STILL HERE?
NICE WORK. NOW LET'S SCRAM BEFORE THEY GET UP.
I KNOW A SAFE PLACE WHERE THOSE WEIRDOS WON'T FOLLOW.
WHERE ARE WE GOING?
IT'S NOT FAR.
HERE WE ARE. WE'LL TAKE THE PRIVATE ELEVATOR.
IS THIS WHERE YOU LIVE?
FAMLY: DISCOVER SECRETS ABOUT YOUR GENES TODAY.
DISCOUNT CODE: OMG OLIVIA.

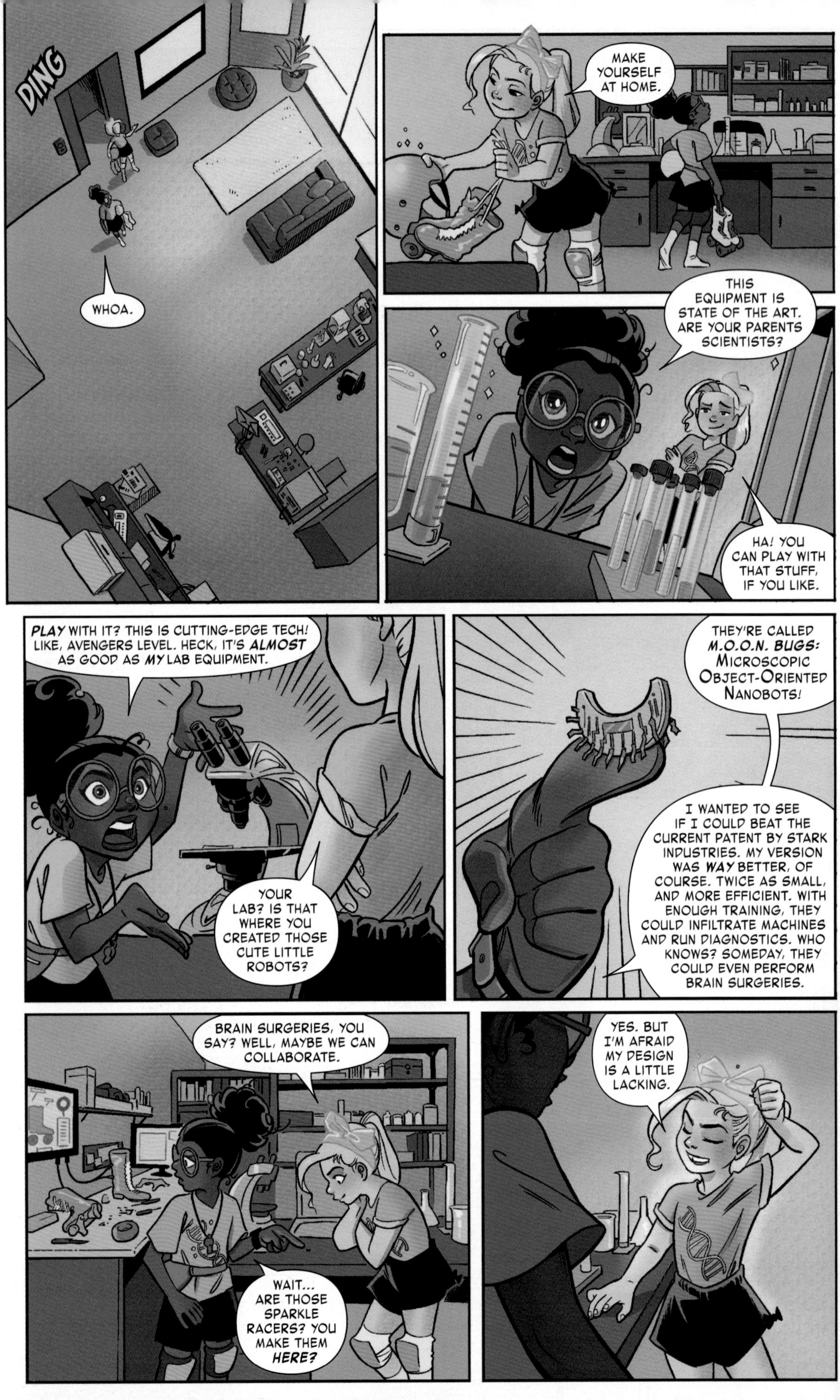
DING
WHOA.
MAKE YOURSELF AT HOME.
THIS EQUIPMENT IS STATE OF THE ART. ARE YOUR PARENTS SCIENTISTS?
HA! YOU CAN PLAY WITH THAT STUFF, IF YOU LIKE.
PLAY WITH IT? THIS IS CUTTING-EDGE TECH! LIKE, AVENGERS LEVEL. HECK, IT'S ALMOST AS GOOD AS MY LAB EQUIPMENT.
YOUR LAB? IS THAT WHERE YOU CREATED THOSE CUTE LITTLE ROBOTS?
THEY'RE CALLED M.O.O.N. BUGS: MICROSCOPIC OBJECT-ORIENTED NANOBOTS!
I WANTED TO SEE IF I COULD BEAT THE CURRENT PATENT BY STARK INDUSTRIES. MY VERSION WAS WAY BETTER, OF COURSE. TWICE AS SMALL, AND MORE EFFICIENT. WITH ENOUGH TRAINING, THEY COULD INFILTRATE MACHINES AND RUN DIAGNOSTICS. WHO KNOWS? SOMEDAY, THEY COULD EVEN PERFORM BRAIN SURGERIES.
BRAIN SURGERIES, YOU SAY? WELL, MAYBE WE CAN COLLABORATE.
WAIT... ARE THOSE SPARKLE RACERS? YOU MAKE THEM HERE?
YES. BUT I'M AFRAID MY DESIGN IS A LITTLE LACKING.

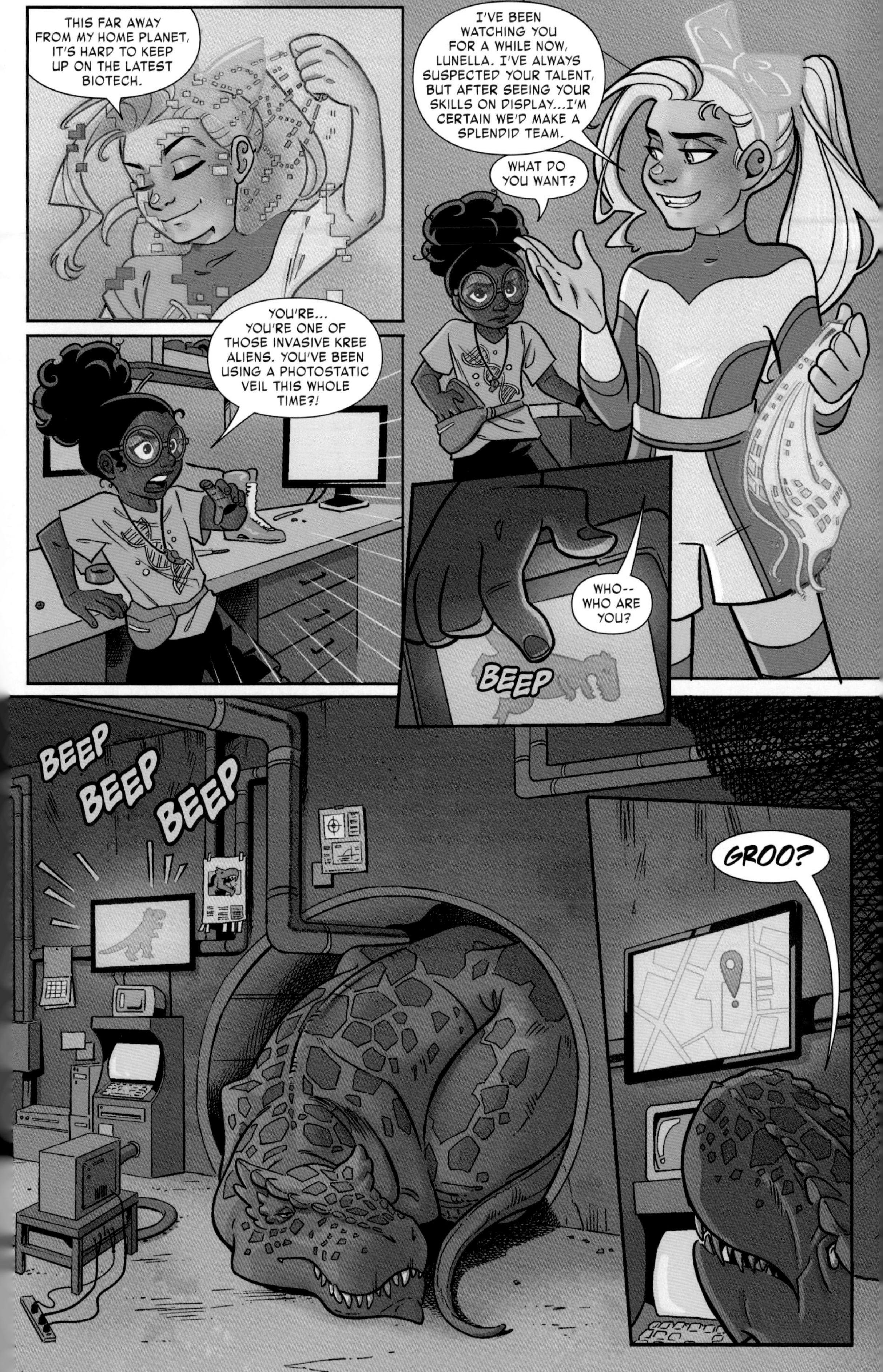
THIS FAR AWAY FROM MY HOME PLANET, IT'S HARD TO KEEP UP ON THE LATEST BIOTECH.
I'VE BEEN WATCHING YOU FOR A WHILE NOW, LUNELLA. I'VE ALWAYS SUSPECTED YOUR TALENT, BUT AFTER SEEING YOUR SKILLS ON DISPLAY...I'M CERTAIN WE'D MAKE A SPLENDID TEAM.
WHAT DO YOU WANT?
YOU'RE... YOU'RE ONE OF THOSE INVASIVE KREE ALIENS. YOU'VE BEEN USING A PHOTOSTATIC VEIL THIS WHOLE TIME?!
WHO-- WHO ARE YOU?
BEEP
BEEP
BEEP
BEEP
GROO?

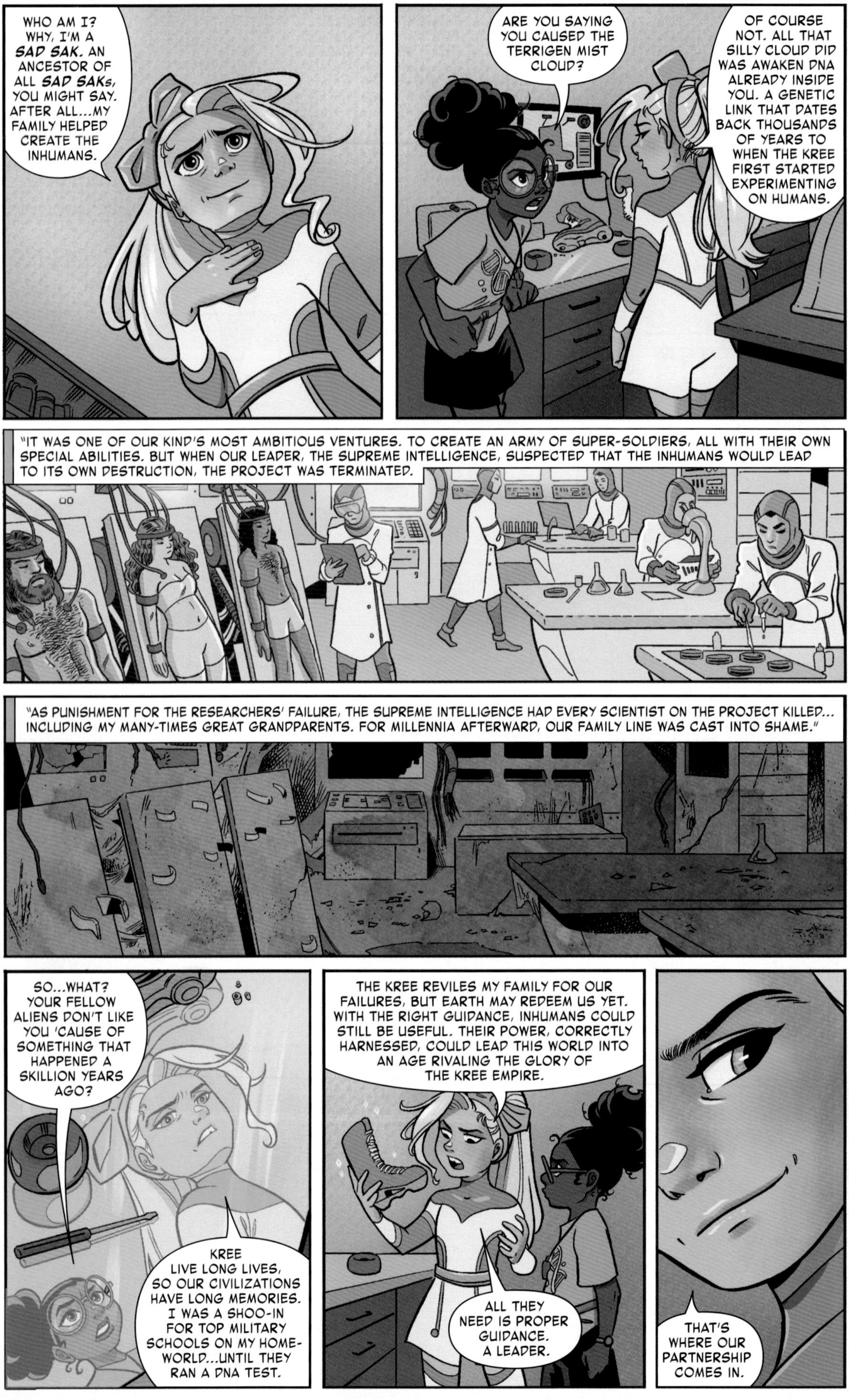
WHO AM I? WHY, I'M A SAD SAK. AN ANCESTOR OF ALL SAD SAKs, YOU MIGHT SAY. AFTER ALL...MY FAMILY HELPED CREATE THE INHUMANS.
ARE YOU SAYING YOU CAUSED THE TERRIGEN MIST CLOUD?
OF COURSE NOT. ALL THAT SILLY CLOUD DID WAS AWAKEN DNA ALREADY INSIDE YOU. A GENETIC LINK THAT DATES BACK THOUSANDS OF YEARS TO WHEN THE KREE FIRST STARTED EXPERIMENTING ON HUMANS.
"IT WAS ONE OF OUR KIND'S MOST AMBITIOUS VENTURES. TO CREATE AN ARMY OF SUPER-SOLDIERS, ALL WITH THEIR OWN SPECIAL ABILITIES. BUT WHEN OUR LEADER, THE SUPREME INTELLIGENCE, SUSPECTED THAT THE INHUMANS WOULD LEAD TO ITS OWN DESTRUCTION, THE PROJECT WAS TERMINATED.
"AS PUNISHMENT FOR THE RESEARCHERS' FAILURE, THE SUPREME INTELLIGENCE HAD EVERY SCIENTIST ON THE PROJECT KILLED... INCLUDING MY MANY-TIMES GREAT GRANDPARENTS. FOR MILLENNIA AFTERWARD, OUR FAMILY LINE WAS CAST INTO SHAME."
SO...WHAT? YOUR FELLOW ALIENS DON'T LIKE YOU 'CAUSE OF SOMETHING THAT HAPPENED A SKILLION YEARS AGO?
KREE LIVE LONG LIVES, SO OUR CIVILIZATIONS HAVE LONG MEMORIES. I WAS A SHOO-IN FOR TOP MILITARY SCHOOLS ON MY HOME-WORLD...UNTIL THEY RAN A DNA TEST.
THE KREE REVILES MY FAMILY FOR OUR FAILURES, BUT EARTH MAY REDEEM US YET. WITH THE RIGHT GUIDANCE, INHUMANS COULD STILL BE USEFUL. THEIR POWER, CORRECTLY HARNESSED, COULD LEAD THIS WORLD INTO AN AGE RIVALING THE GLORY OF THE KREE EMPIRE.
ALL THEY NEED IS PROPER GUIDANCE. A LEADER.
THAT'S WHERE OUR PARTNERSHIP COMES IN.

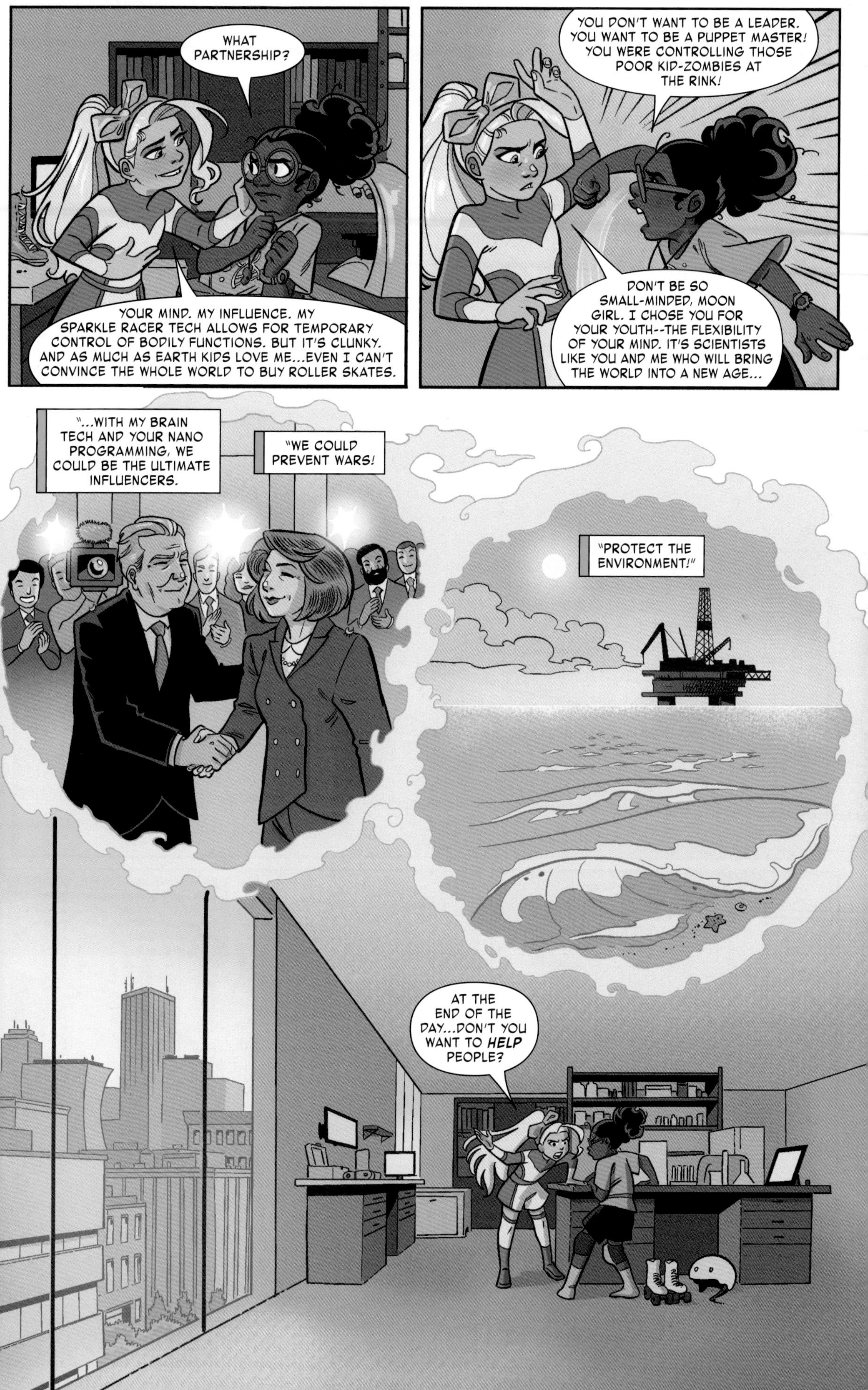
WHAT PARTNERSHIP?
YOUR MIND. MY INFLUENCE. MY SPARKLE RACER TECH ALLOWS FOR TEMPORARY CONTROL OF BODILY FUNCTIONS. BUT IT'S CLUNKY. AND AS MUCH AS EARTH KIDS LOVE ME...EVEN I CAN'T CONVINCE THE WHOLE WORLD TO BUY ROLLER SKATES.
YOU DON'T WANT TO BE A LEADER. YOU WANT TO BE A PUPPET MASTER! YOU WERE CONTROLLING THOSE POOR KID-ZOMBIES AT THE RINK!
DON'T BE SO SMALL-MINDED, MOON GIRL. I CHOSE YOU FOR YOUR YOUTH--THE FLEXIBILITY OF YOUR MIND. IT'S SCIENTISTS LIKE YOU AND ME WHO WILL BRING THE WORLD INTO A NEW AGE...
"...WITH MY BRAIN TECH AND YOUR NANO PROGRAMMING, WE COULD BE THE ULTIMATE INFLUENCERS.
"WE COULD PREVENT WARS!
"PROTECT THE ENVIRONMENT!"
AT THE END OF THE DAY...DON'T YOU WANT TO *HELP* PEOPLE?

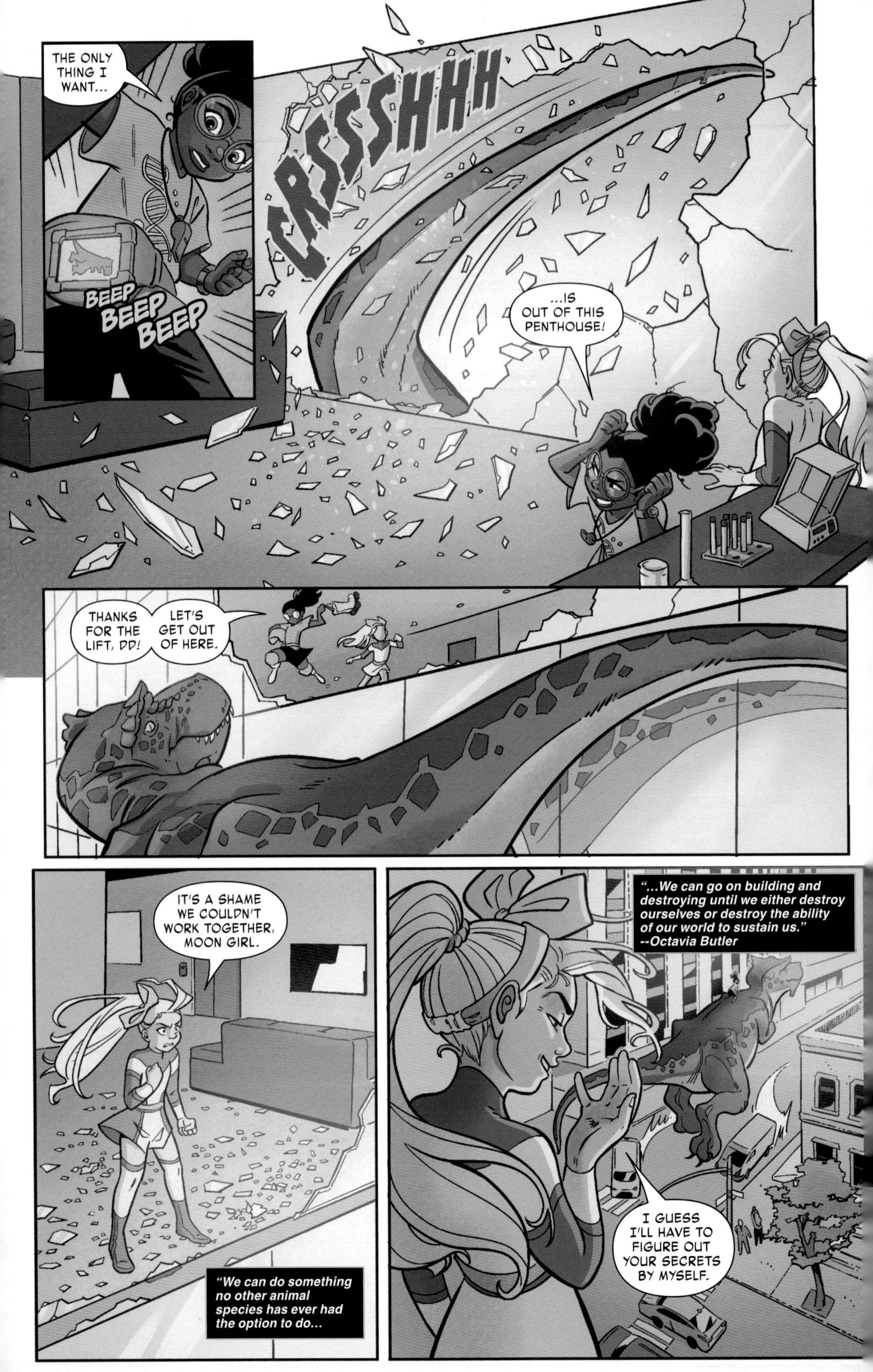
THE ONLY THING I WANT...
BEEP BEEP BEEP
CRSSSHHH
...IS OUT OF THIS PENTHOUSE!
THANKS FOR THE LIFT, DD!
LET'S GET OUT OF HERE.
IT'S A SHAME WE COULDN'T WORK TOGETHER, MOON GIRL.
"We can do something no other animal species has ever had the option to do...
"...We can go on building and destroying until we either destroy ourselves or destroy the ability of our world to sustain us."
--Octavia Butler
I GUESS I'LL HAVE TO FIGURE OUT YOUR SECRETS BY MYSELF.

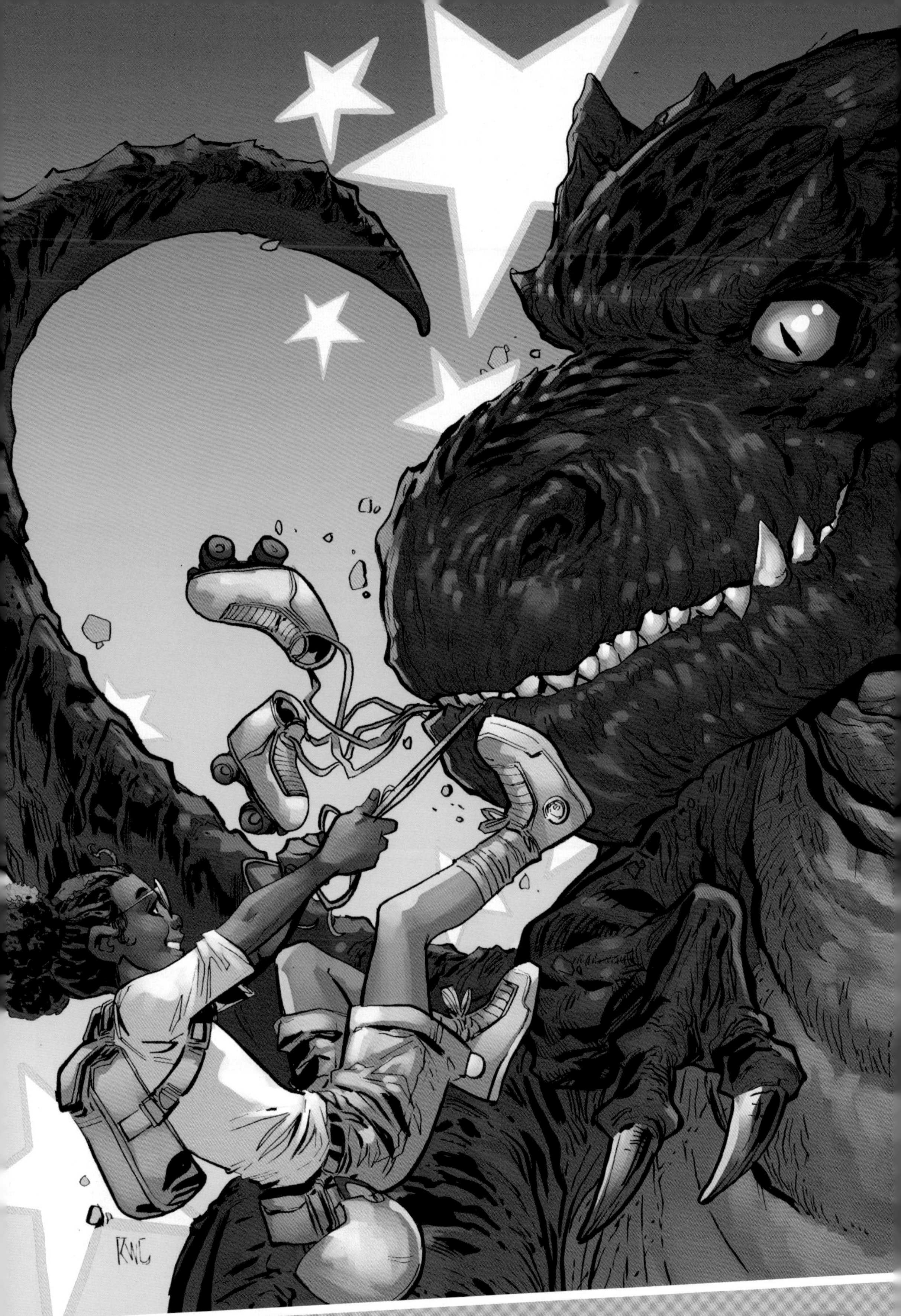

2

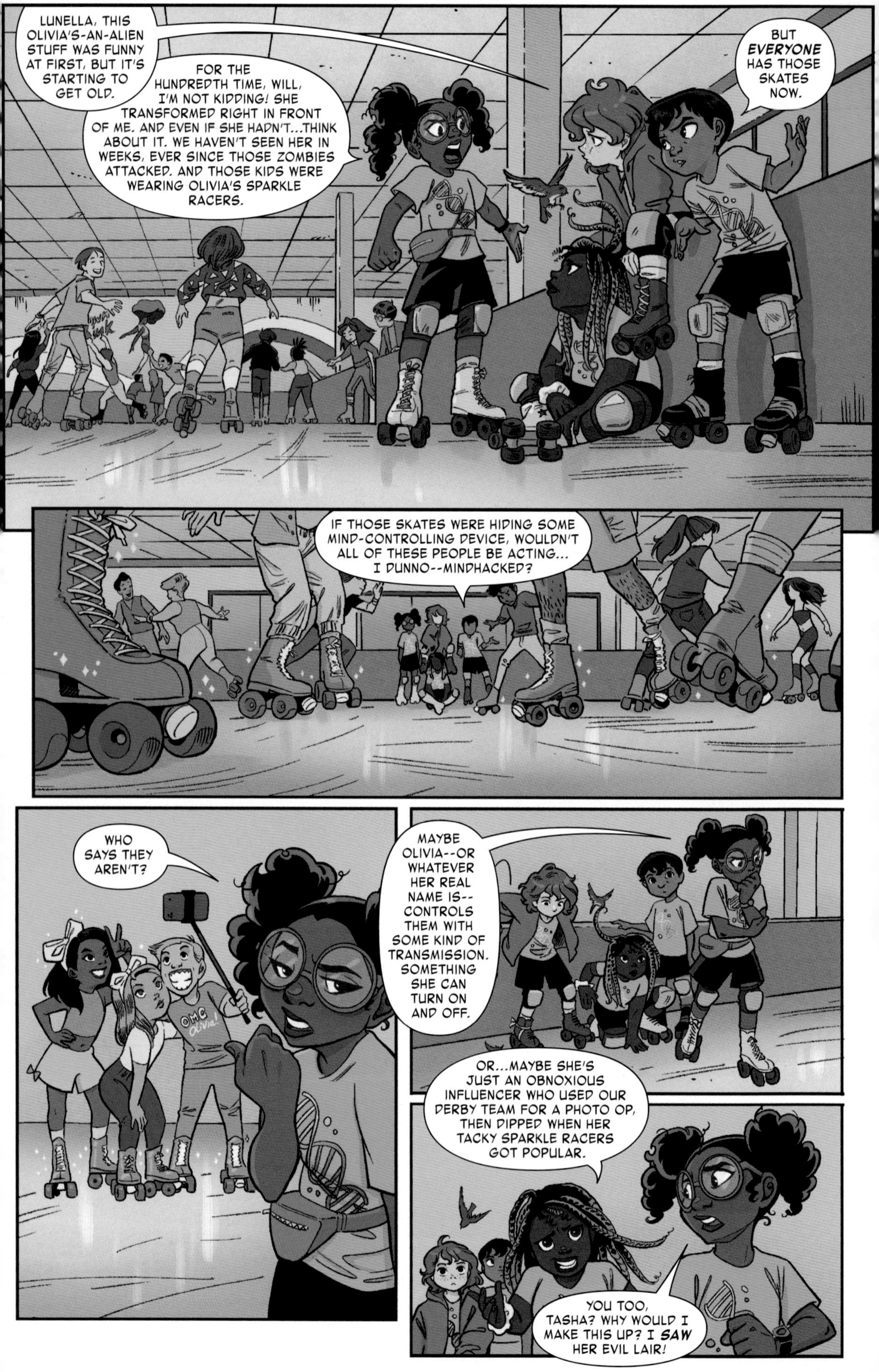
LUNELLA, THIS OLIVIA'S-AN-ALIEN STUFF WAS FUNNY AT FIRST, BUT IT'S STARTING TO GET OLD.
FOR THE HUNDREDTH TIME, WILL, I'M NOT KIDDING! SHE TRANSFORMED RIGHT IN FRONT OF ME. AND EVEN IF SHE HADN'T...THINK ABOUT IT. WE HAVEN'T SEEN HER IN WEEKS, EVER SINCE THOSE ZOMBIES ATTACKED. AND THOSE KIDS WERE WEARING OLIVIA'S SPARKLE RACERS.
BUT *EVERYONE* HAS THOSE SKATES NOW.
IF THOSE SKATES WERE HIDING SOME MIND-CONTROLLING DEVICE, WOULDN'T ALL OF THESE PEOPLE BE ACTING... I DUNNO--MINDHACKED?
WHO SAYS THEY AREN'T?
OMG Olivia!
MAYBE OLIVIA--OR WHATEVER HER REAL NAME IS--CONTROLS THEM WITH SOME KIND OF TRANSMISSION. SOMETHING SHE CAN TURN ON AND OFF.
OR...MAYBE SHE'S JUST AN OBNOXIOUS INFLUENCER WHO USED OUR DERBY TEAM FOR A PHOTO OP, THEN DIPPED WHEN HER TACKY SPARKLE RACERS GOT POPULAR.
YOU TOO, TASHA? WHY WOULD I MAKE THIS UP? I *SAW* HER EVIL LAIR!

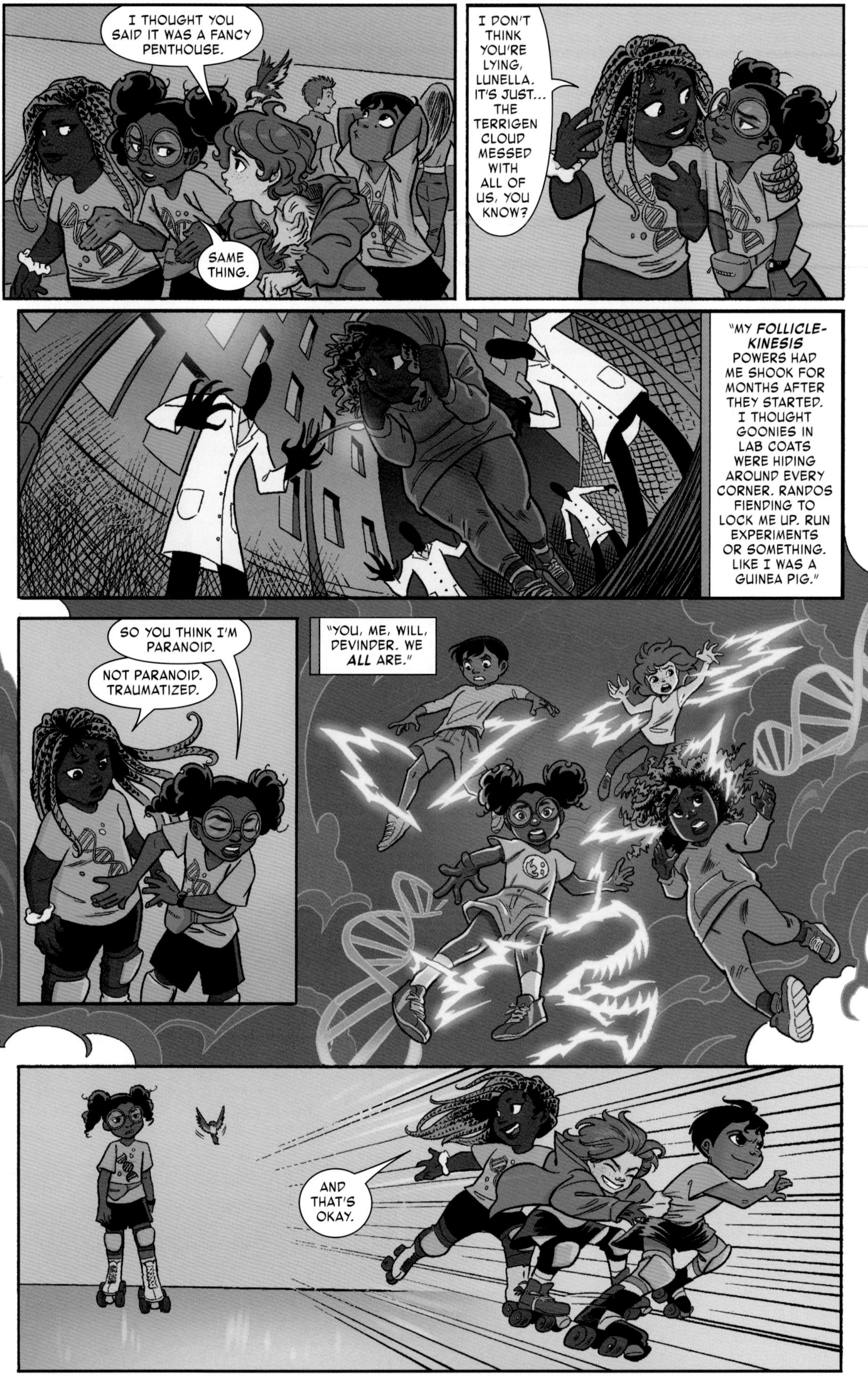

I THOUGHT YOU SAID IT WAS A FANCY PENTHOUSE.
SAME THING.
I DON'T THINK YOU'RE LYING, LUNELLA. IT'S JUST... THE TERRIGEN CLOUD MESSED WITH ALL OF US, YOU KNOW?
"MY FOLLICLE-KINESIS POWERS HAD ME SHOOK FOR MONTHS AFTER THEY STARTED. I THOUGHT GOONIES IN LAB COATS WERE HIDING AROUND EVERY CORNER. RANDOS FIENDING TO LOCK ME UP. RUN EXPERIMENTS OR SOMETHING. LIKE I WAS A GUINEA PIG."
SO YOU THINK I'M PARANOID.
NOT PARANOID. TRAUMATIZED.
"YOU, ME, WILL, DEVINDER. WE ALL ARE."
AND THAT'S OKAY.

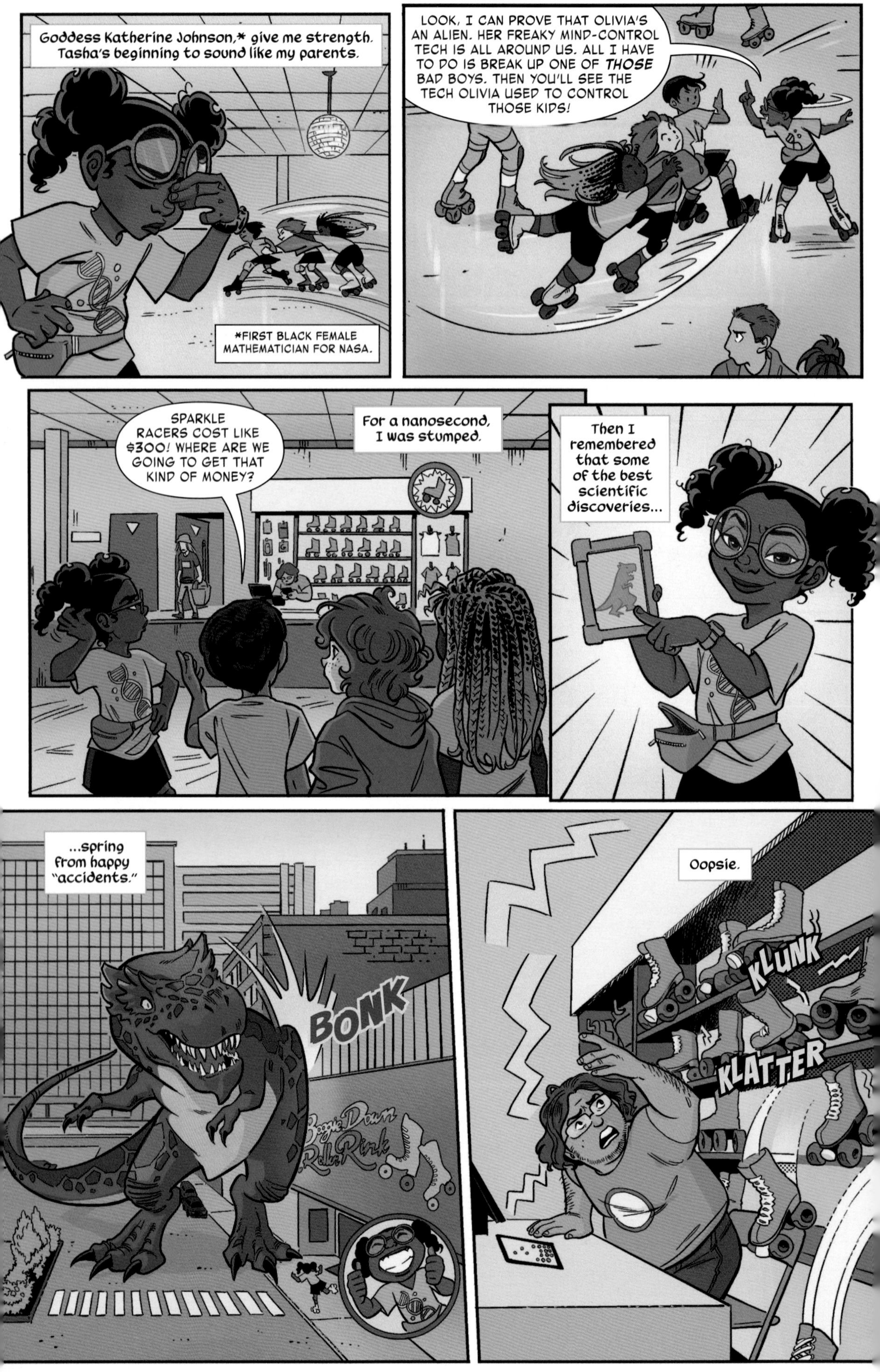

Goddess Katherine Johnson,* give me strength. Tasha's beginning to sound like my parents.
*FIRST BLACK FEMALE MATHEMATICIAN FOR NASA.
LOOK, I CAN PROVE THAT OLIVIA'S AN ALIEN. HER FREAKY MIND-CONTROL TECH IS ALL AROUND US. ALL I HAVE TO DO IS BREAK UP ONE OF THOSE BAD BOYS. THEN YOU'LL SEE THE TECH OLIVIA USED TO CONTROL THOSE KIDS!
SPARKLE RACERS COST LIKE $300! WHERE ARE WE GOING TO GET THAT KIND OF MONEY?
For a nanosecond, I was stumped.
Then I remembered that some of the best scientific discoveries...
...spring from happy "accidents."
BONK
Boogie Down Roller Rink
Oopsie.
KLUNK
KLATTER

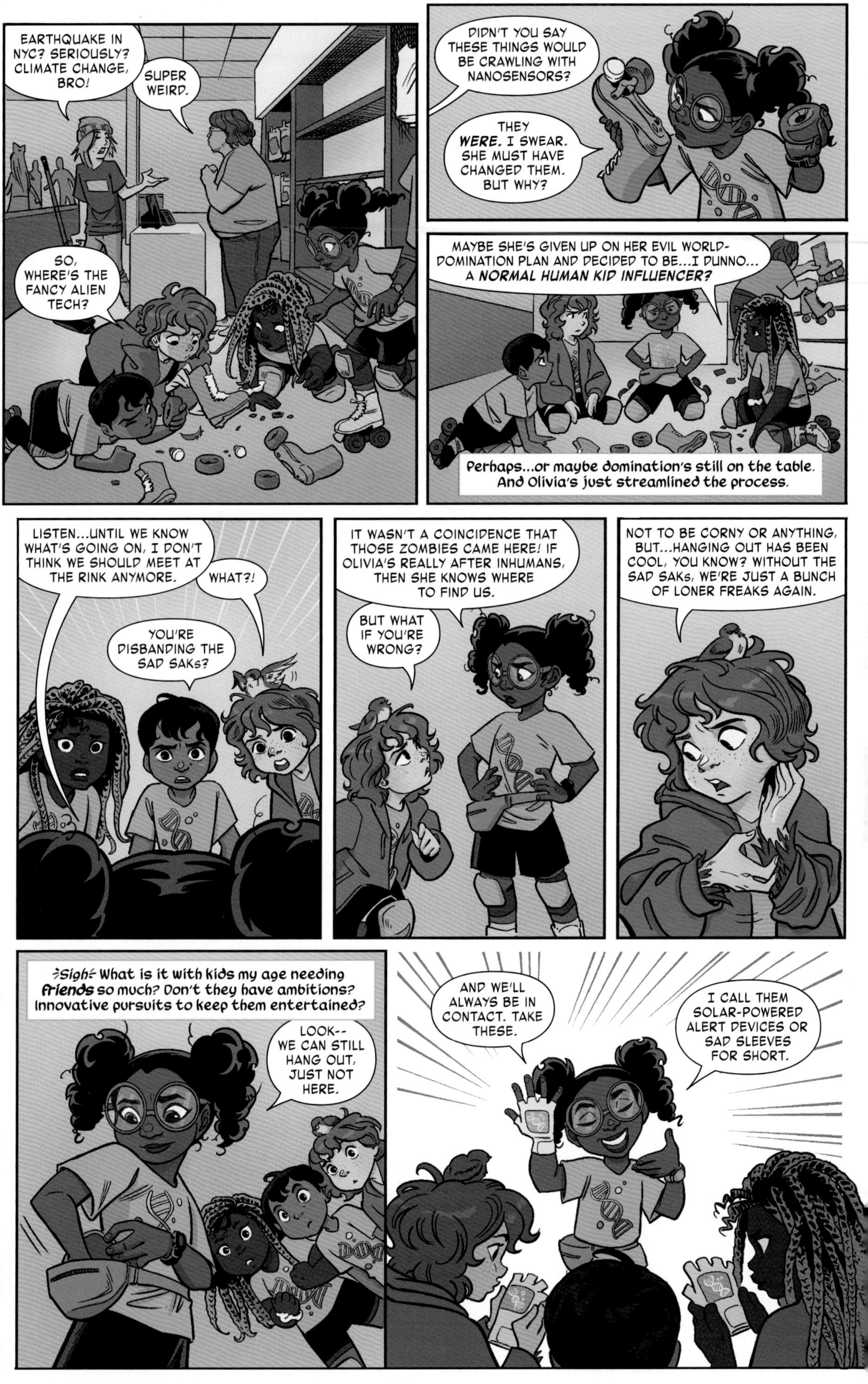

EARTHQUAKE IN NYC? SERIOUSLY? CLIMATE CHANGE, BRO!
SUPER WEIRD.
SO, WHERE'S THE FANCY ALIEN TECH?
DIDN'T YOU SAY THESE THINGS WOULD BE CRAWLING WITH NANOSENSORS?
THEY *WERE.* I SWEAR. SHE MUST HAVE CHANGED THEM. BUT WHY?
MAYBE SHE'S GIVEN UP ON HER EVIL WORLD-DOMINATION PLAN AND DECIDED TO BE...I DUNNO... A ***NORMAL HUMAN KID INFLUENCER?***
Perhaps...or maybe domination's still on the table. And Olivia's just streamlined the process.
LISTEN...UNTIL WE KNOW WHAT'S GOING ON, I DON'T THINK WE SHOULD MEET AT THE RINK ANYMORE.
WHAT?!
YOU'RE DISBANDING THE SAD SAKs?
IT WASN'T A COINCIDENCE THAT THOSE ZOMBIES CAME HERE! IF OLIVIA'S REALLY AFTER INHUMANS, THEN SHE KNOWS WHERE TO FIND US.
BUT WHAT IF YOU'RE WRONG?
NOT TO BE CORNY OR ANYTHING, BUT...HANGING OUT HAS BEEN COOL, YOU KNOW? WITHOUT THE SAD SAKs, WE'RE JUST A BUNCH OF LONER FREAKS AGAIN.
Sigh What is it with kids my age needing *friends* so much? Don't they have ambitions? Innovative pursuits to keep them entertained?
LOOK-- WE CAN STILL HANG OUT, JUST NOT HERE.
AND WE'LL ALWAYS BE IN CONTACT. TAKE THESE.
I CALL THEM SOLAR-POWERED ALERT DEVICES OR SAD SLEEVES FOR SHORT.

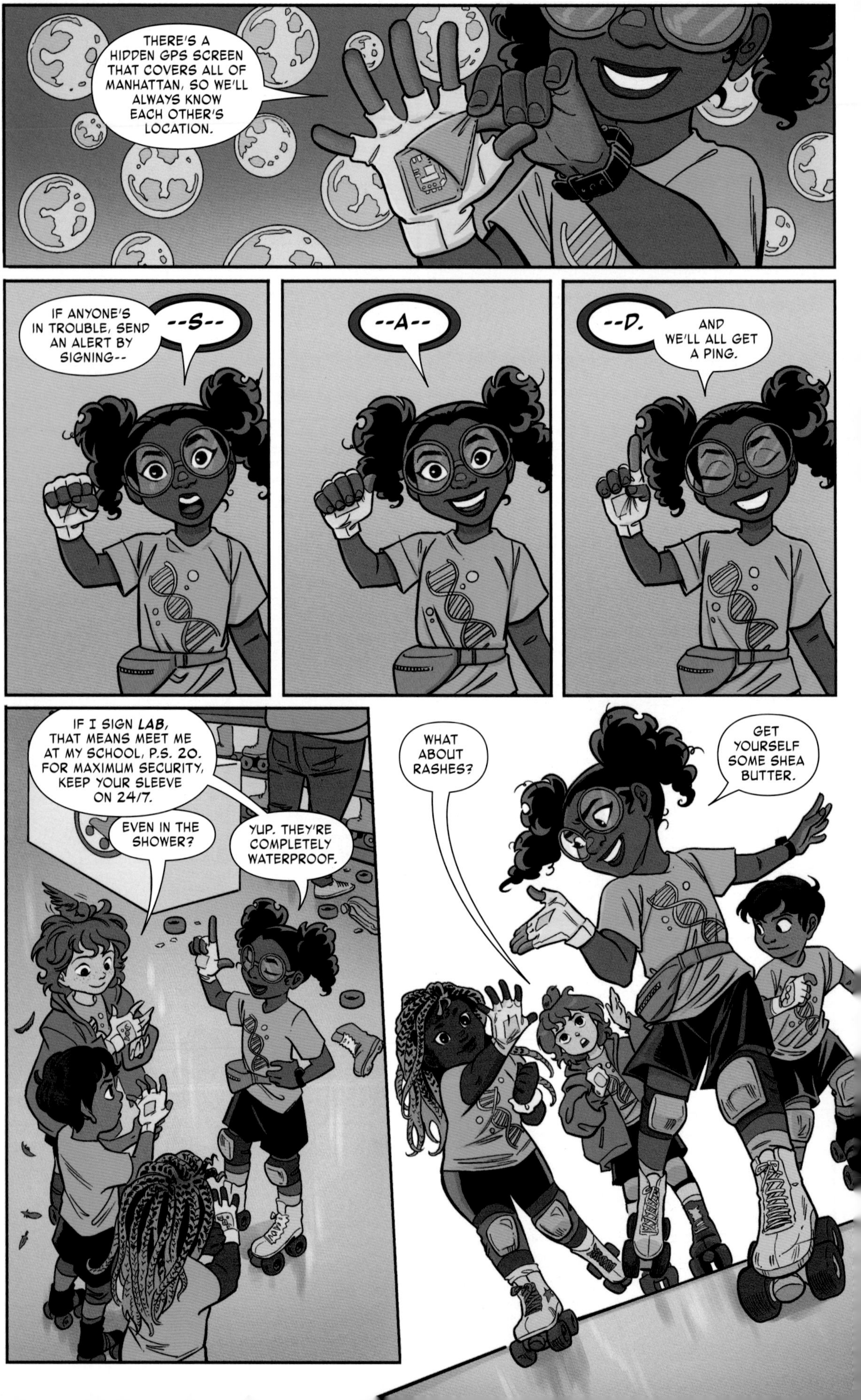
THERE'S A HIDDEN GPS SCREEN THAT COVERS ALL OF MANHATTAN, SO WE'LL ALWAYS KNOW EACH OTHER'S LOCATION.
IF ANYONE'S IN TROUBLE, SEND AN ALERT BY SIGNING--
--S--
--A--
--D.
AND WE'LL ALL GET A PING.
IF I SIGN LAB, THAT MEANS MEET ME AT MY SCHOOL, P.S. 20. FOR MAXIMUM SECURITY, KEEP YOUR SLEEVE ON 24/7.
EVEN IN THE SHOWER?
YUP. THEY'RE COMPLETELY WATERPROOF.
WHAT ABOUT RASHES?
GET YOURSELF SOME SHEA BUTTER.

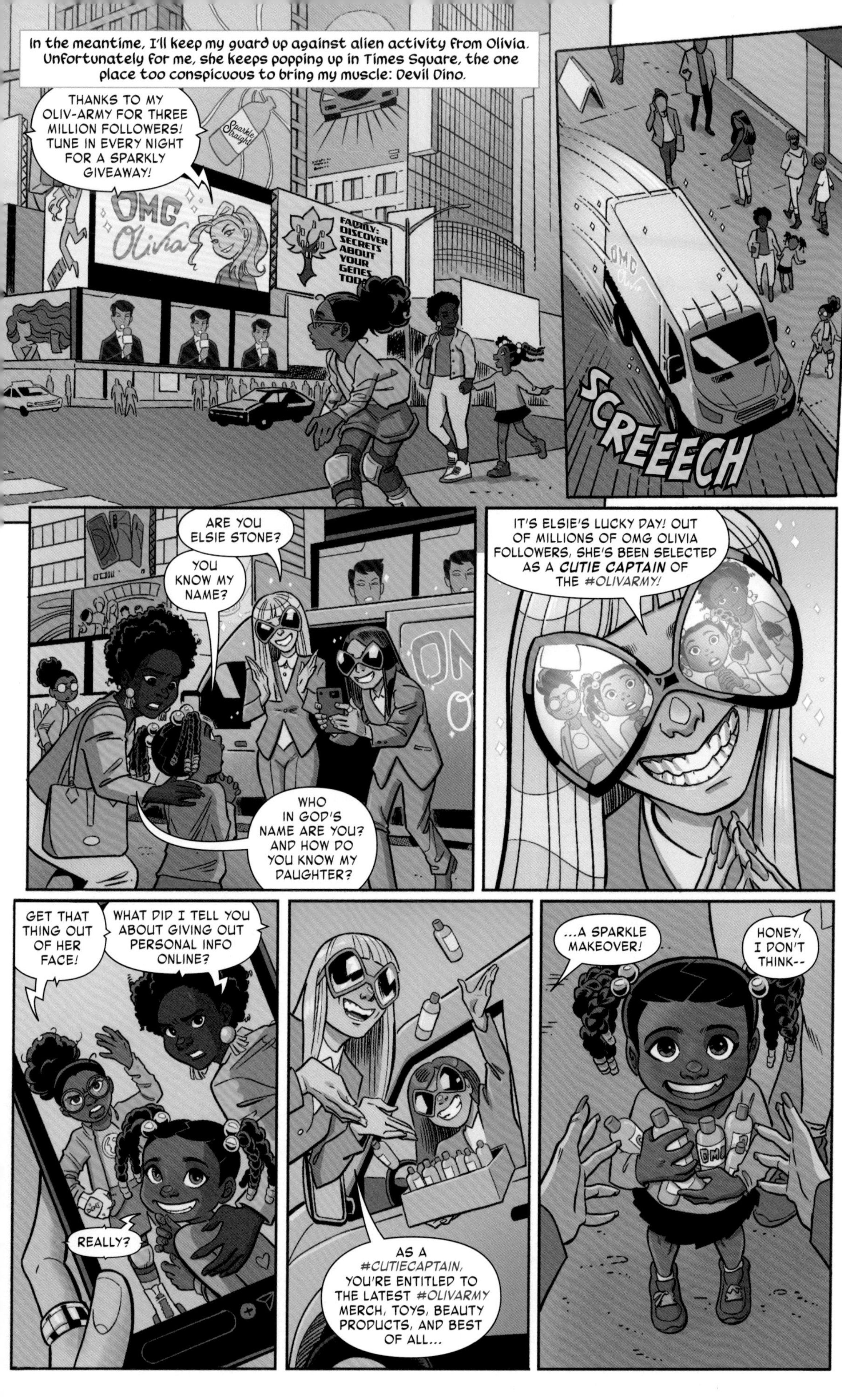
In the meantime, I'll keep my guard up against alien activity from Olivia. Unfortunately for me, she keeps popping up in Times Square, the one place too conspicuous to bring my muscle: Devil Dino.
THANKS TO MY OLIV-ARMY FOR THREE MILLION FOLLOWERS! TUNE IN EVERY NIGHT FOR A SPARKLY GIVEAWAY!
OMG Olivia
Sparkle Straight
FAMILY: DISCOVER SECRETS ABOUT YOUR GENES TODA
SCREEECH
ARE YOU ELSIE STONE?
YOU KNOW MY NAME?
WHO IN GOD'S NAME ARE YOU? AND HOW DO YOU KNOW MY DAUGHTER?
IT'S ELSIE'S LUCKY DAY! OUT OF MILLIONS OF OMG OLIVIA FOLLOWERS, SHE'S BEEN SELECTED AS A CUTIE CAPTAIN OF THE #OLIVARMY!
GET THAT THING OUT OF HER FACE!
WHAT DID I TELL YOU ABOUT GIVING OUT PERSONAL INFO ONLINE?
REALLY?
AS A #CUTIECAPTAIN, YOU'RE ENTITLED TO THE LATEST #OLIVARMY MERCH, TOYS, BEAUTY PRODUCTS, AND BEST OF ALL...
...A SPARKLE MAKEOVER!
HONEY, I DON'T THINK--

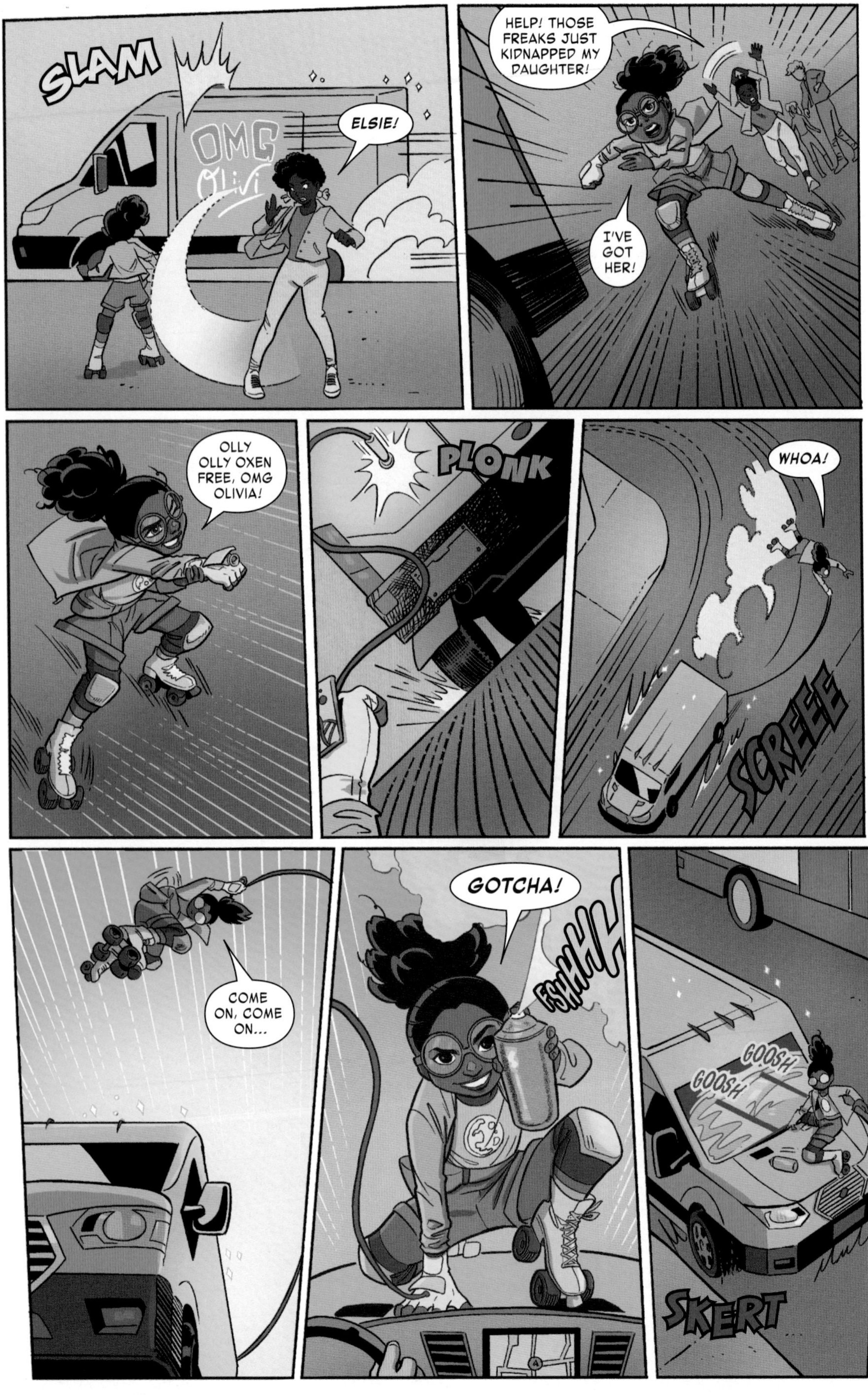
SLAM
OMG
ELSIE!
HELP! THOSE FREAKS JUST KIDNAPPED MY DAUGHTER!
I'VE GOT HER!
OLLY OLLY OXEN FREE, OMG OLIVIA!
PLONK
WHOA!
SCREEE
COME ON, COME ON...
GOTCHA!
FSHHHH
GOOSH
GOOSH
SKERT

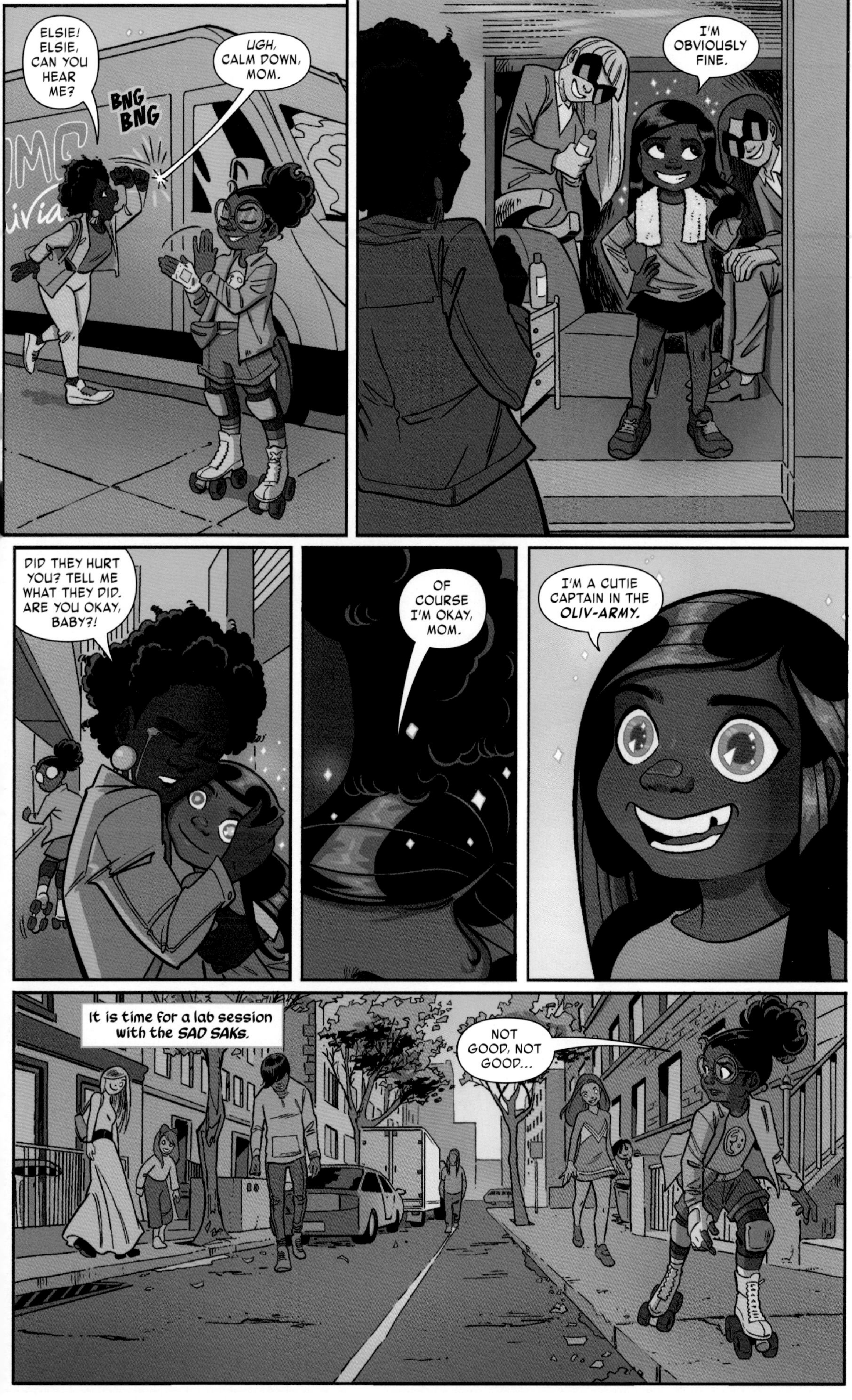
ELSIE! ELSIE, CAN YOU HEAR ME?
BNG BNG
UGH, CALM DOWN, MOM.
I'M OBVIOUSLY FINE.
DID THEY HURT YOU? TELL ME WHAT THEY DID. ARE YOU OKAY, BABY?!
OF COURSE I'M OKAY, MOM.
I'M A CUTIE CAPTAIN IN THE OLIV-ARMY.
It is time for a lab session with the SAD SAKS.
NOT GOOD, NOT GOOD...

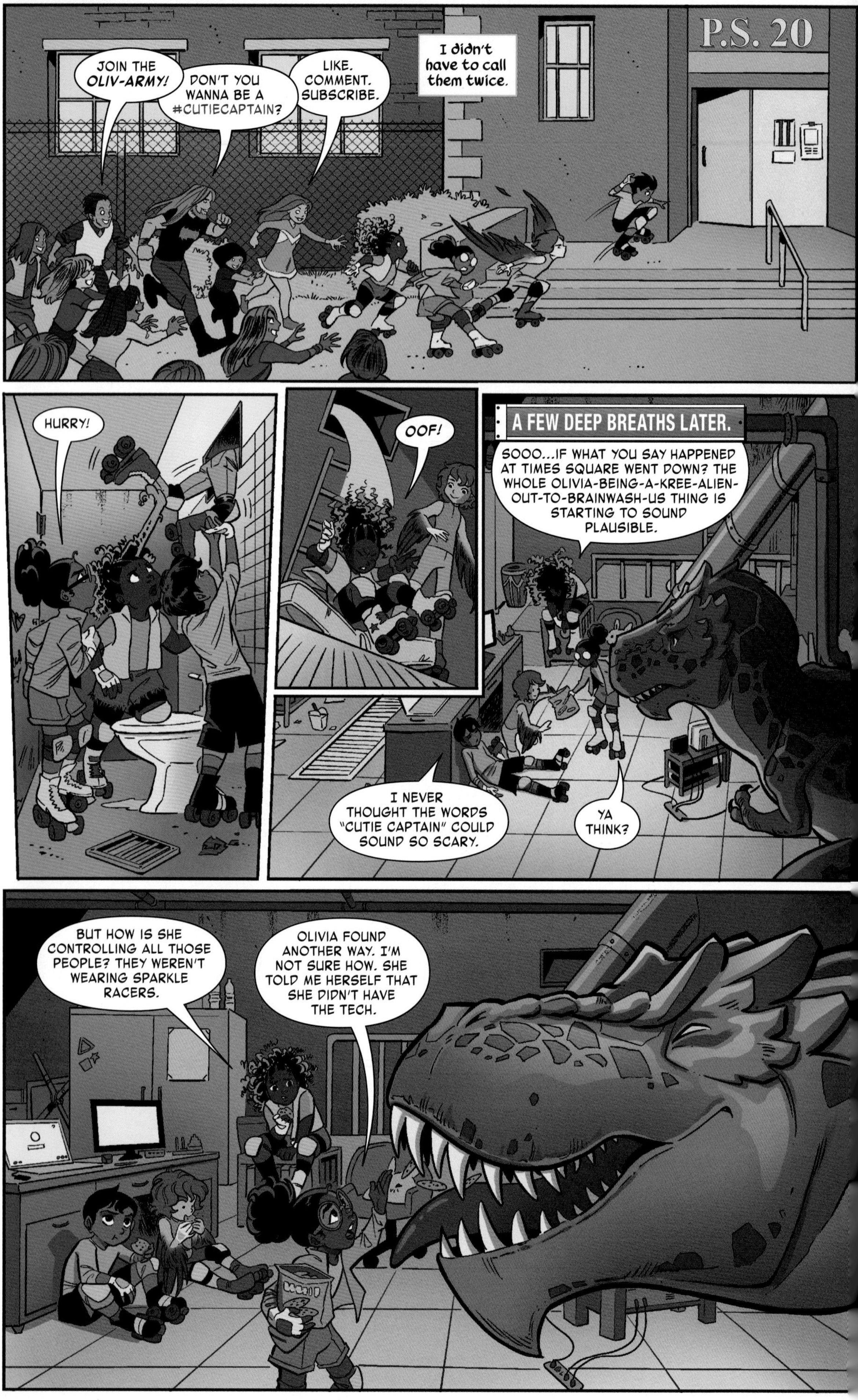
P.S. 20
JOIN THE OLIV-ARMY!
DON'T YOU WANNA BE A #CUTIECAPTAIN?
LIKE. COMMENT. SUBSCRIBE.
I didn't have to call them twice.
HURRY!
OOF!
A FEW DEEP BREATHS LATER.
SOOO...IF WHAT YOU SAY HAPPENED AT TIMES SQUARE WENT DOWN? THE WHOLE OLIVIA-BEING-A-KREE-ALIEN-OUT-TO-BRAINWASH-US THING IS STARTING TO SOUND PLAUSIBLE.
I NEVER THOUGHT THE WORDS "CUTIE CAPTAIN" COULD SOUND SO SCARY.
YA THINK?
BUT HOW IS SHE CONTROLLING ALL THOSE PEOPLE? THEY WEREN'T WEARING SPARKLE RACERS.
OLIVIA FOUND ANOTHER WAY. I'M NOT SURE HOW. SHE TOLD ME HERSELF THAT SHE DIDN'T HAVE THE TECH.

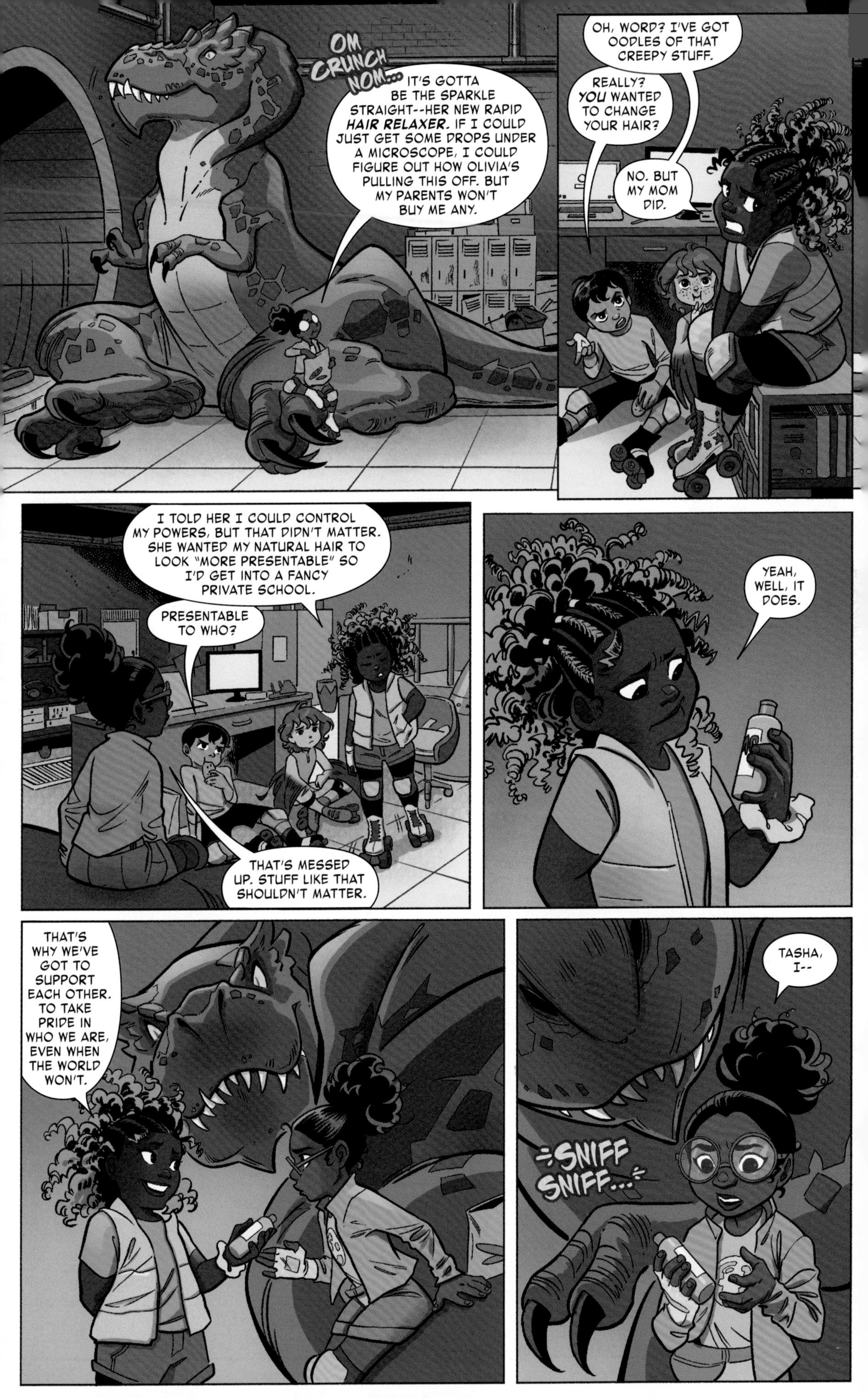
OM CRUNCH NOM...
IT'S GOTTA BE THE SPARKLE STRAIGHT--HER NEW RAPID **HAIR RELAXER.** IF I COULD JUST GET SOME DROPS UNDER A MICROSCOPE, I COULD FIGURE OUT HOW OLIVIA'S PULLING THIS OFF. BUT MY PARENTS WON'T BUY ME ANY.
OH, WORD? I'VE GOT OODLES OF THAT CREEPY STUFF.
REALLY? *YOU* WANTED TO CHANGE YOUR HAIR?
NO. BUT MY MOM DID.
I TOLD HER I COULD CONTROL MY POWERS, BUT THAT DIDN'T MATTER. SHE WANTED MY NATURAL HAIR TO LOOK "MORE PRESENTABLE" SO I'D GET INTO A FANCY PRIVATE SCHOOL.
PRESENTABLE TO WHO?
THAT'S MESSED UP. STUFF LIKE THAT SHOULDN'T MATTER.
YEAH, WELL, IT DOES.
THAT'S WHY WE'VE GOT TO SUPPORT EACH OTHER. TO TAKE PRIDE IN WHO WE ARE, EVEN WHEN THE WORLD WON'T.
TASHA, I--
SNIFF SNIFF...

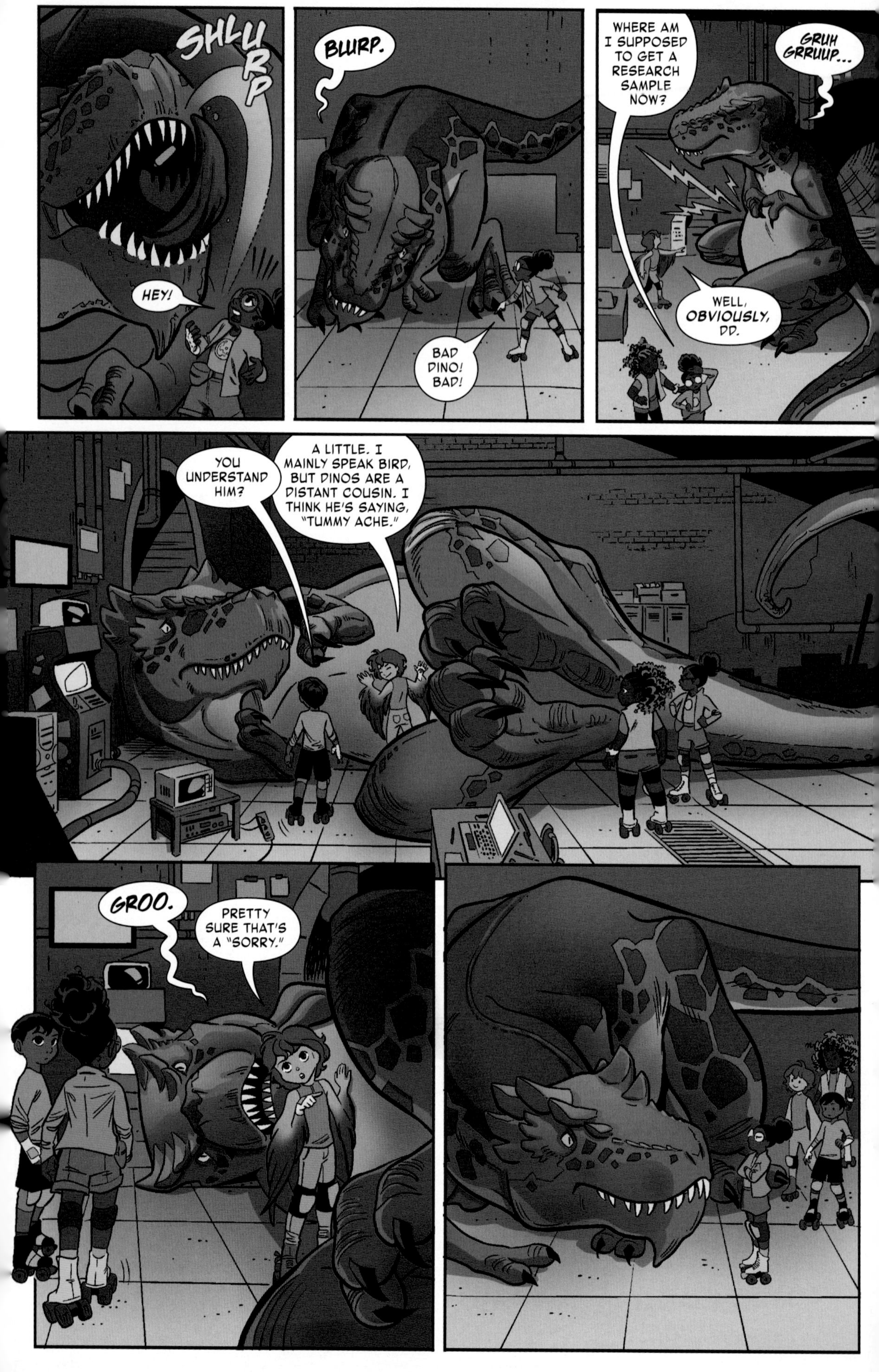
SHLURP
HEY!
BLURP.
BAD DINO! BAD!
WHERE AM I SUPPOSED TO GET A RESEARCH SAMPLE NOW?
GRUH GRRUUP...
WELL, OBVIOUSLY, DD.
YOU UNDERSTAND HIM?
A LITTLE. I MAINLY SPEAK BIRD, BUT DINOS ARE A DISTANT COUSIN. I THINK HE'S SAYING, "TUMMY ACHE."
GROO.
PRETTY SURE THAT'S A "SORRY."

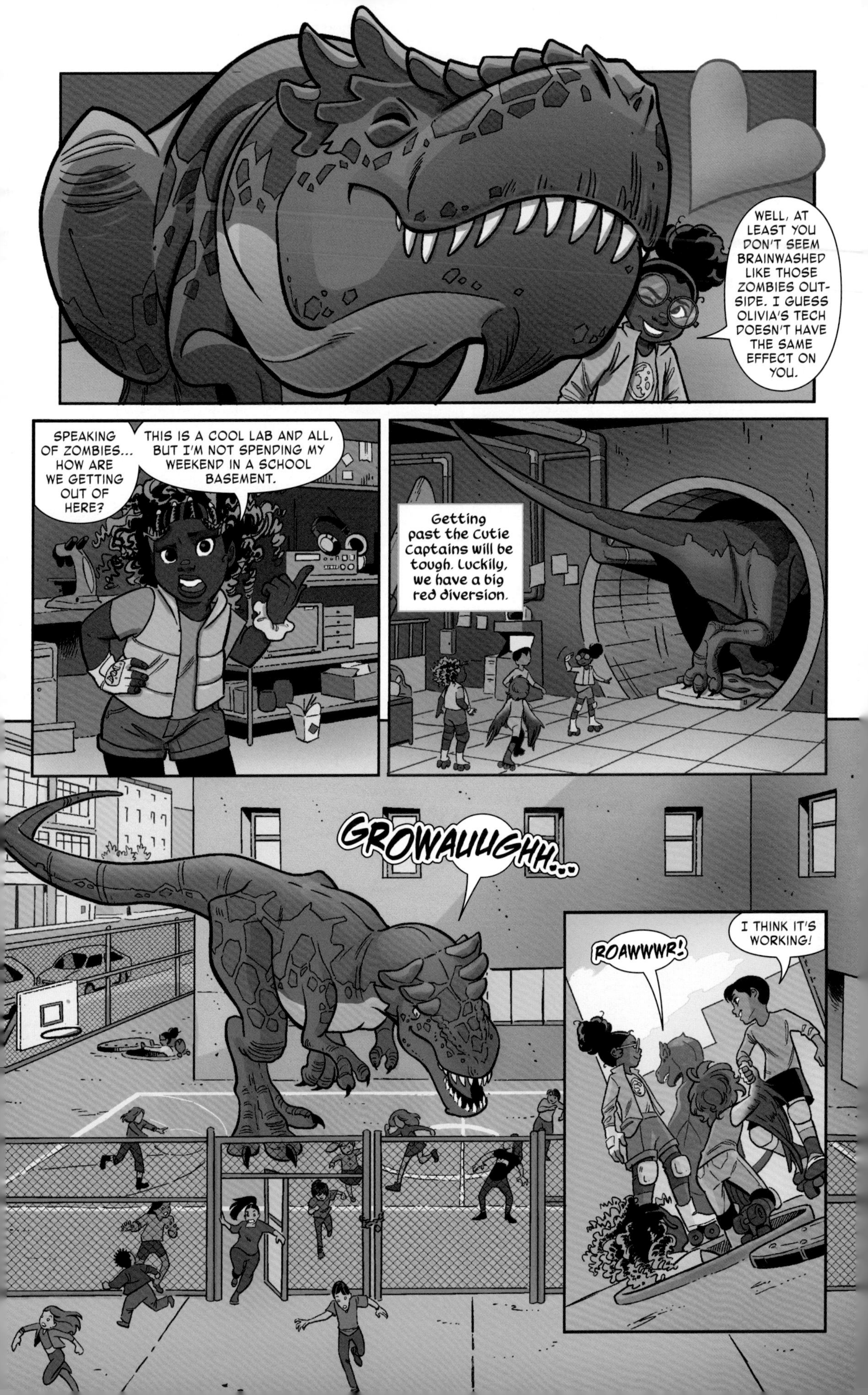
WELL, AT LEAST YOU DON'T SEEM BRAINWASHED LIKE THOSE ZOMBIES OUT-SIDE. I GUESS OLIVIA'S TECH DOESN'T HAVE THE SAME EFFECT ON YOU.
SPEAKING OF ZOMBIES... HOW ARE WE GETTING OUT OF HERE?
THIS IS A COOL LAB AND ALL, BUT I'M NOT SPENDING MY WEEKEND IN A SCHOOL BASEMENT.
Getting past the Cutie Captains will be tough. Luckily, we have a big red diversion.
GROWAUUGHH...
ROAWWWR!
I THINK IT'S WORKING!

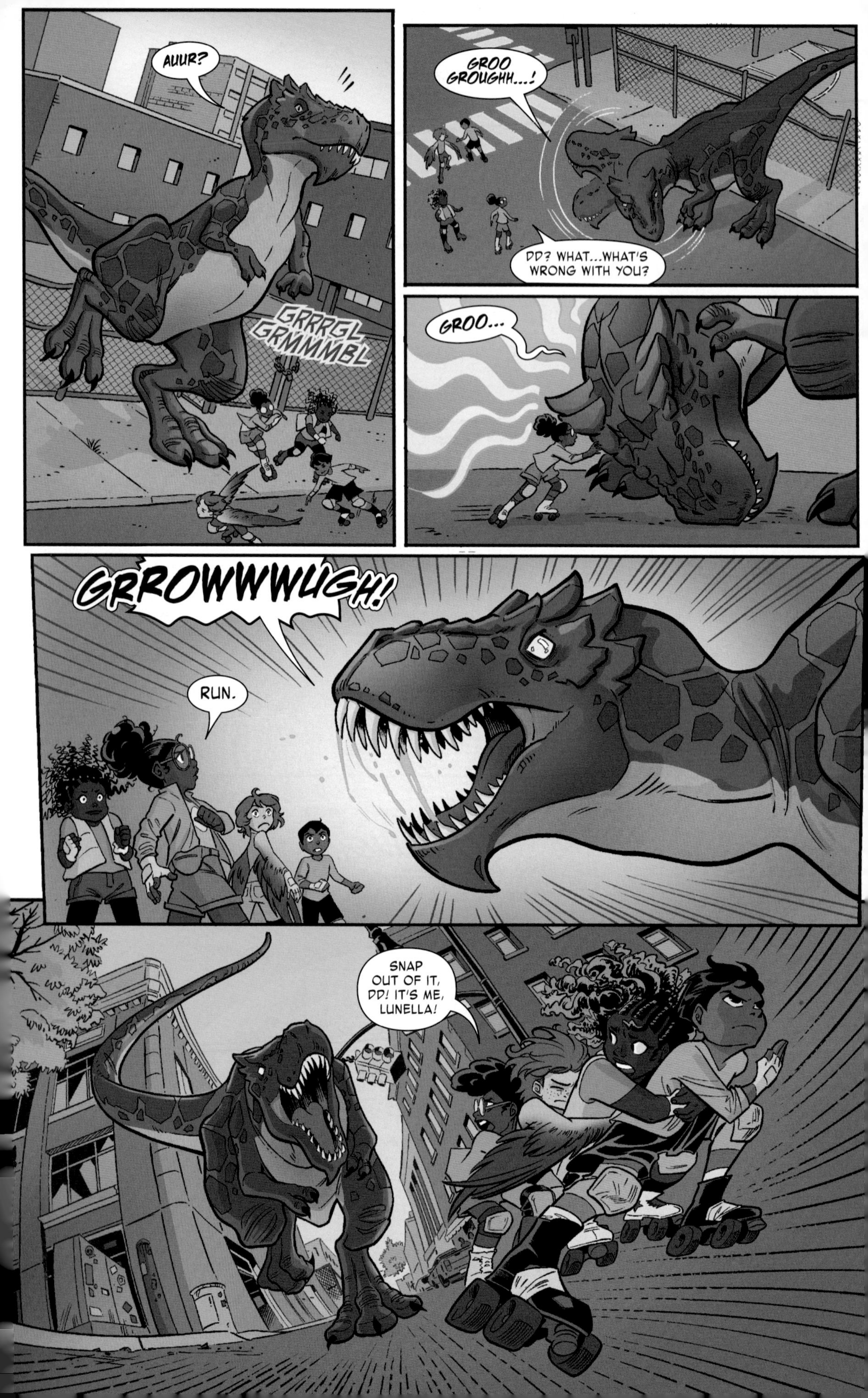
AUUR?
GRRRGL GRMMMBL
GROO GROUGHH...!
DD? WHAT...WHAT'S WRONG WITH YOU?
GROO...
GRROWWWUGH!
RUN.
SNAP OUT OF IT, DD! IT'S ME, LUNELLA!

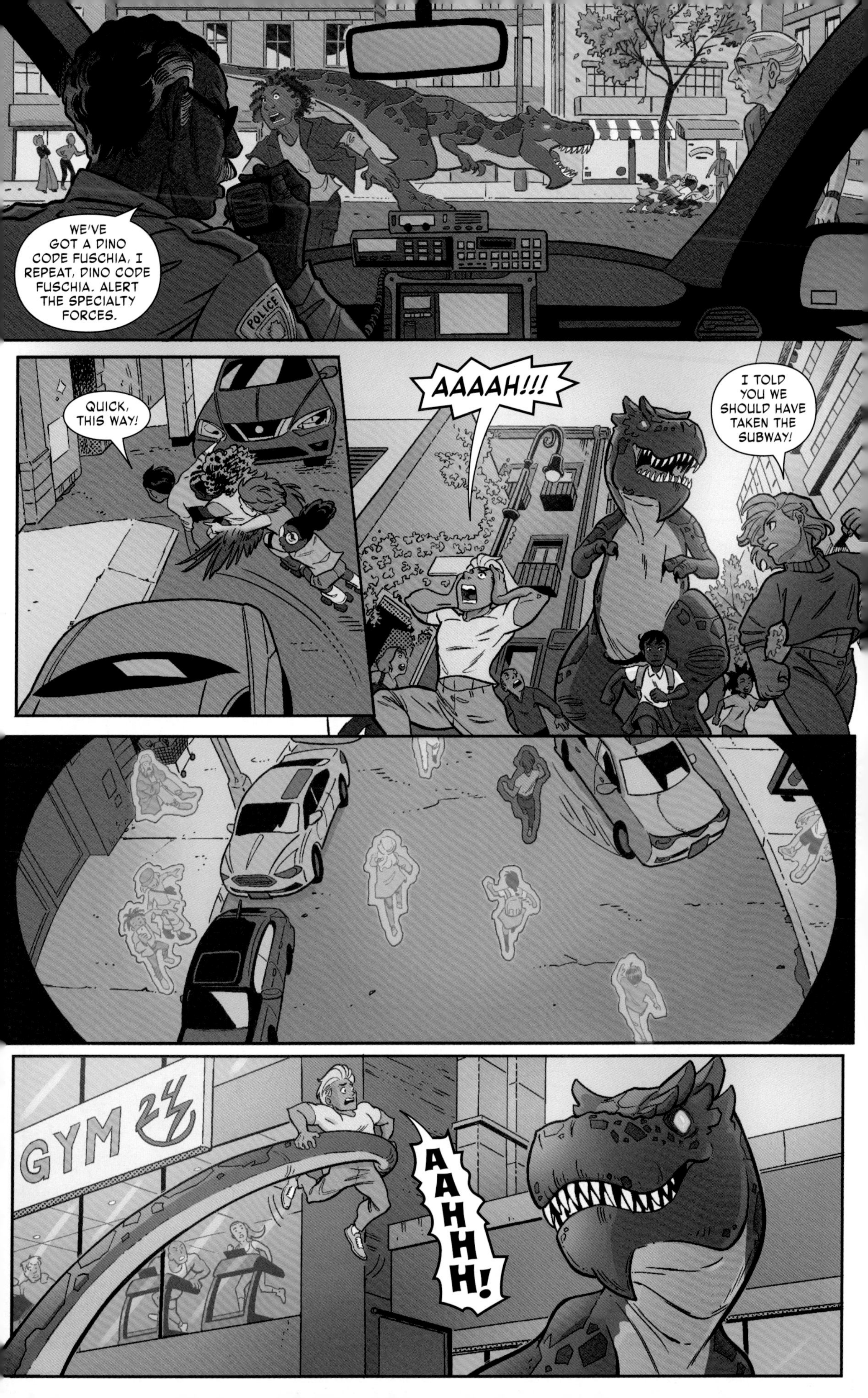
WE'VE GOT A DINO CODE FUSCHIA, I REPEAT, DINO CODE FUSCHIA. ALERT THE SPECIALTY FORCES.
QUICK, THIS WAY!
AAAAH!!!
I TOLD YOU WE SHOULD HAVE TAKEN THE SUBWAY!
GYM
AAHHH!

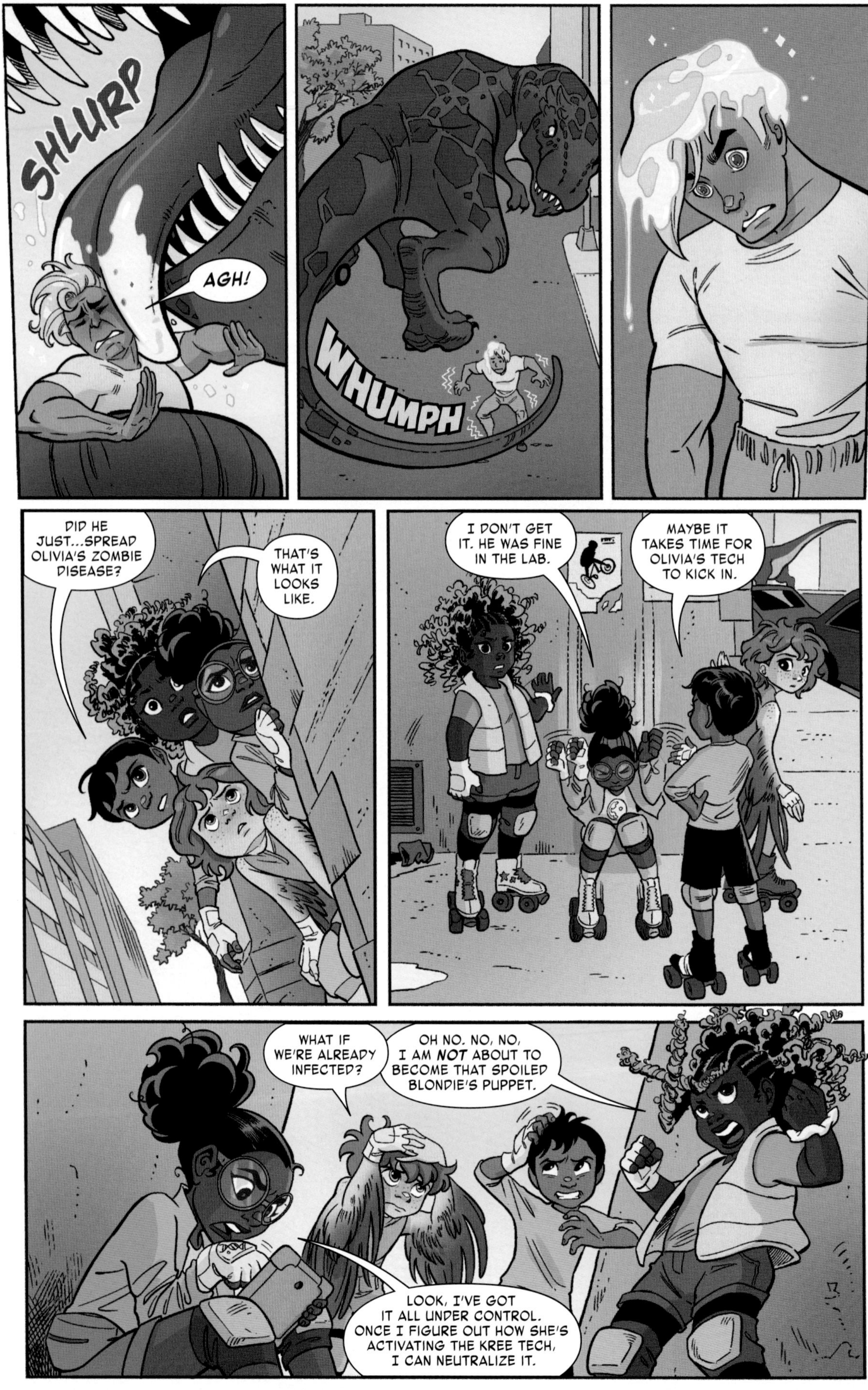
SHLURP
AGH!
WHUMPH
DID HE JUST...SPREAD OLIVIA'S ZOMBIE DISEASE?
THAT'S WHAT IT LOOKS LIKE.
I DON'T GET IT. HE WAS FINE IN THE LAB.
MAYBE IT TAKES TIME FOR OLIVIA'S TECH TO KICK IN.
WHAT IF WE'RE ALREADY INFECTED?
OH NO. NO, NO, I AM **NOT** ABOUT TO BECOME THAT SPOILED BLONDIE'S PUPPET.
LOOK, I'VE GOT IT ALL UNDER CONTROL. ONCE I FIGURE OUT HOW SHE'S ACTIVATING THE KREE TECH, I CAN NEUTRALIZE IT.

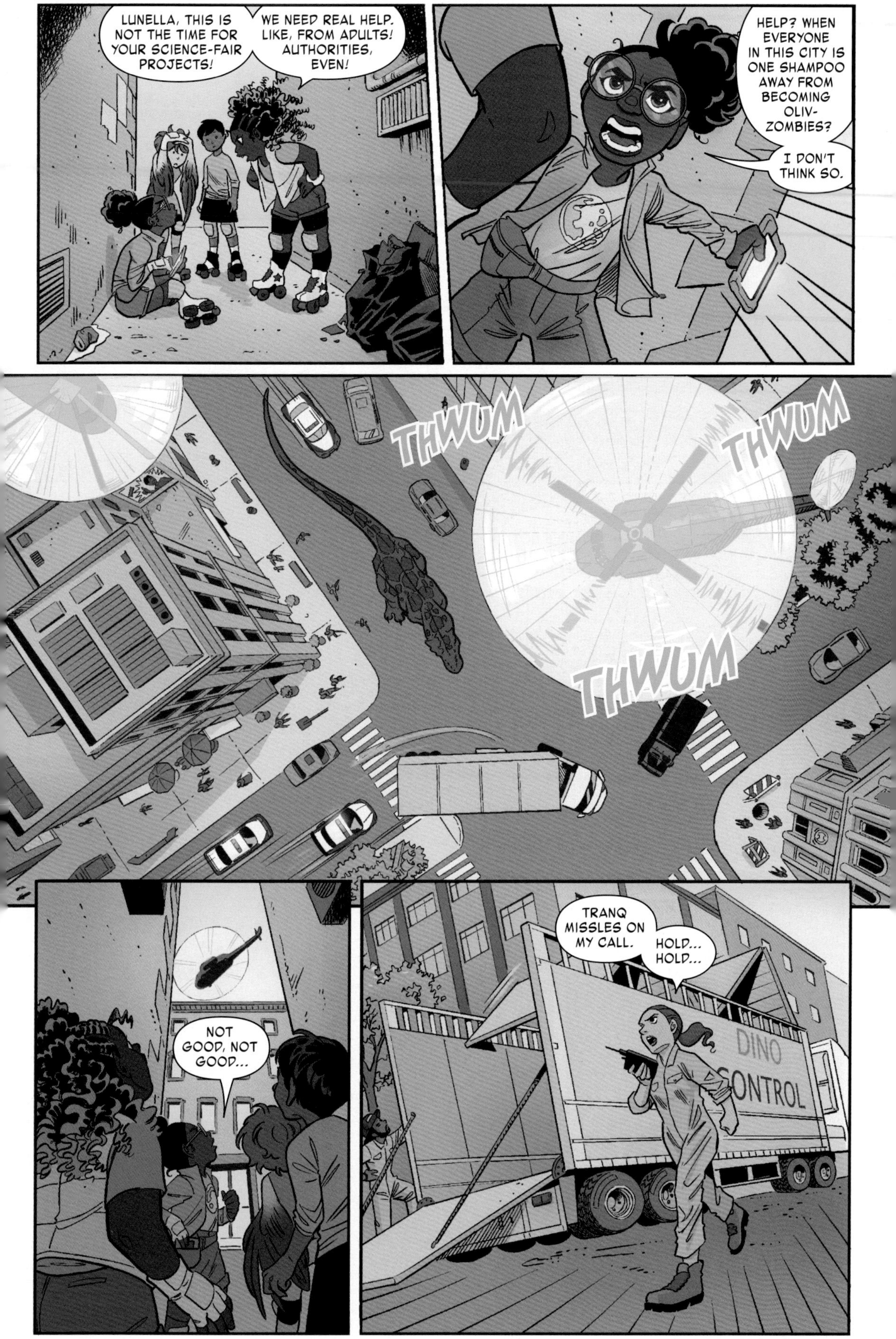
LUNELLA, THIS IS NOT THE TIME FOR YOUR SCIENCE-FAIR PROJECTS!
WE NEED REAL HELP. LIKE, FROM ADULTS! AUTHORITIES, EVEN!
HELP? WHEN EVERYONE IN THIS CITY IS ONE SHAMPOO AWAY FROM BECOMING OLIV-ZOMBIES?
I DON'T THINK SO.
THWUM
THWUM
THWUM
NOT GOOD, NOT GOOD...
TRANQ MISSLES ON MY CALL.
HOLD... HOLD...
DINO CONTROL

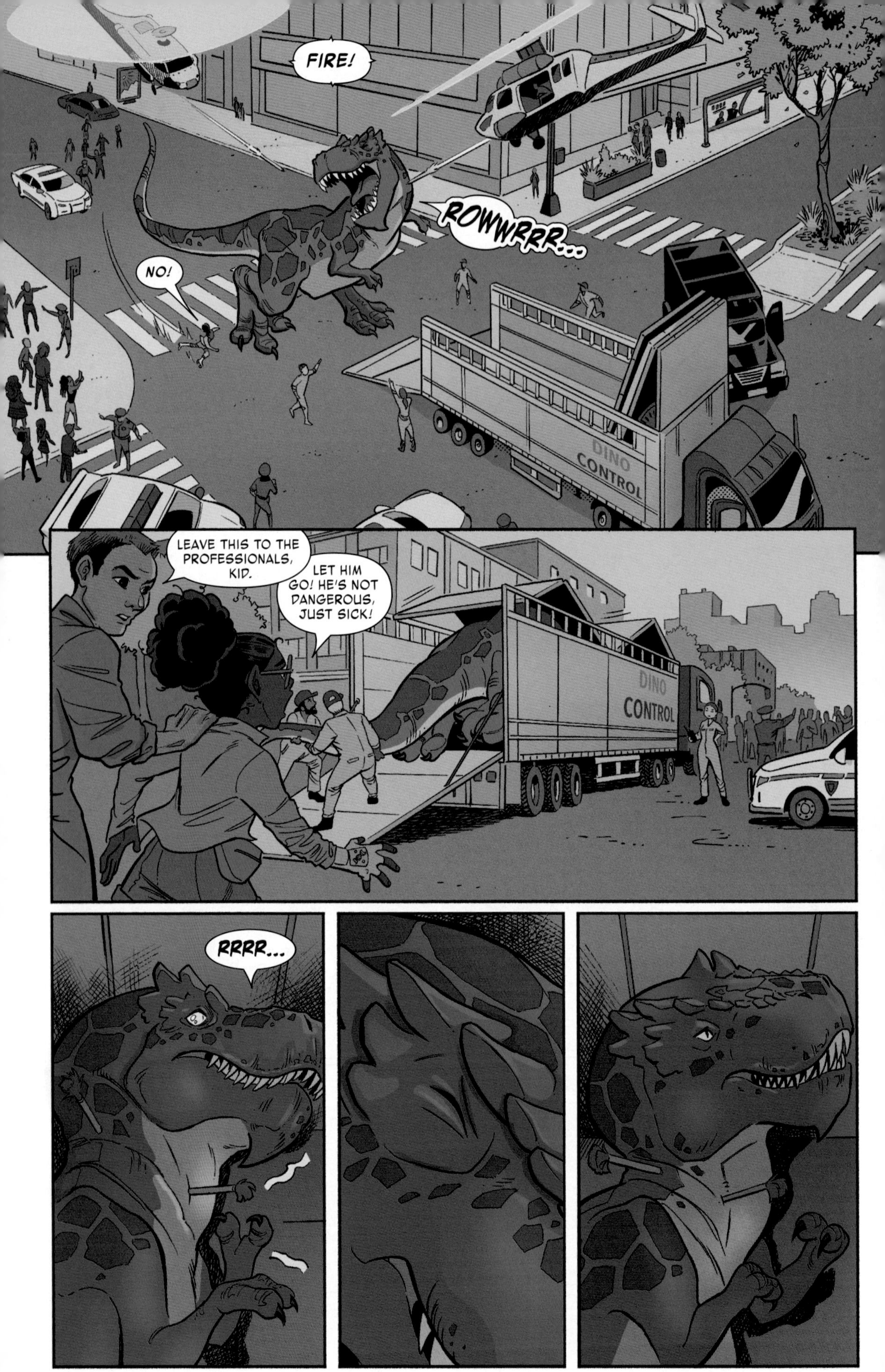
FIRE!
ROWWRRR...
NO!
DINO CONTROL
LEAVE THIS TO THE PROFESSIONALS, KID.
LET HIM GO! HE'S NOT DANGEROUS, JUST SICK!
DINO CONTROL
RRRR...

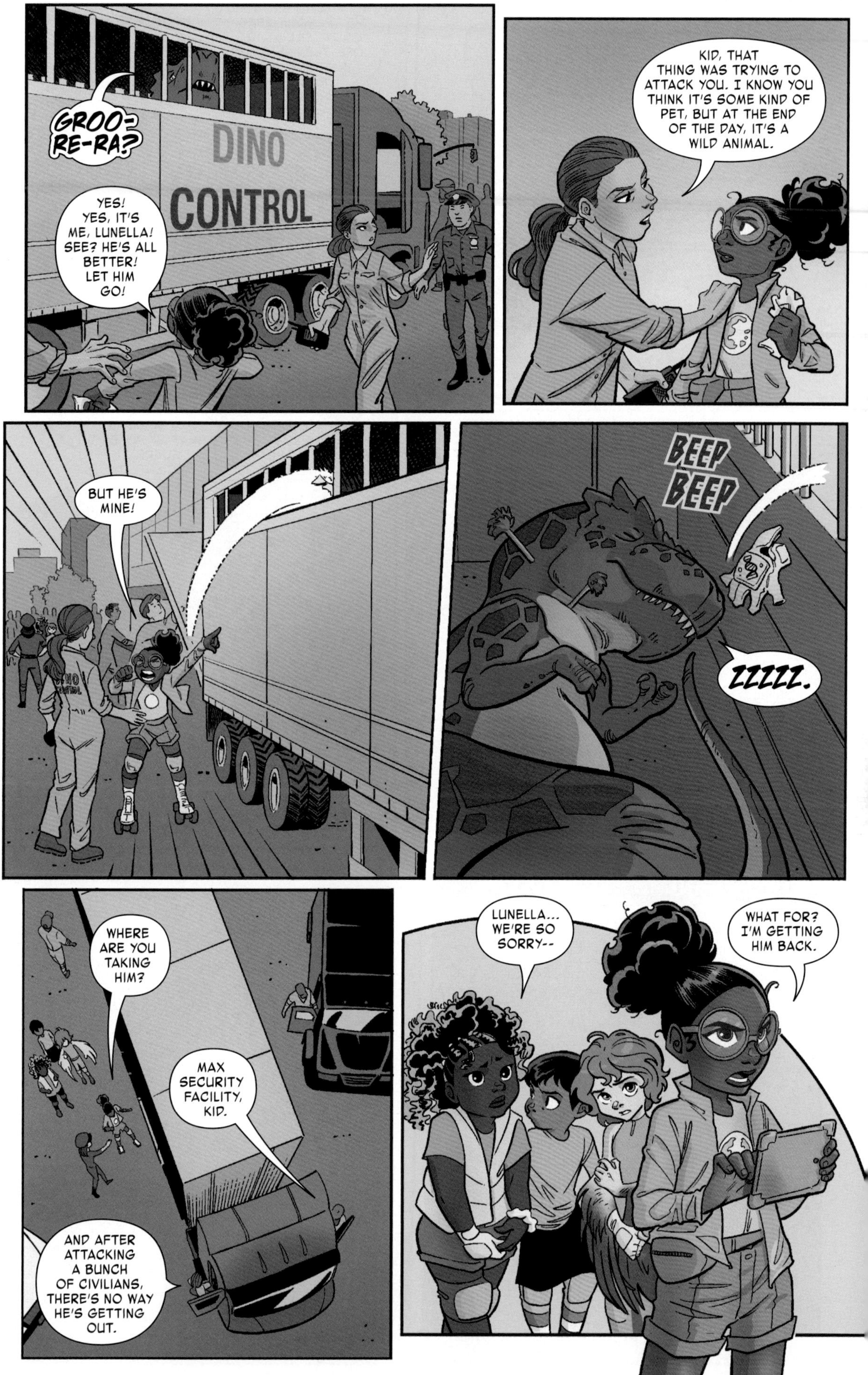
GROO-RE-RA?
DINO CONTROL
YES! YES, IT'S ME, LUNELLA! SEE? HE'S ALL BETTER! LET HIM GO!
KID, THAT THING WAS TRYING TO ATTACK YOU. I KNOW YOU THINK IT'S SOME KIND OF PET, BUT AT THE END OF THE DAY, IT'S A WILD ANIMAL.
BUT HE'S MINE!
BEEP BEEP
ZZZZZ.
WHERE ARE YOU TAKING HIM?
MAX SECURITY FACILITY, KID.
AND AFTER ATTACKING A BUNCH OF CIVILIANS, THERE'S NO WAY HE'S GETTING OUT.
LUNELLA... WE'RE SO SORRY--
WHAT FOR? I'M GETTING HIM BACK.

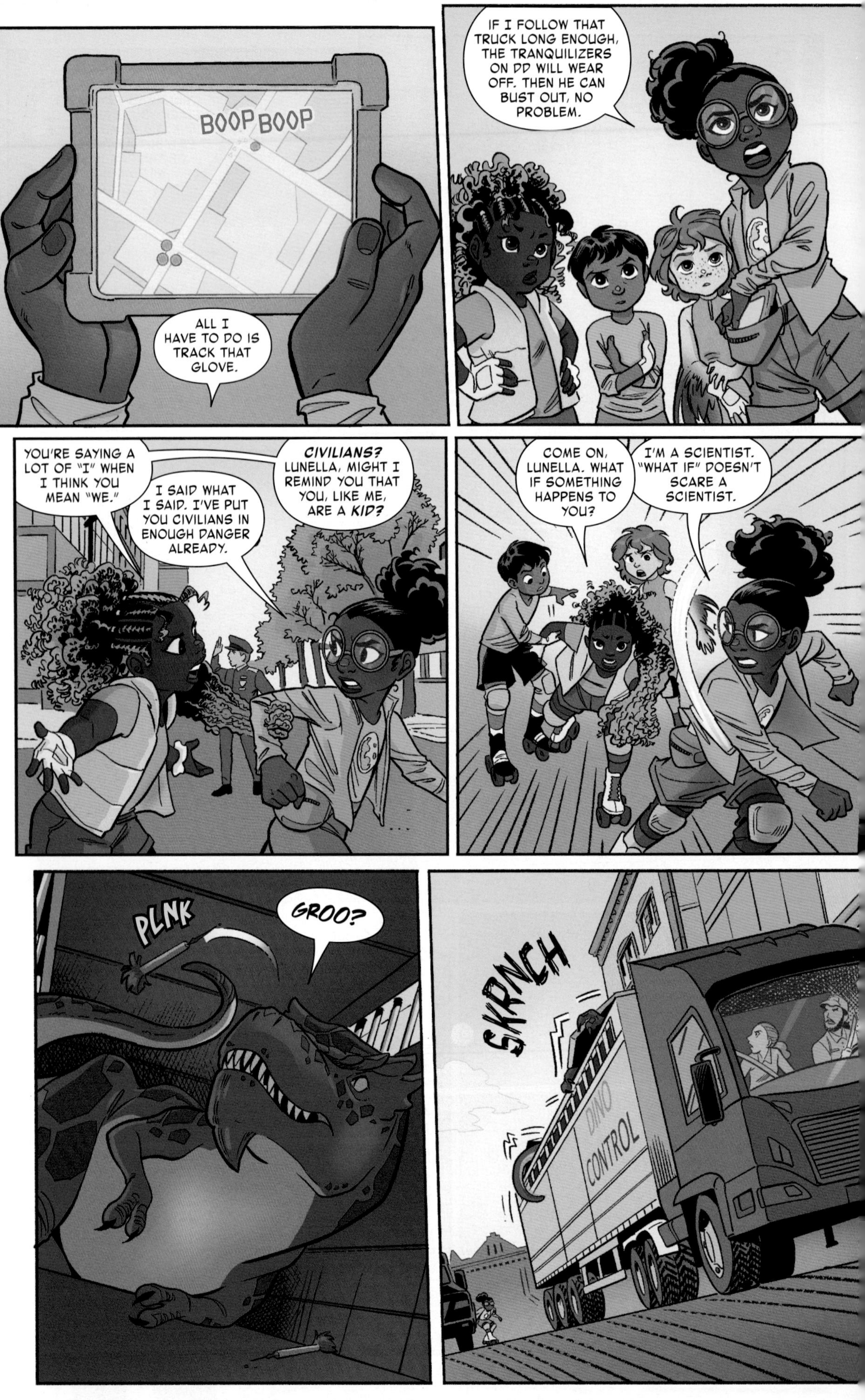
BOOP BOOP
ALL I HAVE TO DO IS TRACK THAT GLOVE.
IF I FOLLOW THAT TRUCK LONG ENOUGH, THE TRANQUILIZERS ON DD WILL WEAR OFF. THEN HE CAN BUST OUT, NO PROBLEM.
YOU'RE SAYING A LOT OF "I" WHEN I THINK YOU MEAN "WE."
I SAID WHAT I SAID. I'VE PUT YOU CIVILIANS IN ENOUGH DANGER ALREADY.
CIVILIANS? LUNELLA, MIGHT I REMIND YOU THAT YOU, LIKE ME, ARE A KID?
COME ON, LUNELLA. WHAT IF SOMETHING HAPPENS TO YOU?
I'M A SCIENTIST. "WHAT IF" DOESN'T SCARE A SCIENTIST.
PLNK
GROO?
SKRNCH
DINO CONTROL

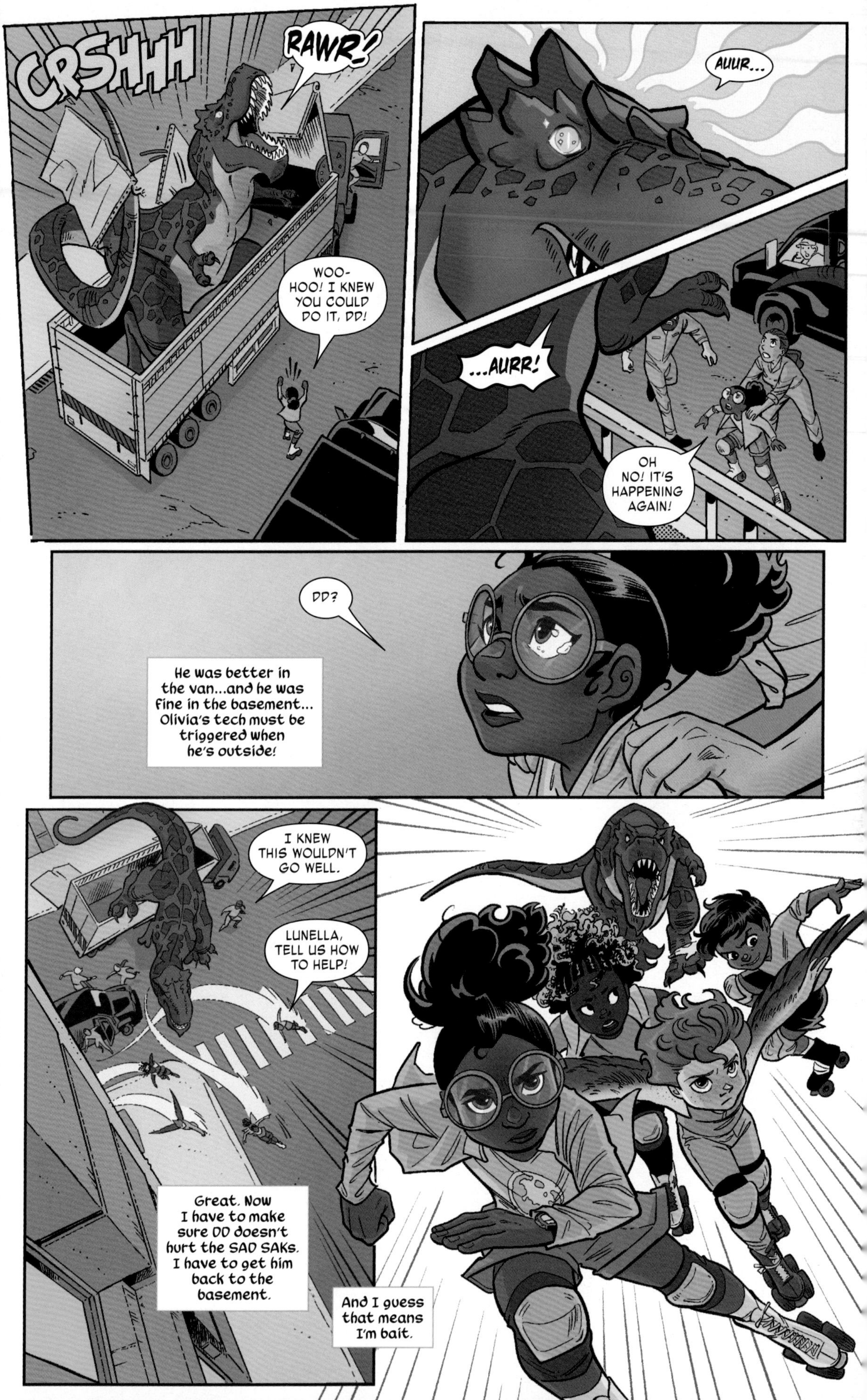
CRSHHH
RAWR!
WOO-HOO! I KNEW YOU COULD DO IT, DD!
AUUR...
...AURR!
OH NO! IT'S HAPPENING AGAIN!
DD?
He was better in the van...and he was fine in the basement... Olivia's tech must be triggered when he's outside!
I KNEW THIS WOULDN'T GO WELL.
LUNELLA, TELL US HOW TO HELP!
Great. Now I have to make sure DD doesn't hurt the SAD SAKS. I have to get him back to the basement.
And I guess that means I'm bait.

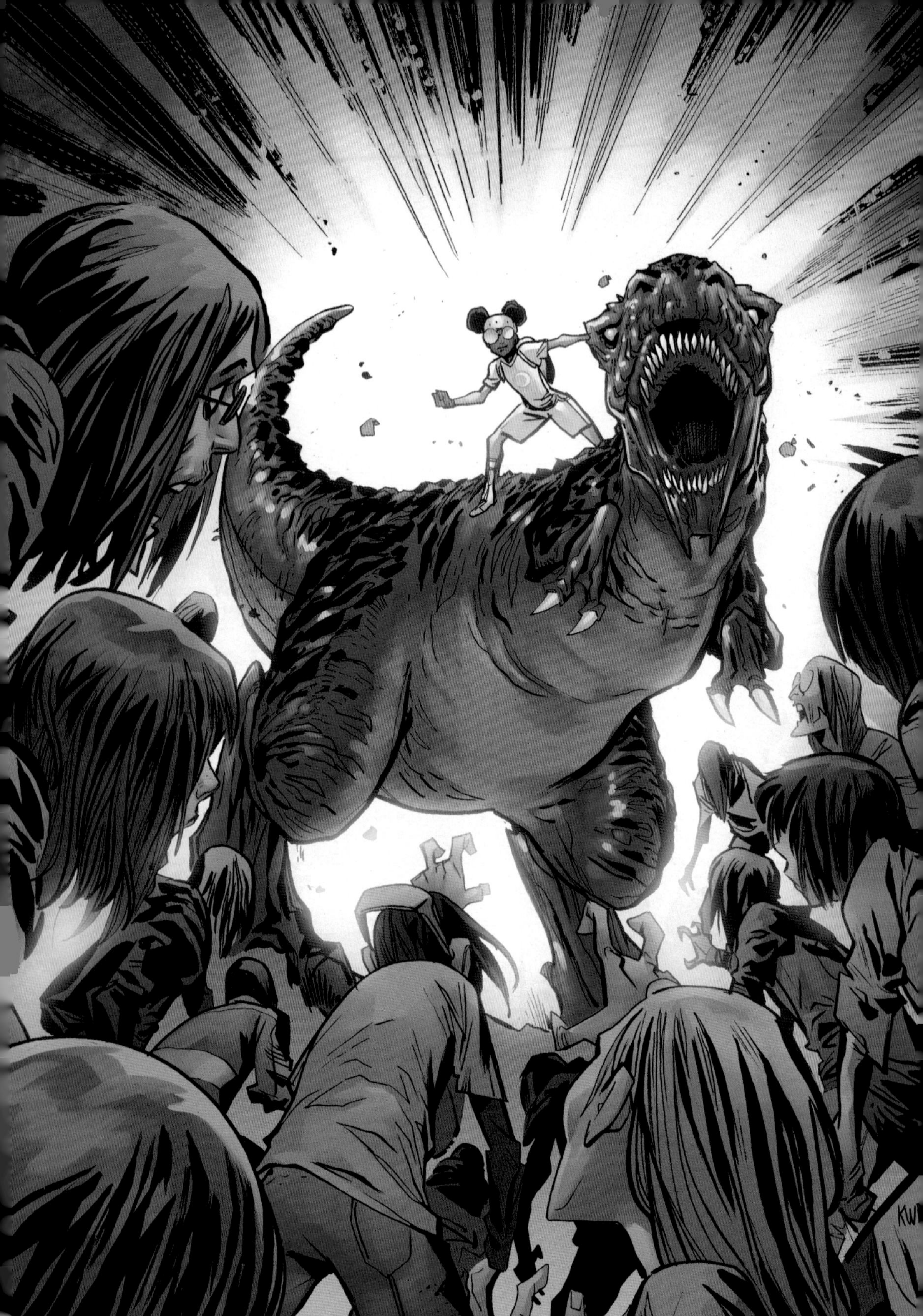

3

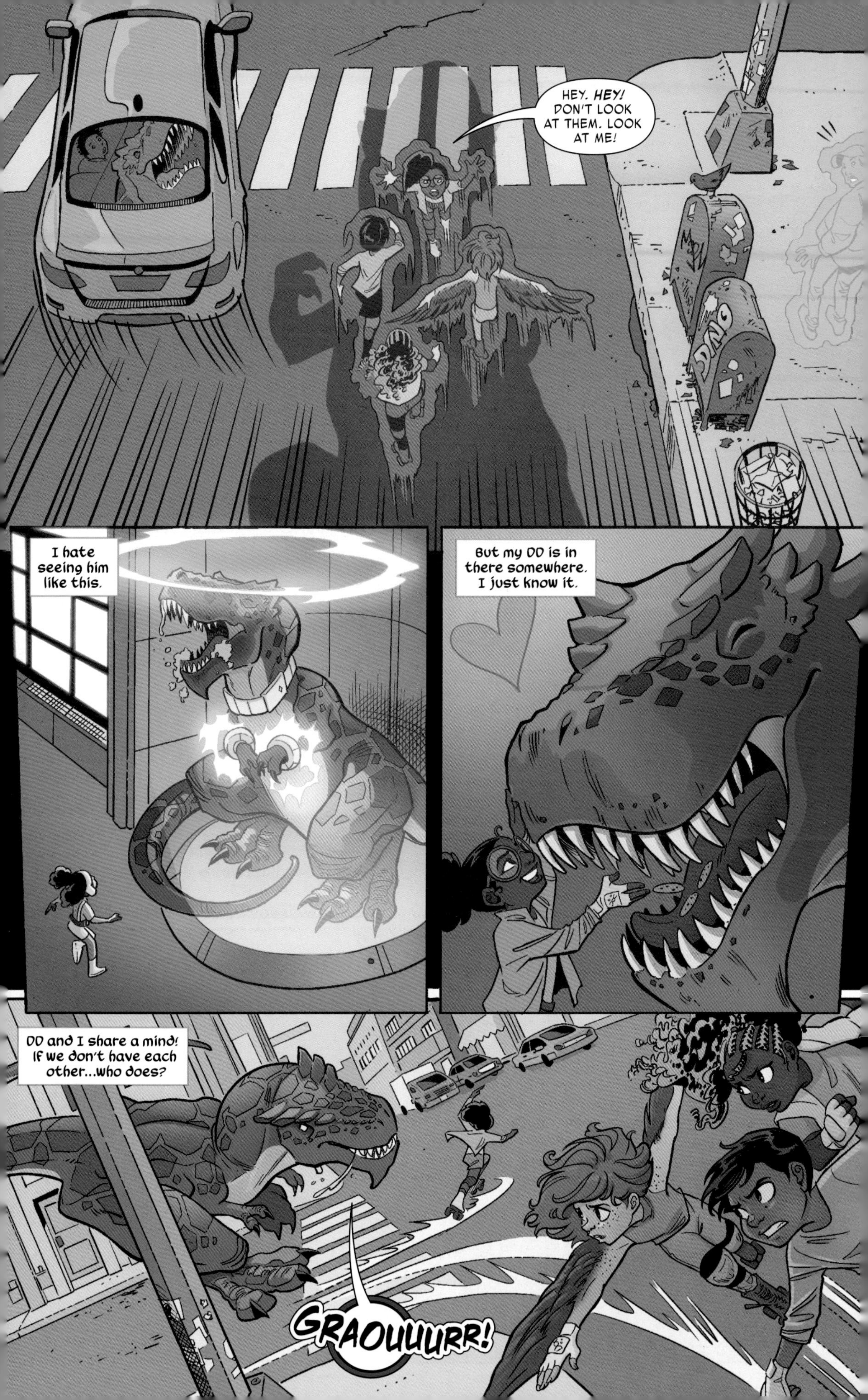
HEY. HEY! DON'T LOOK AT THEM. LOOK AT ME!
DINO
I hate seeing him like this.
But my DD is in there somewhere. I just know it.
DD and I share a mind! If we don't have each other...who does?
GRAOUUUURR!

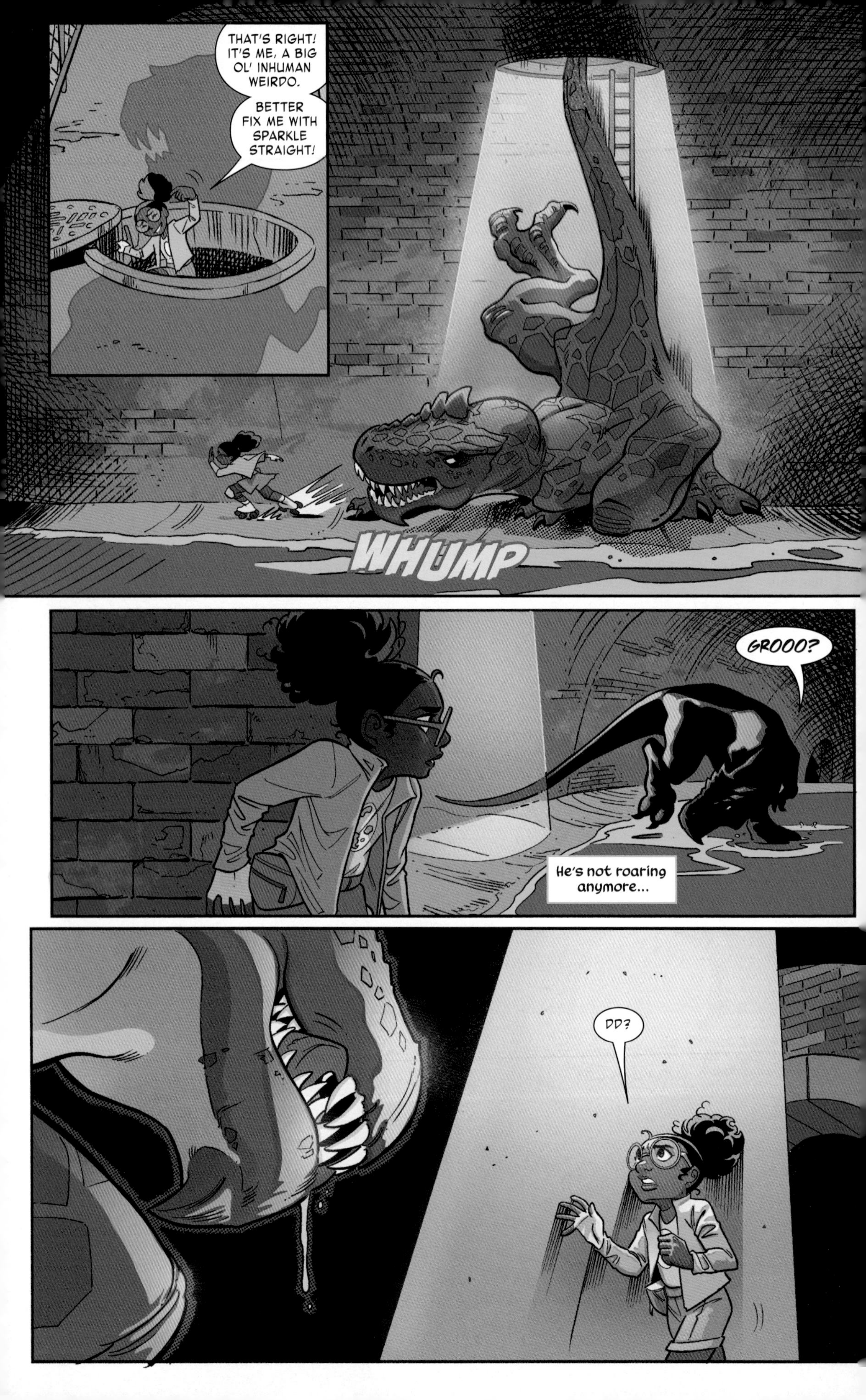
THAT'S RIGHT! IT'S ME, A BIG OL' INHUMAN WEIRDO.
BETTER FIX ME WITH SPARKLE STRAIGHT!
WHUMP
GROOO?
He's not roaring anymore...
DD?

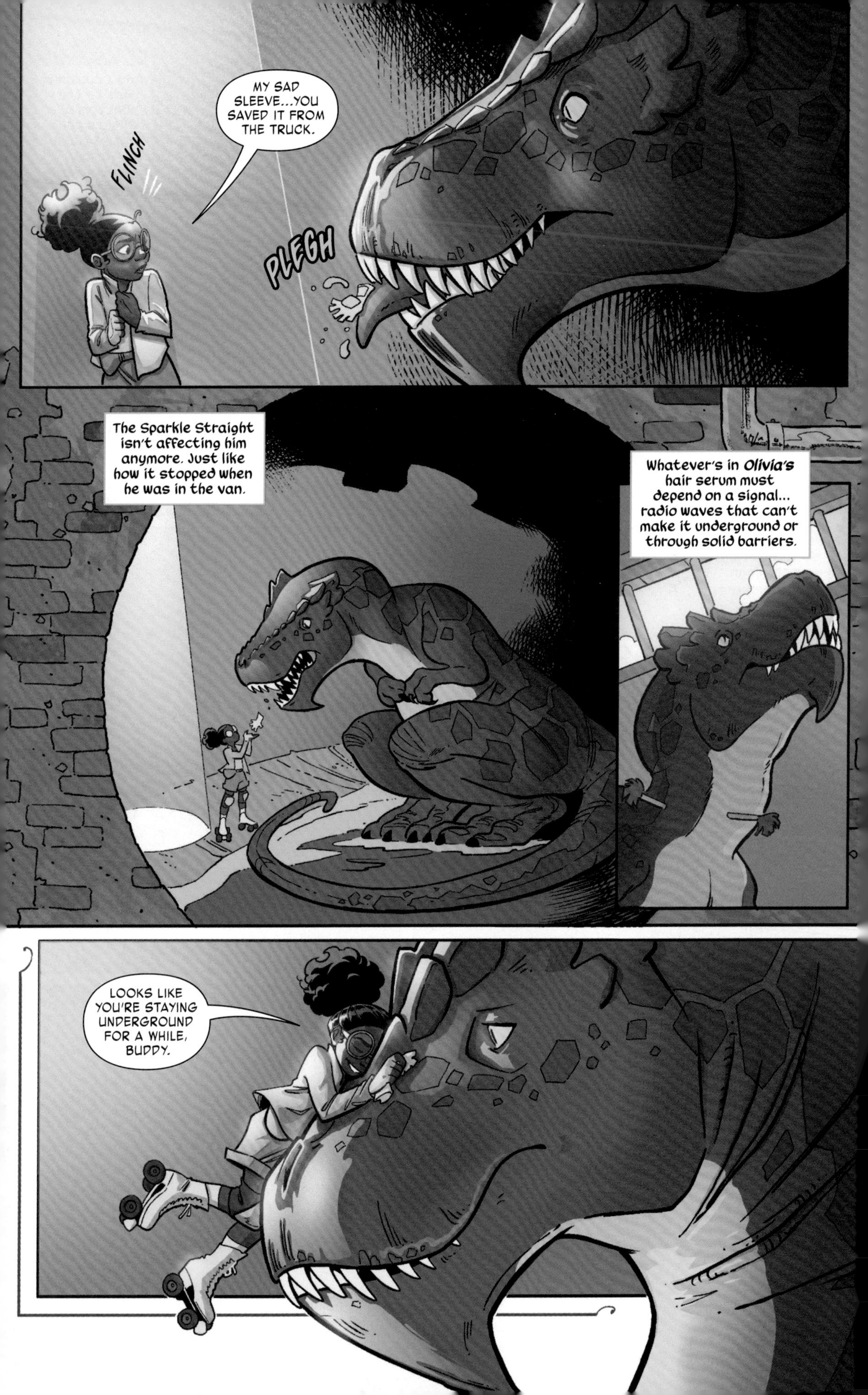
MY SAD SLEEVE...YOU SAVED IT FROM THE TRUCK.
FLINCH
PLEGH
The Sparkle Straight isn't affecting him anymore. Just like how it stopped when he was in the van.
Whatever's in *Olivia's* hair serum must depend on a signal... radio waves that can't make it underground or through solid barriers.
LOOKS LIKE YOU'RE STAYING UNDERGROUND FOR A WHILE, BUDDY.

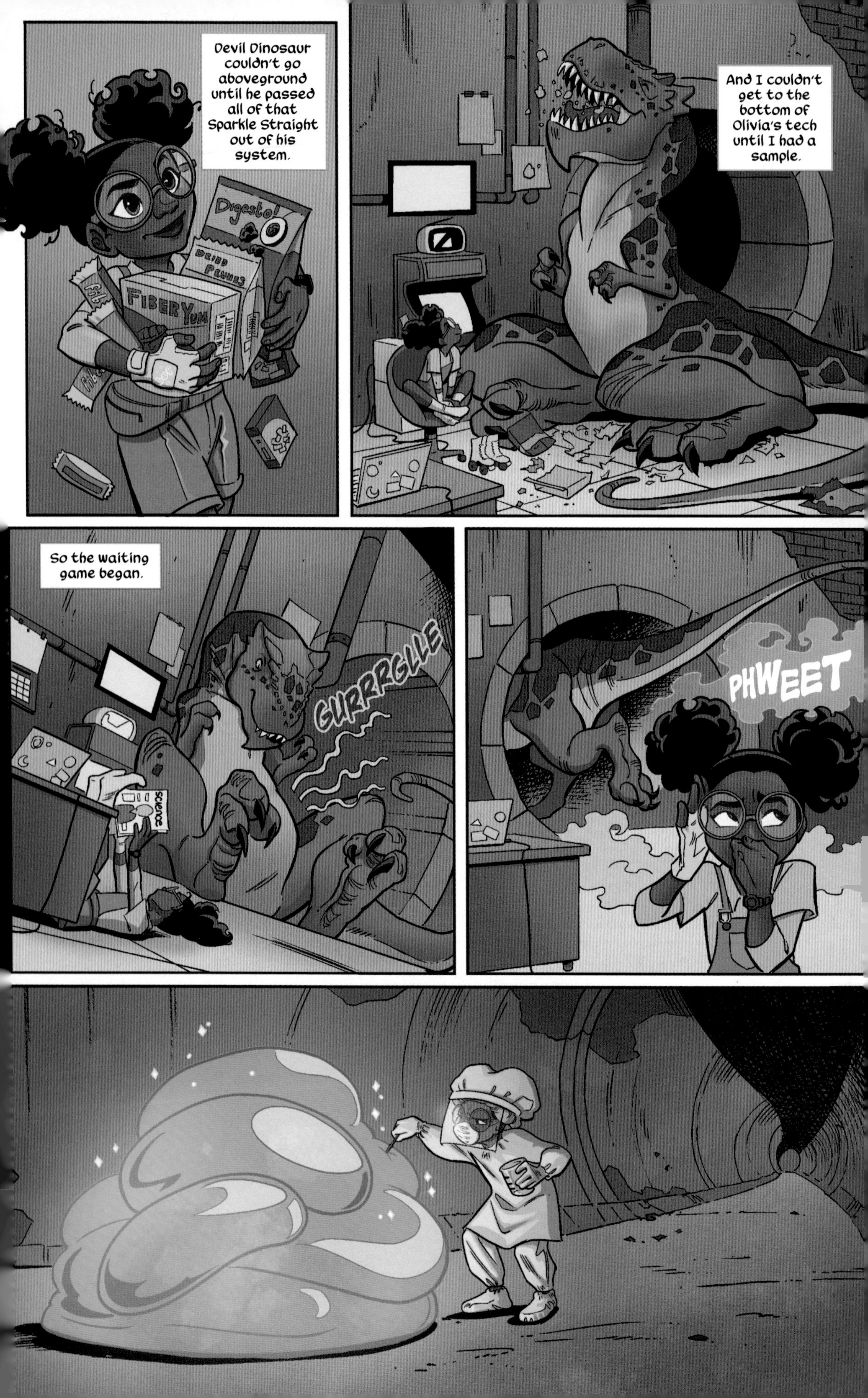
Devil Dinosaur couldn't go aboveground until he passed all of that Sparkle Straight out of his system.
Digesto!
Dried Prunes
FiberYum
And I couldn't get to the bottom of Olivia's tech until I had a sample.
So the waiting game began.
GURRRGLLE
Science
PHWEET

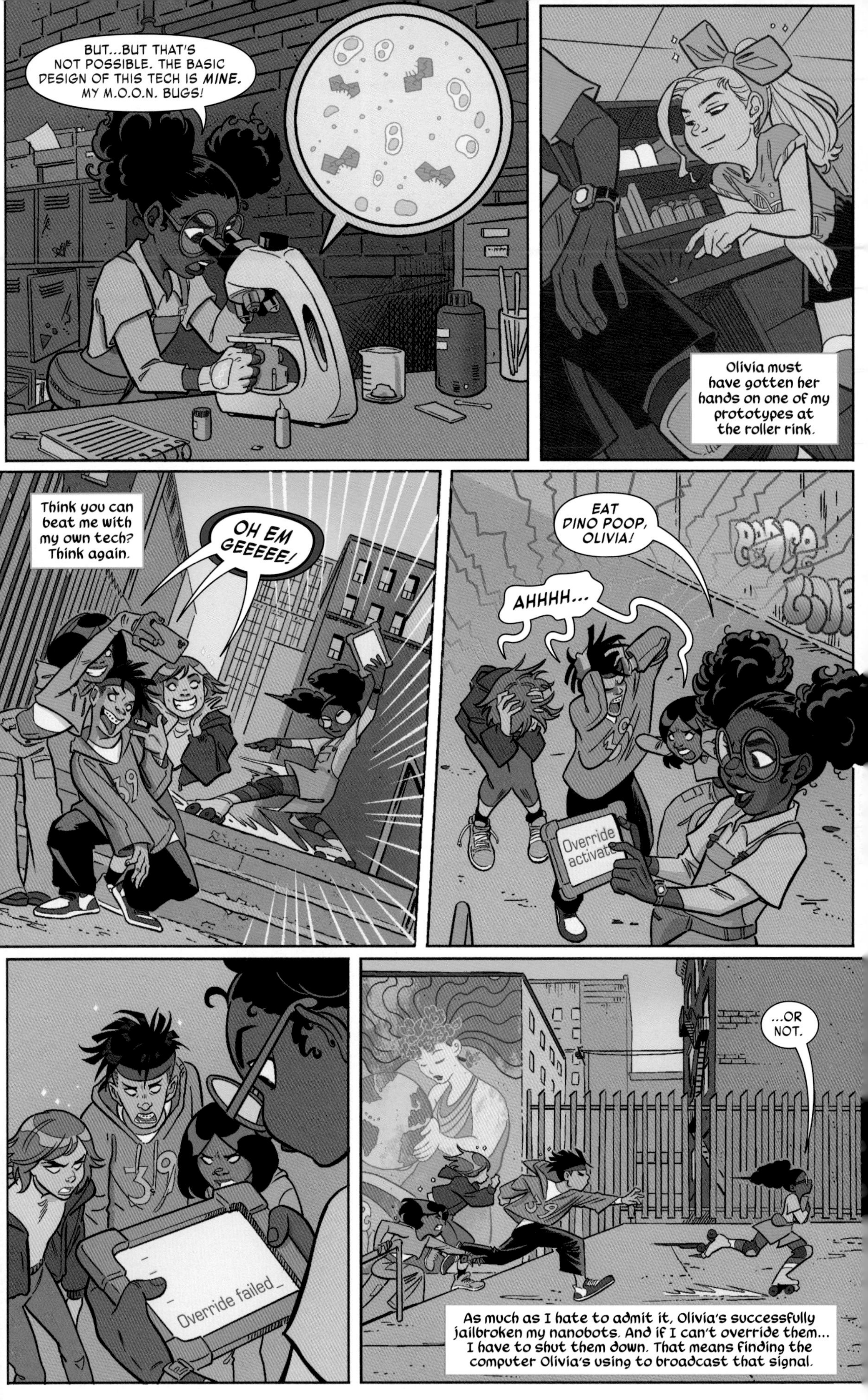
BUT...BUT THAT'S NOT POSSIBLE. THE BASIC DESIGN OF THIS TECH IS *MINE.* MY M.O.O.N. BUGS!
Olivia must have gotten her hands on one of my prototypes at the roller rink.
Think you can beat me with my own tech? Think again.
OH EM GEEEEE!
EAT DINO POOP, OLIVIA!
AHHHH...
Override activate
Override failed_
...OR NOT.
As much as I hate to admit it, Olivia's successfully jailbroken my nanobots. And if I can't override them... I have to shut them down. That means finding the computer Olivia's using to broadcast that signal.

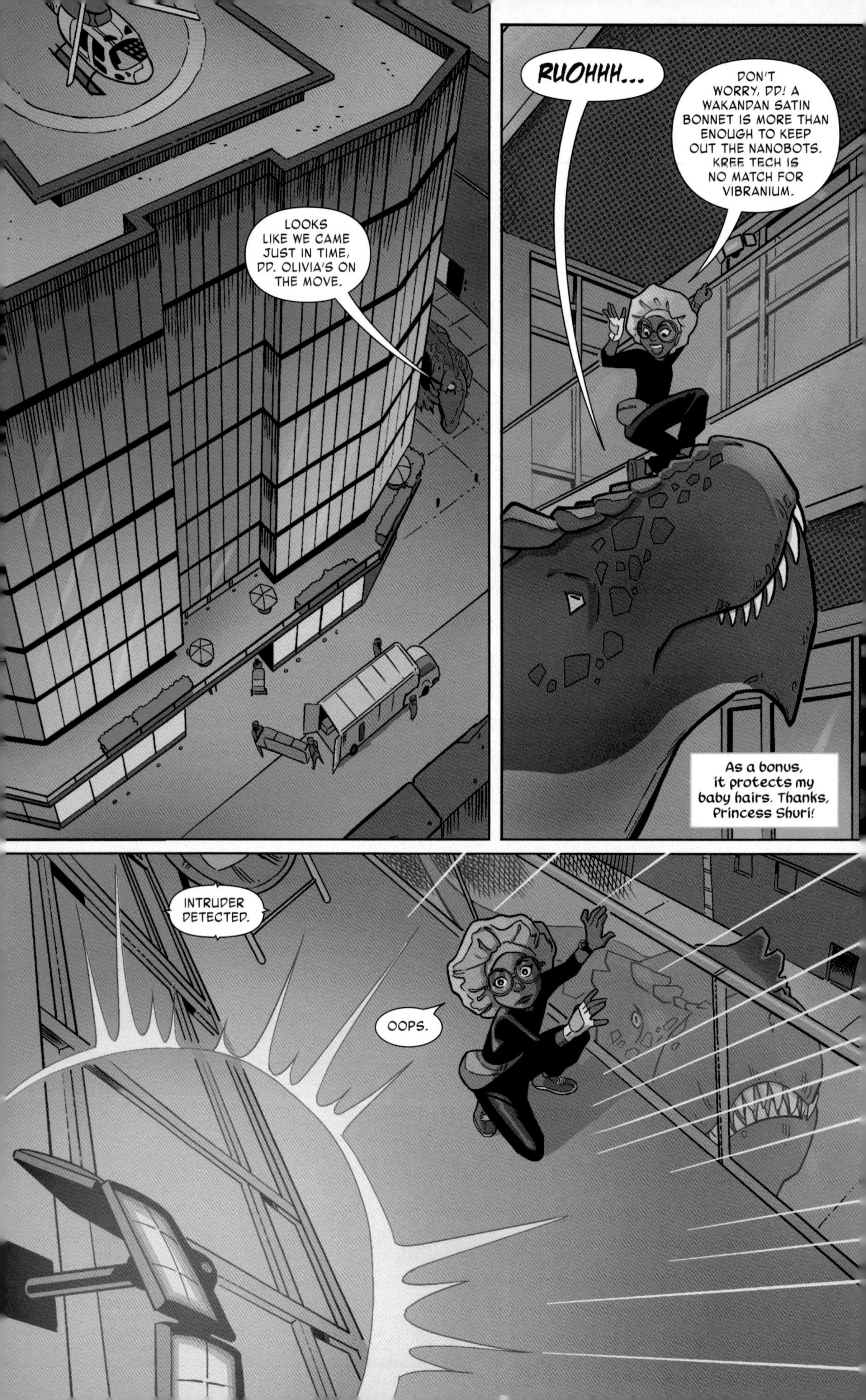
LOOKS LIKE WE CAME JUST IN TIME, DD. OLIVIA'S ON THE MOVE.
RUOHHH...
DON'T WORRY, DD! A WAKANDAN SATIN BONNET IS MORE THAN ENOUGH TO KEEP OUT THE NANOBOTS. KREE TECH IS NO MATCH FOR VIBRANIUM.
As a bonus, it protects my baby hairs. Thanks, Princess Shuri!
INTRUDER DETECTED.
OOPS.

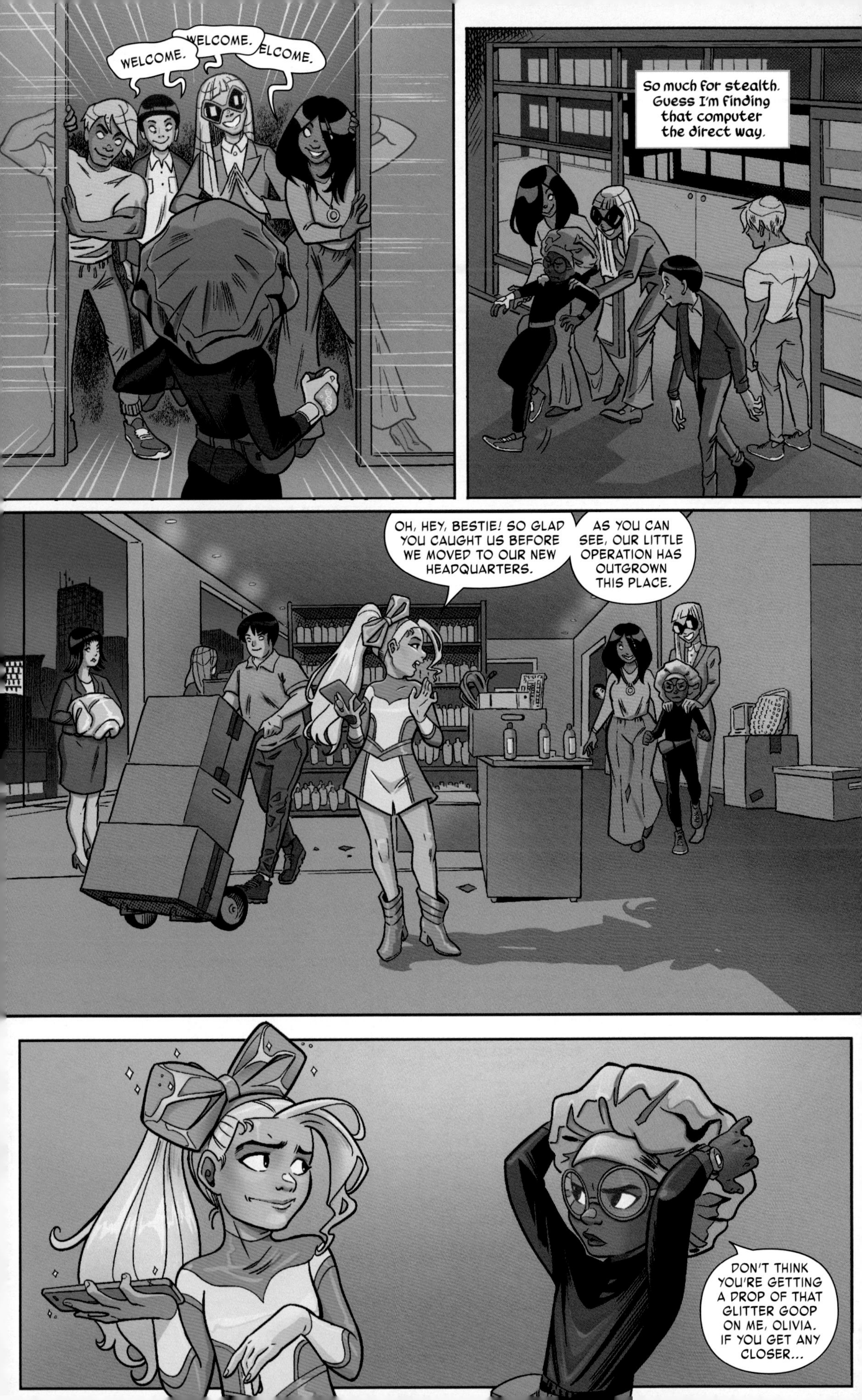
WELCOME.
WELCOME.
WELCOME.
So much for stealth. Guess I'm finding that computer the direct way.
OH, HEY, BESTIE! SO GLAD YOU CAUGHT US BEFORE WE MOVED TO OUR NEW HEADQUARTERS.
AS YOU CAN SEE, OUR LITTLE OPERATION HAS OUTGROWN THIS PLACE.
DON'T THINK YOU'RE GETTING A DROP OF THAT GLITTER GOOP ON ME, OLIVIA. IF YOU GET ANY CLOSER...

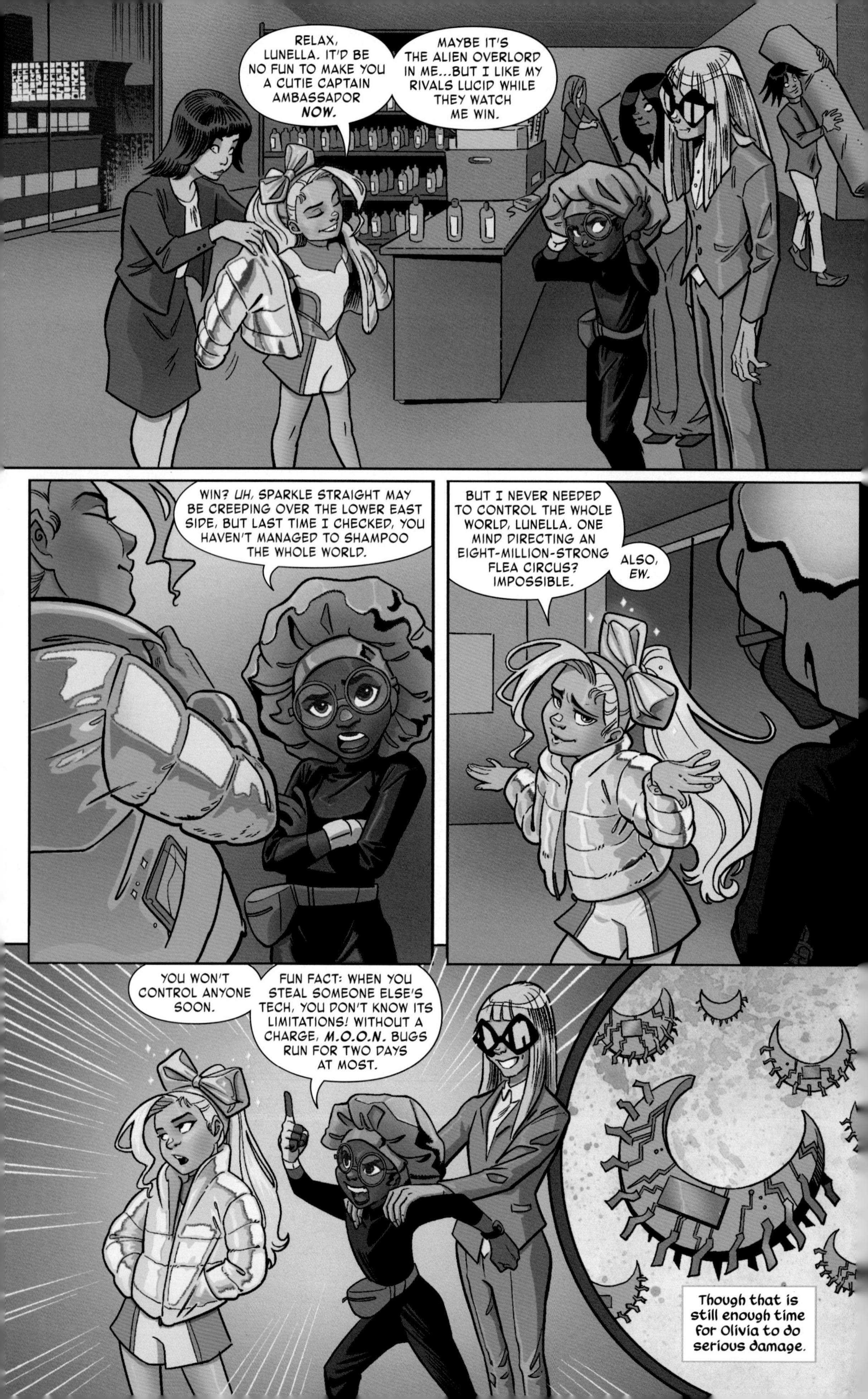
RELAX, LUNELLA. IT'D BE NO FUN TO MAKE YOU A CUTIE CAPTAIN AMBASSADOR *NOW.*
MAYBE IT'S THE ALIEN OVERLORD IN ME...BUT I LIKE MY RIVALS LUCID WHILE THEY WATCH ME WIN.
WIN? *UH,* SPARKLE STRAIGHT MAY BE CREEPING OVER THE LOWER EAST SIDE, BUT LAST TIME I CHECKED, YOU HAVEN'T MANAGED TO SHAMPOO THE WHOLE WORLD.
BUT I NEVER NEEDED TO CONTROL THE WHOLE WORLD, LUNELLA. ONE MIND DIRECTING AN EIGHT-MILLION-STRONG FLEA CIRCUS? IMPOSSIBLE.
ALSO, *EW.*
YOU WON'T CONTROL ANYONE SOON.
FUN FACT: WHEN YOU STEAL SOMEONE ELSE'S TECH, YOU DON'T KNOW ITS LIMITATIONS! WITHOUT A CHARGE, *M.O.O.N.* BUGS RUN FOR TWO DAYS AT MOST.
Though that is still enough time for Olivia to do serious damage.

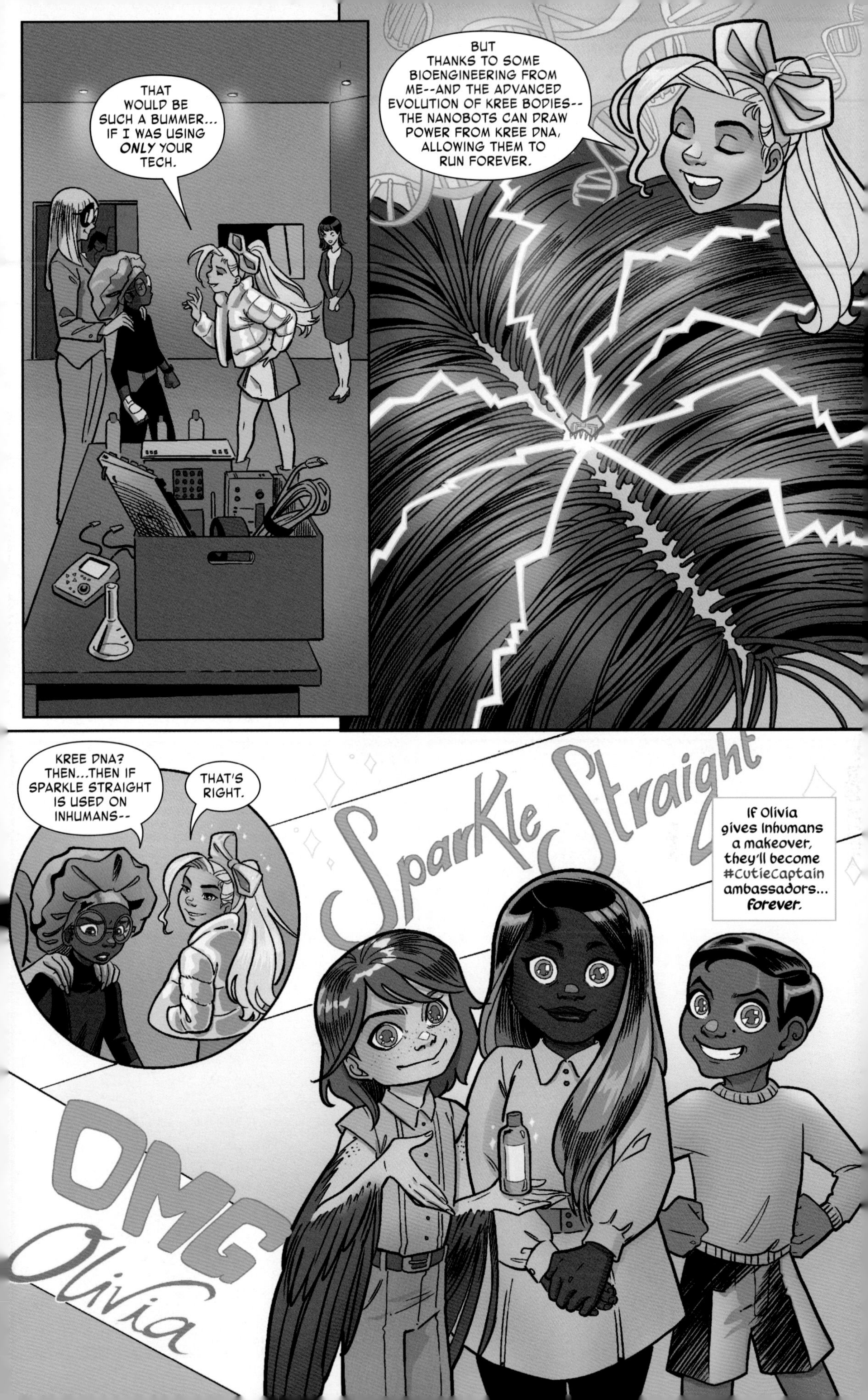

THAT WOULD BE SUCH A BUMMER... IF I WAS USING *ONLY* YOUR TECH.
BUT THANKS TO SOME BIOENGINEERING FROM ME--AND THE ADVANCED EVOLUTION OF KREE BODIES--THE NANOBOTS CAN DRAW POWER FROM KREE DNA, ALLOWING THEM TO RUN FOREVER.
KREE DNA? THEN...THEN IF SPARKLE STRAIGHT IS USED ON INHUMANS--
THAT'S RIGHT.
Sparkle Straight
If Olivia gives Inhumans a makeover, they'll become #CutieCaptain ambassadors... *forever.*
OMG
Olivia

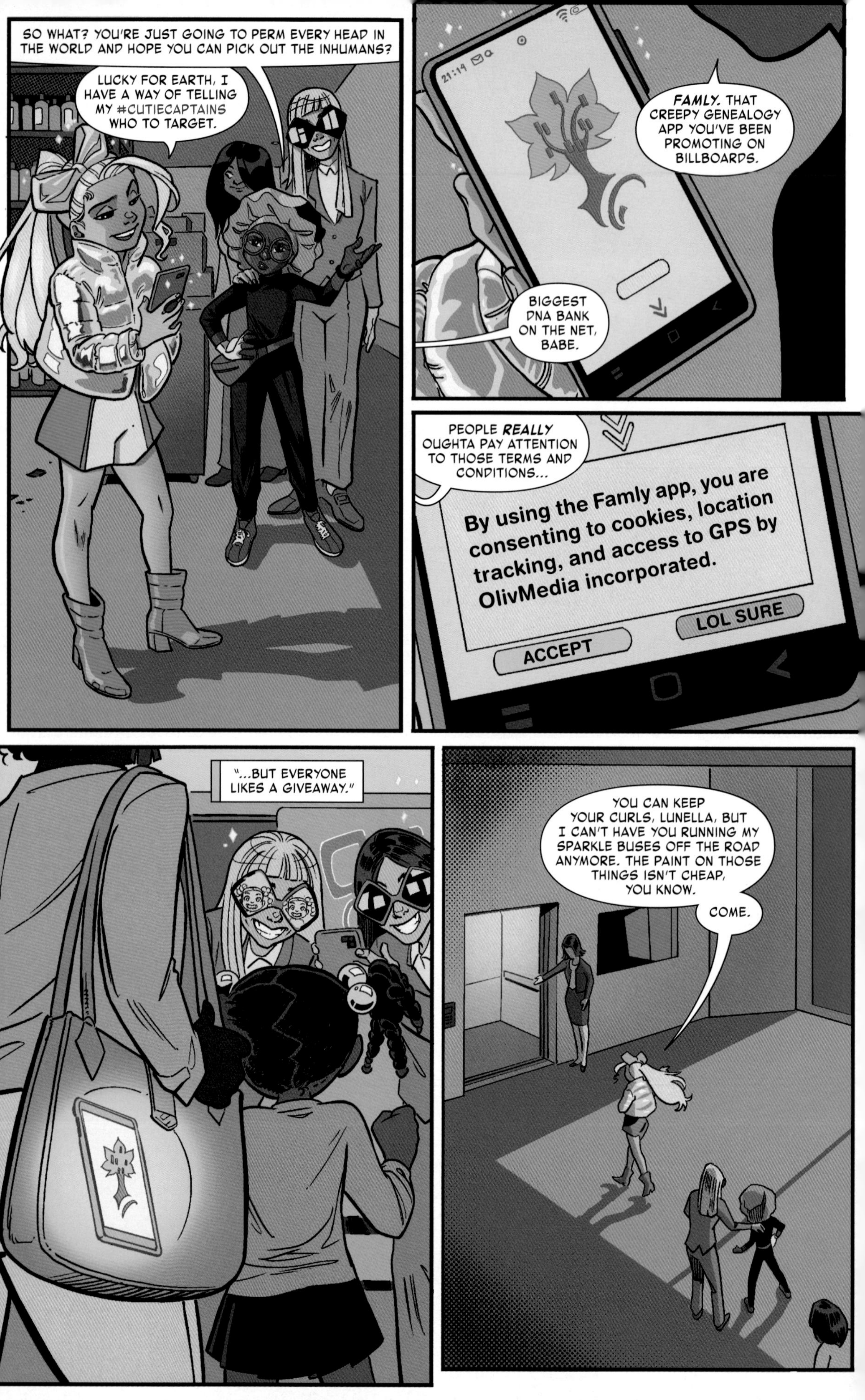
SO WHAT? YOU'RE JUST GOING TO PERM EVERY HEAD IN THE WORLD AND HOPE YOU CAN PICK OUT THE INHUMANS?
LUCKY FOR EARTH, I HAVE A WAY OF TELLING MY #CUTIECAPTAINS WHO TO TARGET.
FAMLY. THAT CREEPY GENEALOGY APP YOU'VE BEEN PROMOTING ON BILLBOARDS.
BIGGEST DNA BANK ON THE NET, BABE.
PEOPLE REALLY OUGHTA PAY ATTENTION TO THOSE TERMS AND CONDITIONS...
By using the Famly app, you are consenting to cookies, location tracking, and access to GPS by OlivMedia incorporated.
ACCEPT
LOL SURE
"...BUT EVERYONE LIKES A GIVEAWAY."
YOU CAN KEEP YOUR CURLS, LUNELLA, BUT I CAN'T HAVE YOU RUNNING MY SPARKLE BUSES OFF THE ROAD ANYMORE. THE PAINT ON THOSE THINGS ISN'T CHEAP, YOU KNOW.
COME.

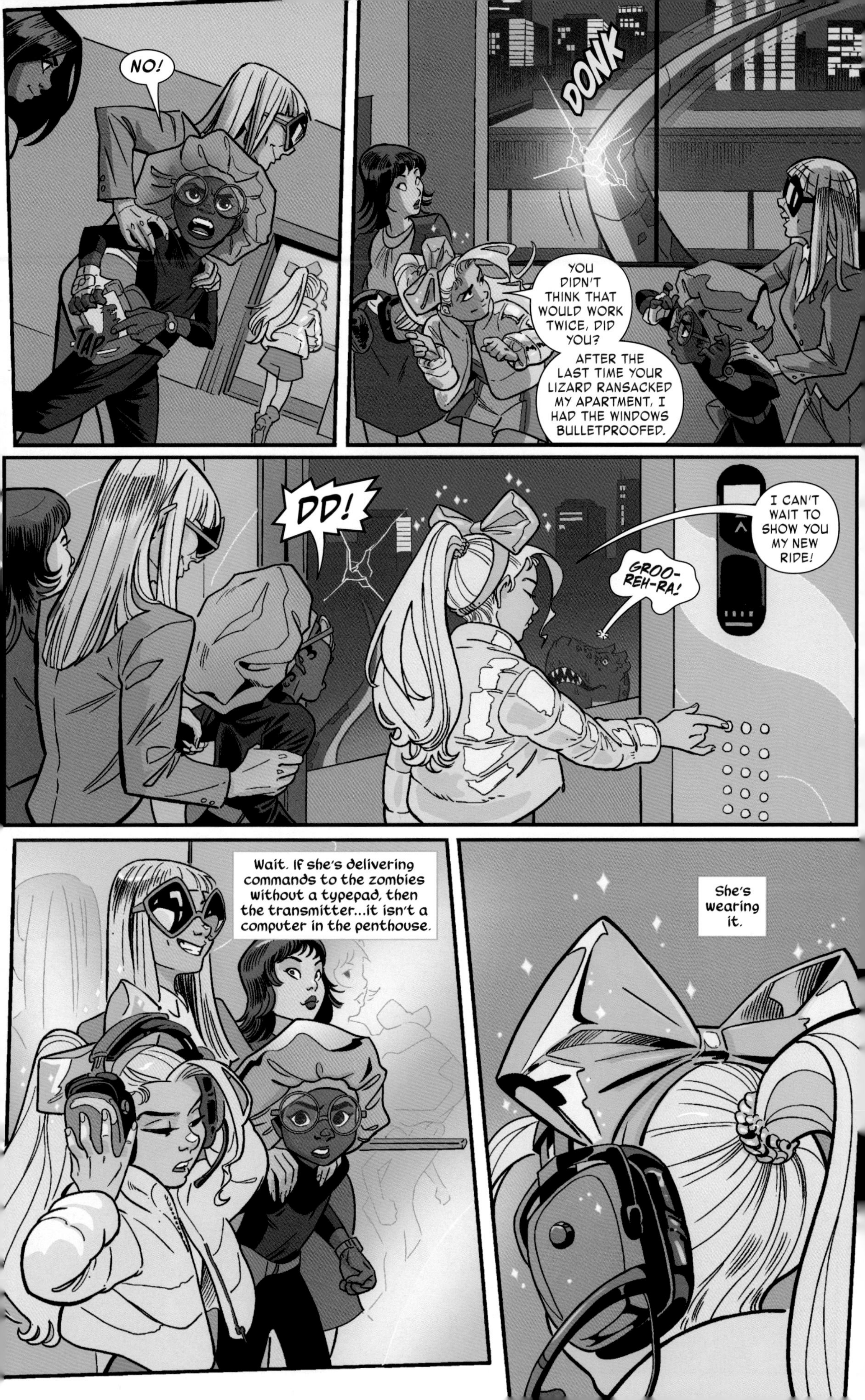
NO!
TAP
DONK
YOU DIDN'T THINK THAT WOULD WORK TWICE, DID YOU?
AFTER THE LAST TIME YOUR LIZARD RANSACKED MY APARTMENT, I HAD THE WINDOWS BULLETPROOFED.
DD!
I CAN'T WAIT TO SHOW YOU MY NEW RIDE!
GROO-REH-RA!
Wait. If she's delivering commands to the zombies without a typepad, then the transmitter...it isn't a computer in the penthouse.
She's wearing it.

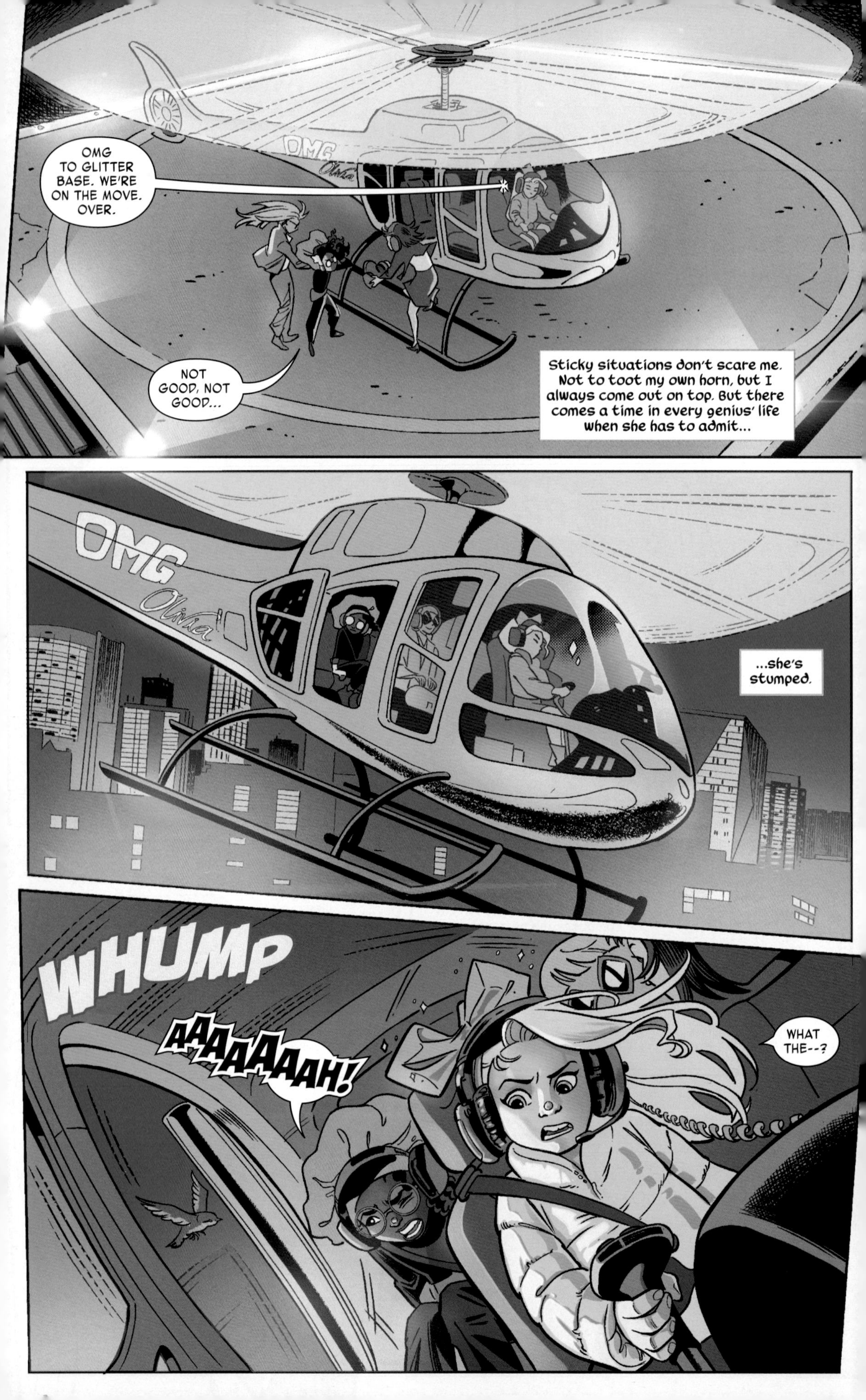
OMG TO GLITTER BASE. WE'RE ON THE MOVE. OVER.
NOT GOOD, NOT GOOD...
Sticky situations don't scare me. Not to toot my own horn, but I always come out on top. But there comes a time in every genius' life when she has to admit...
OMG
Olivia
...she's stumped.
WHUMP
AAAAAAAAH!
WHAT THE--?

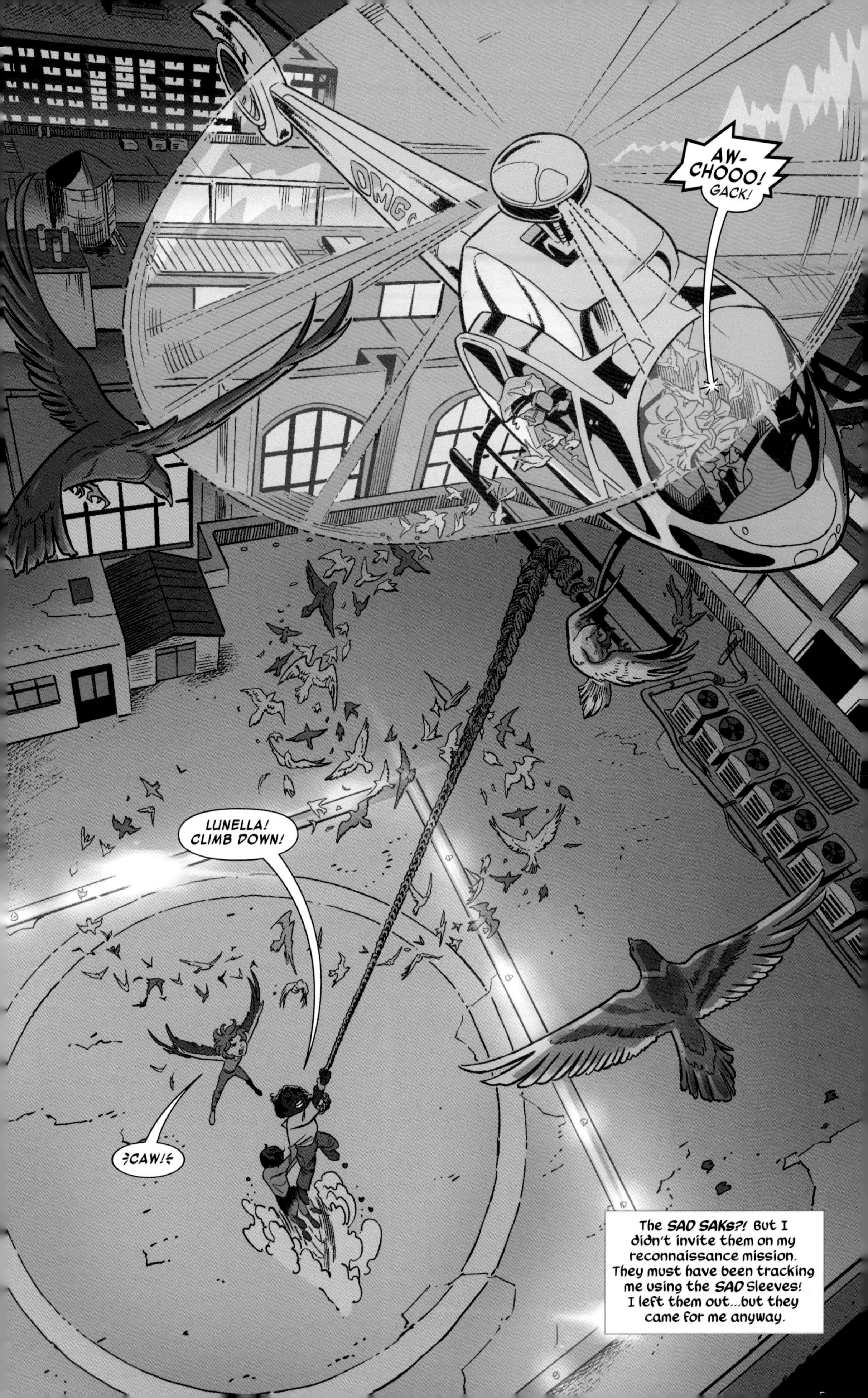
AW-CHOOO! GACK!
LUNELLA! CLIMB DOWN!
CAW!
The SAD SAKs?! But I didn't invite them on my reconnaissance mission. They must have been tracking me using the SAD Sleeves! I left them out...but they came for me anyway.

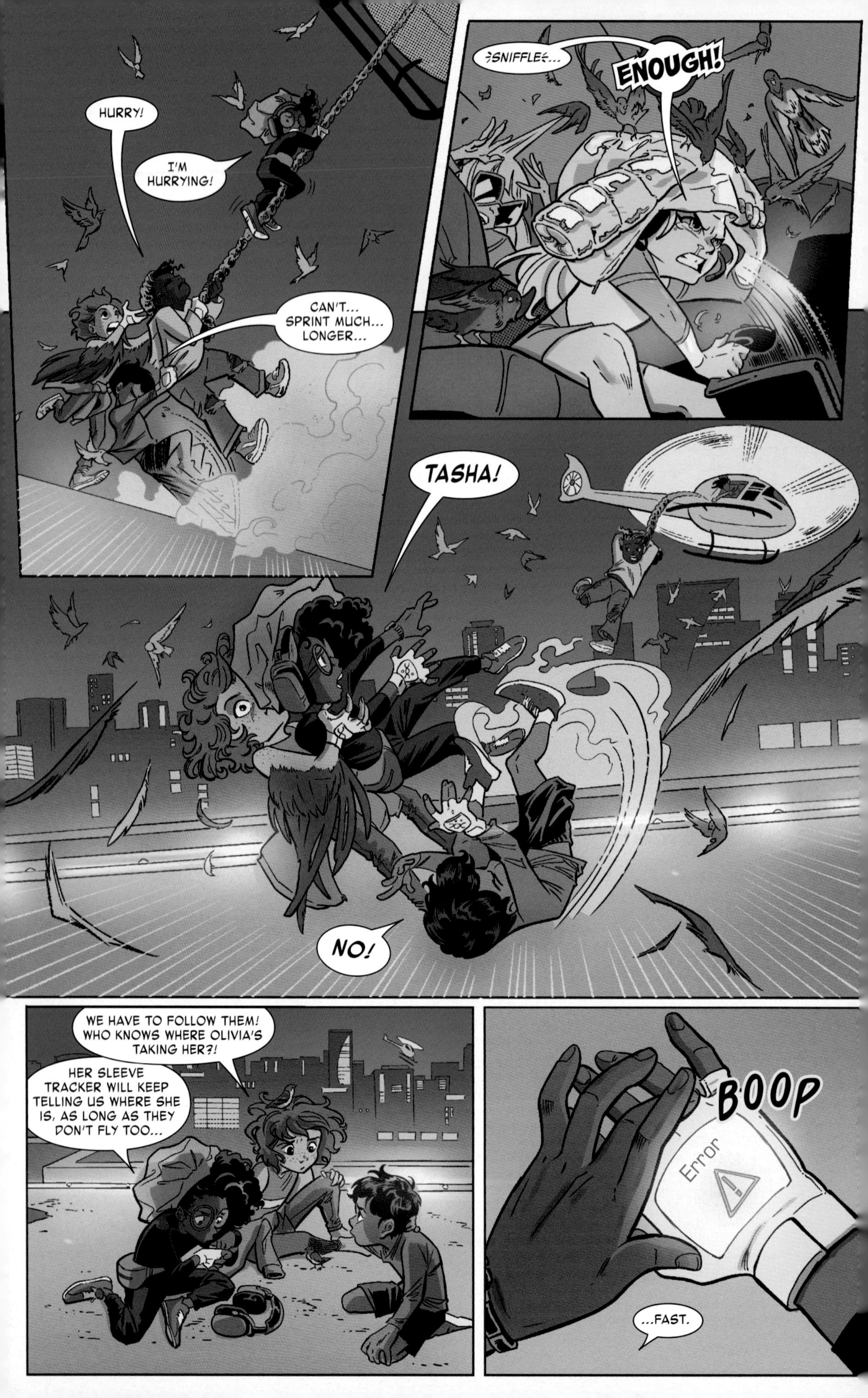

HURRY!
I'M HURRYING!
CAN'T... SPRINT MUCH... LONGER...
SNIFFLE...
ENOUGH!
TASHA!
NO!
WE HAVE TO FOLLOW THEM! WHO KNOWS WHERE OLIVIA'S TAKING HER?!
HER SLEEVE TRACKER WILL KEEP TELLING US WHERE SHE IS, AS LONG AS THEY DON'T FLY TOO...
BOOP
Error
...FAST.

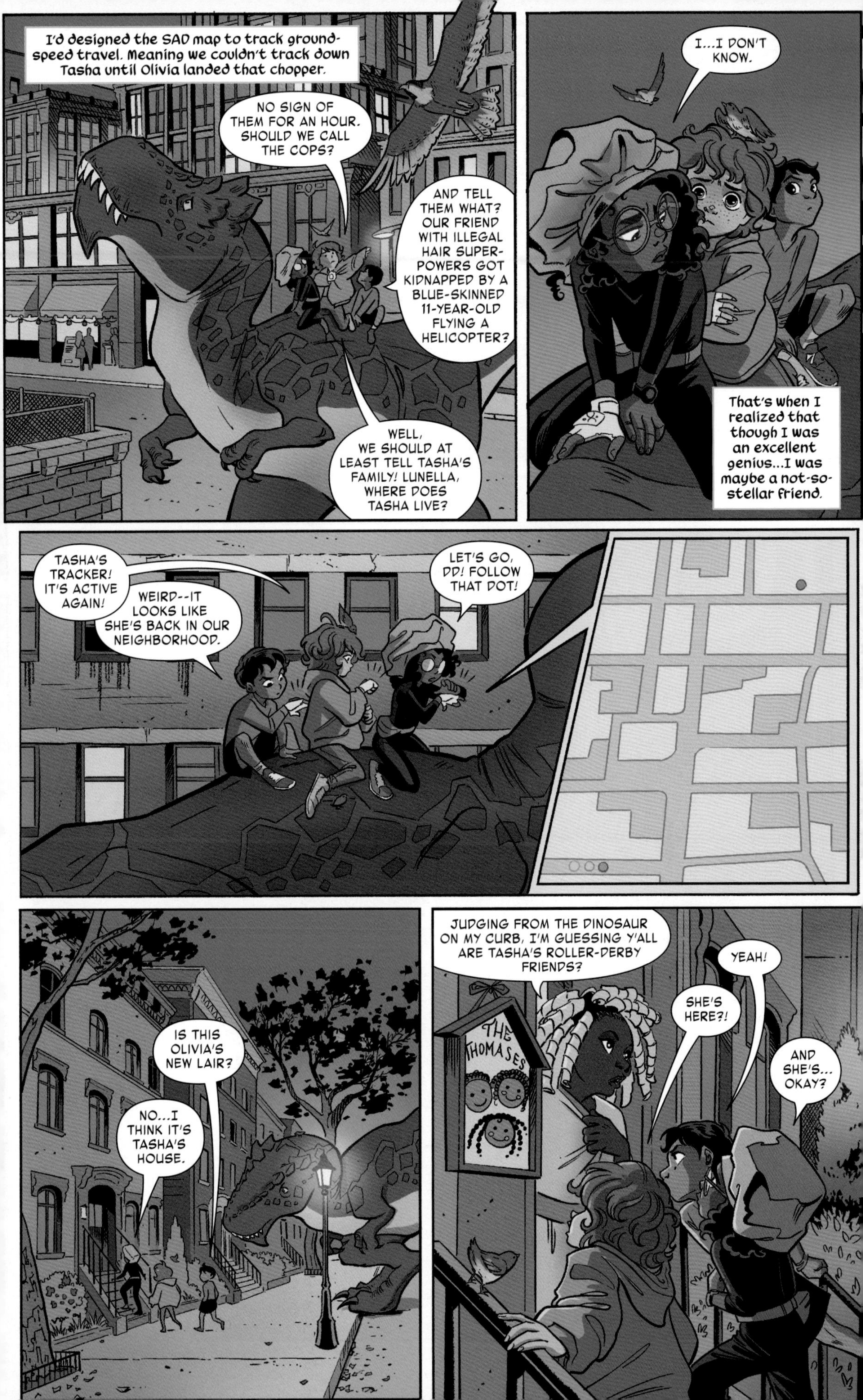

I'd designed the SAD map to track ground-speed travel. Meaning we couldn't track down Tasha until Olivia landed that chopper.
NO SIGN OF THEM FOR AN HOUR. SHOULD WE CALL THE COPS?
AND TELL THEM WHAT? OUR FRIEND WITH ILLEGAL HAIR SUPER-POWERS GOT KIDNAPPED BY A BLUE-SKINNED 11-YEAR-OLD FLYING A HELICOPTER?
WELL, WE SHOULD AT LEAST TELL TASHA'S FAMILY! LUNELLA, WHERE DOES TASHA LIVE?
I...I DON'T KNOW.
That's when I realized that though I was an excellent genius...I was maybe a not-so-stellar friend.
TASHA'S TRACKER! IT'S ACTIVE AGAIN!
WEIRD--IT LOOKS LIKE SHE'S BACK IN OUR NEIGHBORHOOD.
LET'S GO, DD! FOLLOW THAT DOT!
IS THIS OLIVIA'S NEW LAIR?
NO...I THINK IT'S TASHA'S HOUSE.
JUDGING FROM THE DINOSAUR ON MY CURB, I'M GUESSING Y'ALL ARE TASHA'S ROLLER-DERBY FRIENDS?
THE THOMASES
YEAH!
SHE'S HERE?!
AND SHE'S... OKAY?

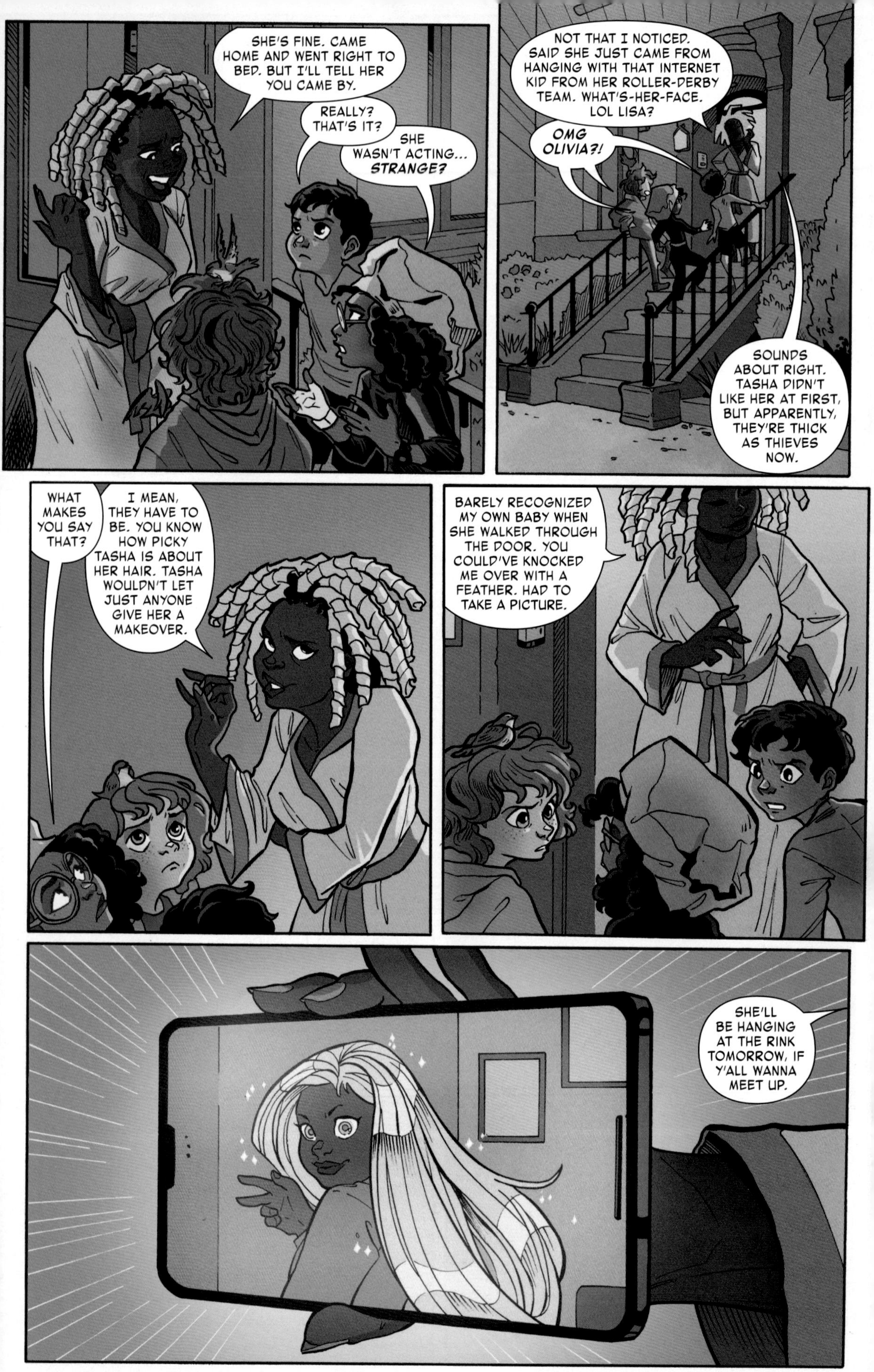
SHE'S FINE. CAME HOME AND WENT RIGHT TO BED. BUT I'LL TELL HER YOU CAME BY.
REALLY? THAT'S IT?
SHE WASN'T ACTING... *STRANGE?*
NOT THAT I NOTICED. SAID SHE JUST CAME FROM HANGING WITH THAT INTERNET KID FROM HER ROLLER-DERBY TEAM. WHAT'S-HER-FACE. LOL LISA?
OMG OLIVIA?!
SOUNDS ABOUT RIGHT. TASHA DIDN'T LIKE HER AT FIRST, BUT APPARENTLY, THEY'RE THICK AS THIEVES NOW.
WHAT MAKES YOU SAY THAT?
I MEAN, THEY HAVE TO BE. YOU KNOW HOW PICKY TASHA IS ABOUT HER HAIR. TASHA WOULDN'T LET JUST ANYONE GIVE HER A MAKEOVER.
BARELY RECOGNIZED MY OWN BABY WHEN SHE WALKED THROUGH THE DOOR. YOU COULD'VE KNOCKED ME OVER WITH A FEATHER. HAD TO TAKE A PICTURE.
SHE'LL BE HANGING AT THE RINK TOMORROW, IF Y'ALL WANNA MEET UP.

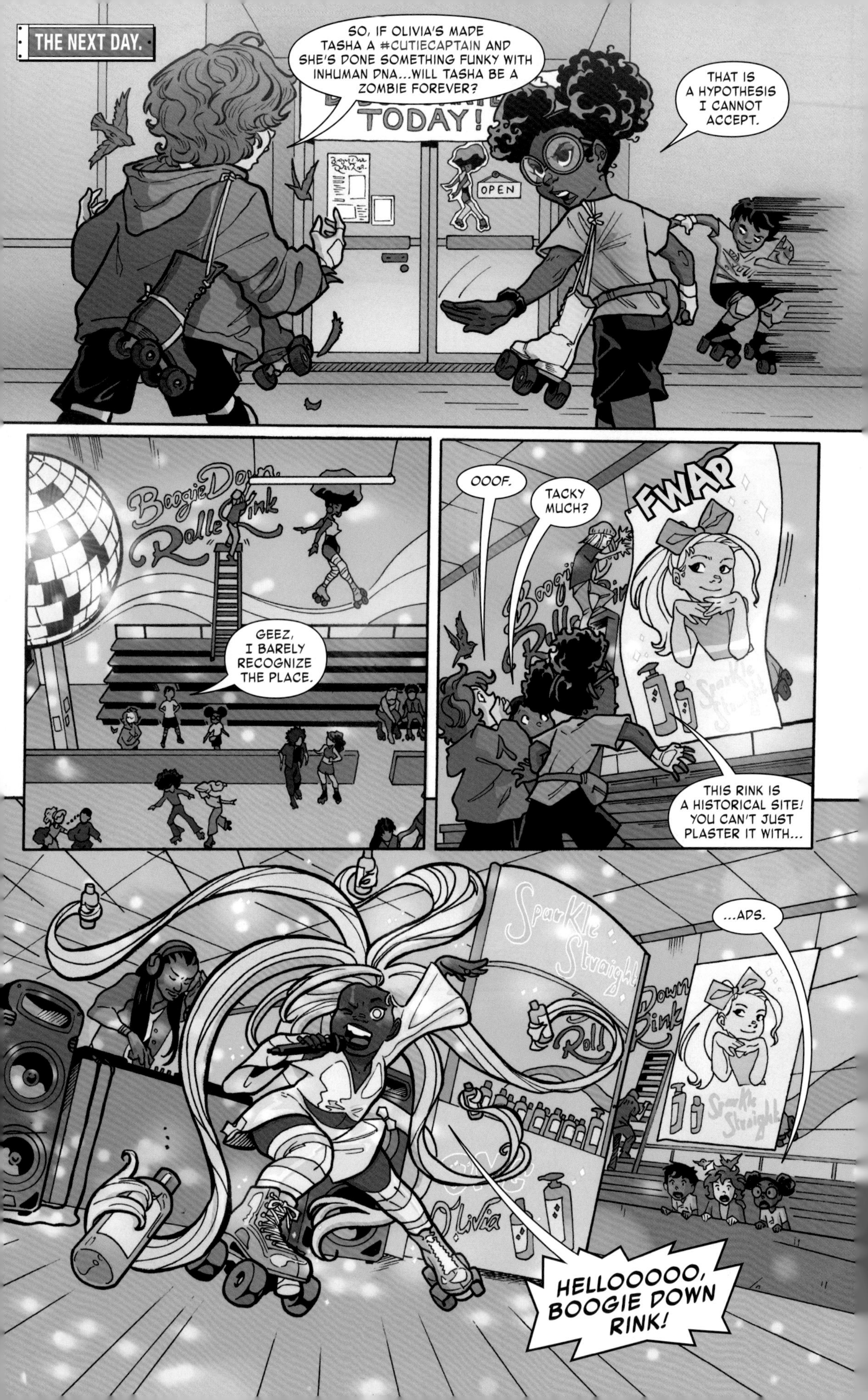
THE NEXT DAY.
SO, IF OLIVIA'S MADE TASHA A #CUTIECAPTAIN AND SHE'S DONE SOMETHING FUNKY WITH INHUMAN DNA...WILL TASHA BE A ZOMBIE FOREVER?
TODAY!
OPEN
THAT IS A HYPOTHESIS I CANNOT ACCEPT.
Boogie Down Roller Rink
GEEZ, I BARELY RECOGNIZE THE PLACE.
OOOF.
TACKY MUCH?
FWAP
Sparkle Straight
THIS RINK IS A HISTORICAL SITE! YOU CAN'T JUST PLASTER IT WITH...
Sparkle Straight
...ADS.
Olivia
Sparkle Straight
HELLOOOOO, BOOGIE DOWN RINK!

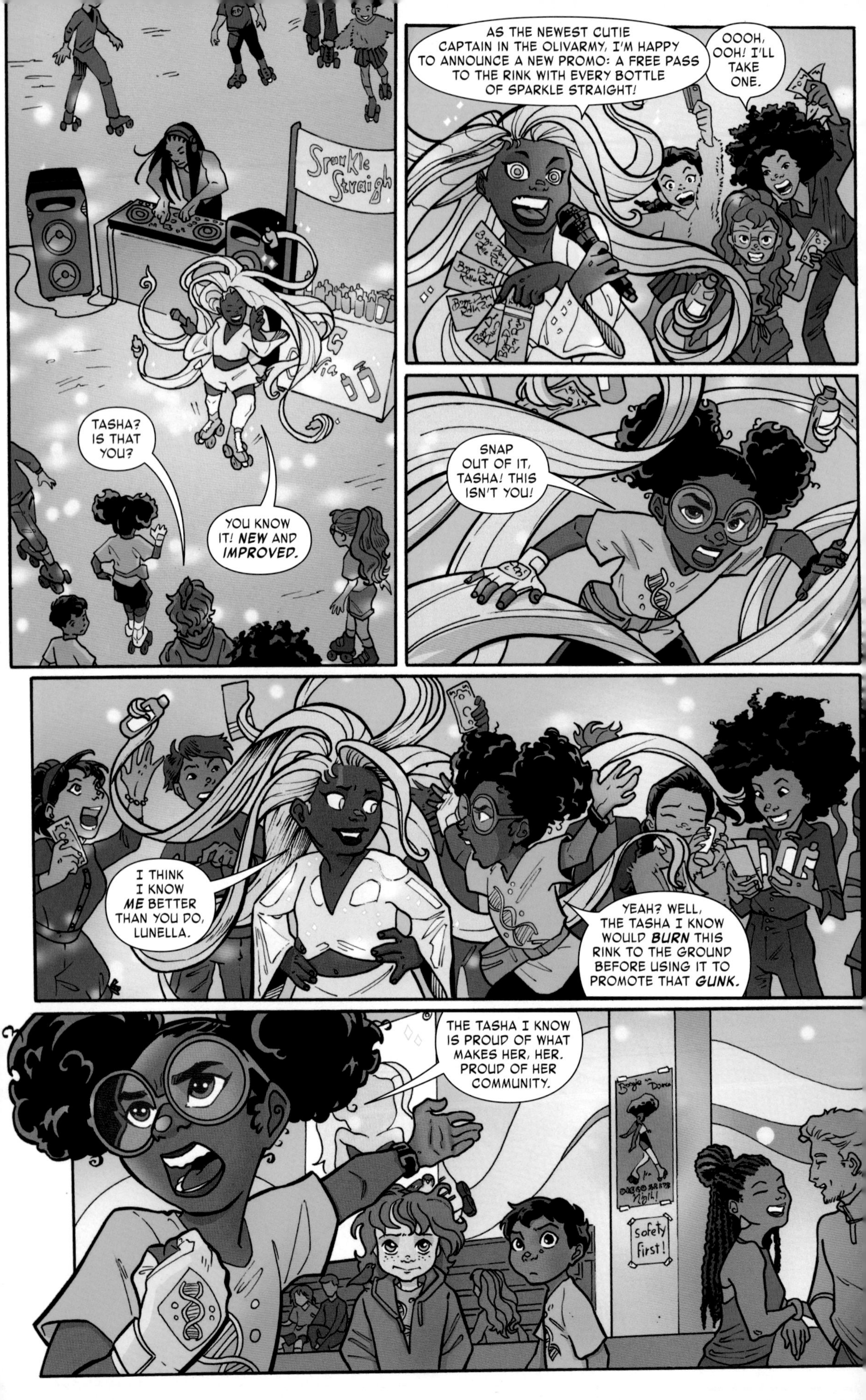
Sparkle Straigh
TASHA? IS THAT YOU?
YOU KNOW IT! NEW AND IMPROVED.
AS THE NEWEST CUTIE CAPTAIN IN THE OLIVARMY, I'M HAPPY TO ANNOUNCE A NEW PROMO: A FREE PASS TO THE RINK WITH EVERY BOTTLE OF SPARKLE STRAIGHT!
OOOH, OOH! I'LL TAKE ONE.
SNAP OUT OF IT, TASHA! THIS ISN'T YOU!
I THINK I KNOW ME BETTER THAN YOU DO, LUNELLA.
YEAH? WELL, THE TASHA I KNOW WOULD BURN THIS RINK TO THE GROUND BEFORE USING IT TO PROMOTE THAT GUNK.
THE TASHA I KNOW IS PROUD OF WHAT MAKES HER, HER. PROUD OF HER COMMUNITY.
Safety first!

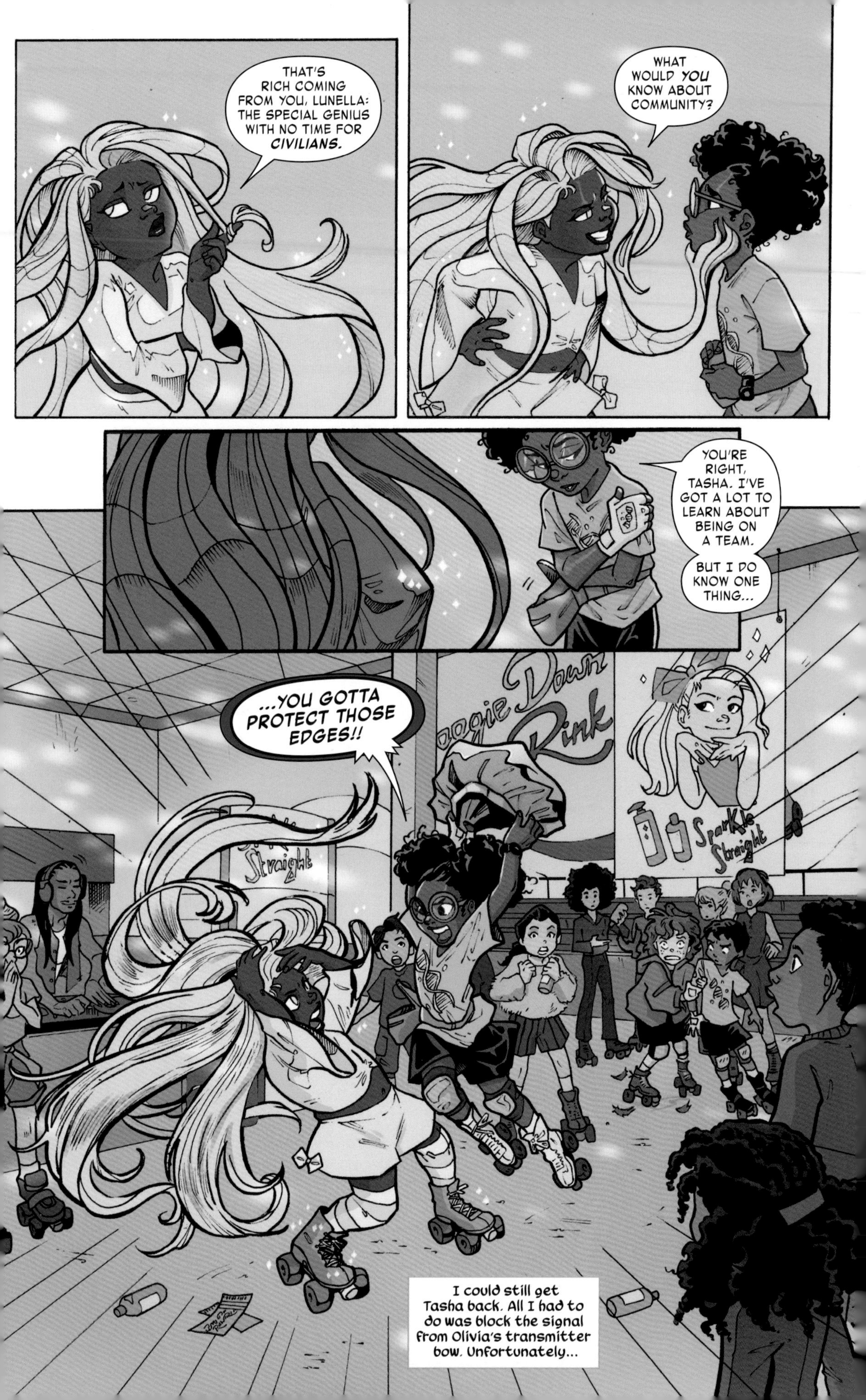
THAT'S RICH COMING FROM YOU, LUNELLA: THE SPECIAL GENIUS WITH NO TIME FOR *CIVILIANS.*
WHAT WOULD *YOU* KNOW ABOUT COMMUNITY?
YOU'RE RIGHT, TASHA. I'VE GOT A LOT TO LEARN ABOUT BEING ON A TEAM.
BUT I DO KNOW ONE THING...
...YOU GOTTA PROTECT THOSE EDGES!!
oogie Down Rink
Sparkle Straight
I could still get Tasha back. All I had to do was block the signal from Olivia's transmitter bow. Unfortunately...

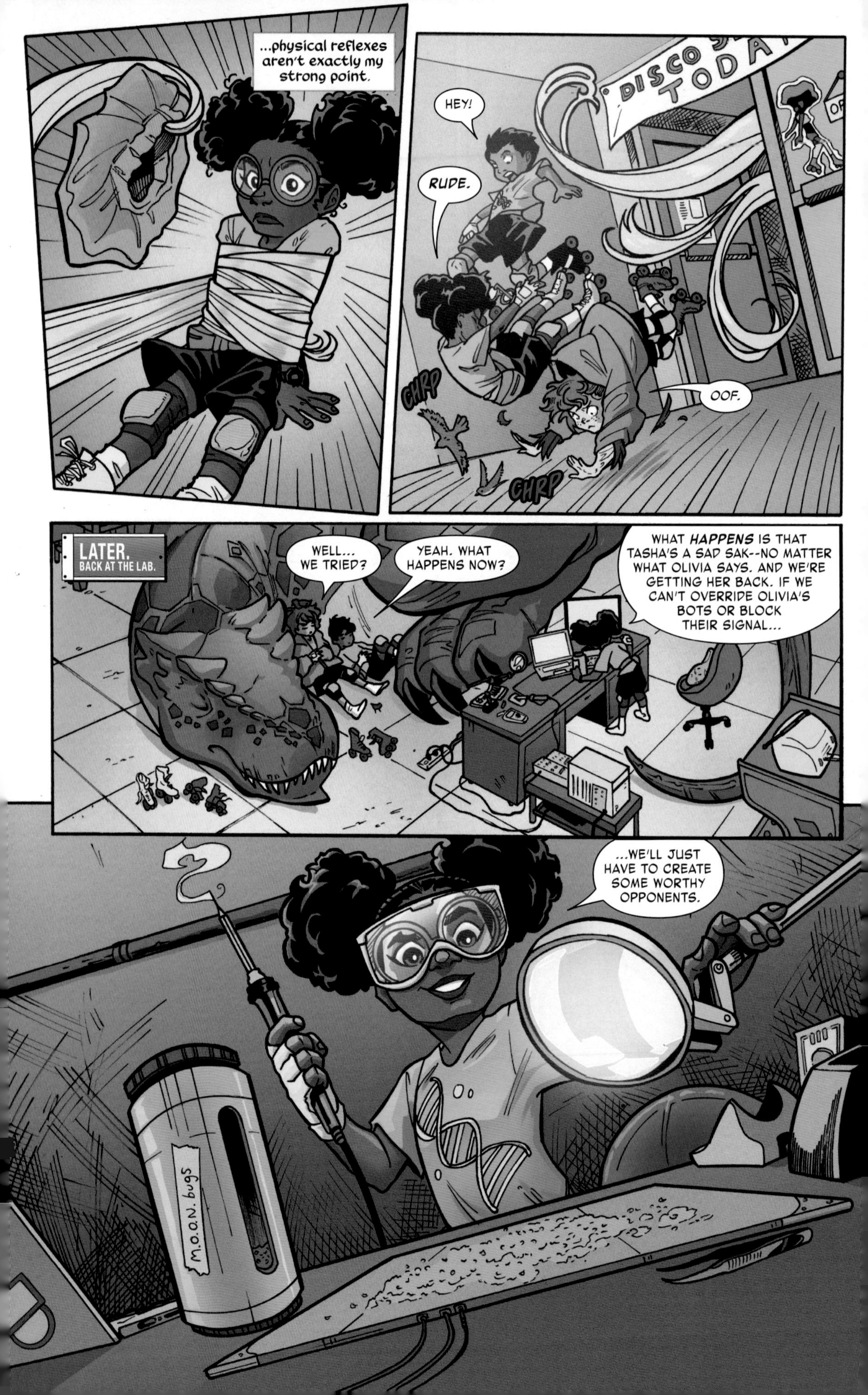
...physical reflexes aren't exactly my strong point.
HEY!
RUDE.
DISCO
TODA
CHRP
OOF.
CHRP
LATER. BACK AT THE LAB.
WELL... WE TRIED?
YEAH. WHAT HAPPENS NOW?
WHAT HAPPENS IS THAT TASHA'S A SAD SAK--NO MATTER WHAT OLIVIA SAYS. AND WE'RE GETTING HER BACK. IF WE CAN'T OVERRIDE OLIVIA'S BOTS OR BLOCK THEIR SIGNAL...
...WE'LL JUST HAVE TO CREATE SOME WORTHY OPPONENTS.
M.O.O.N. bugs

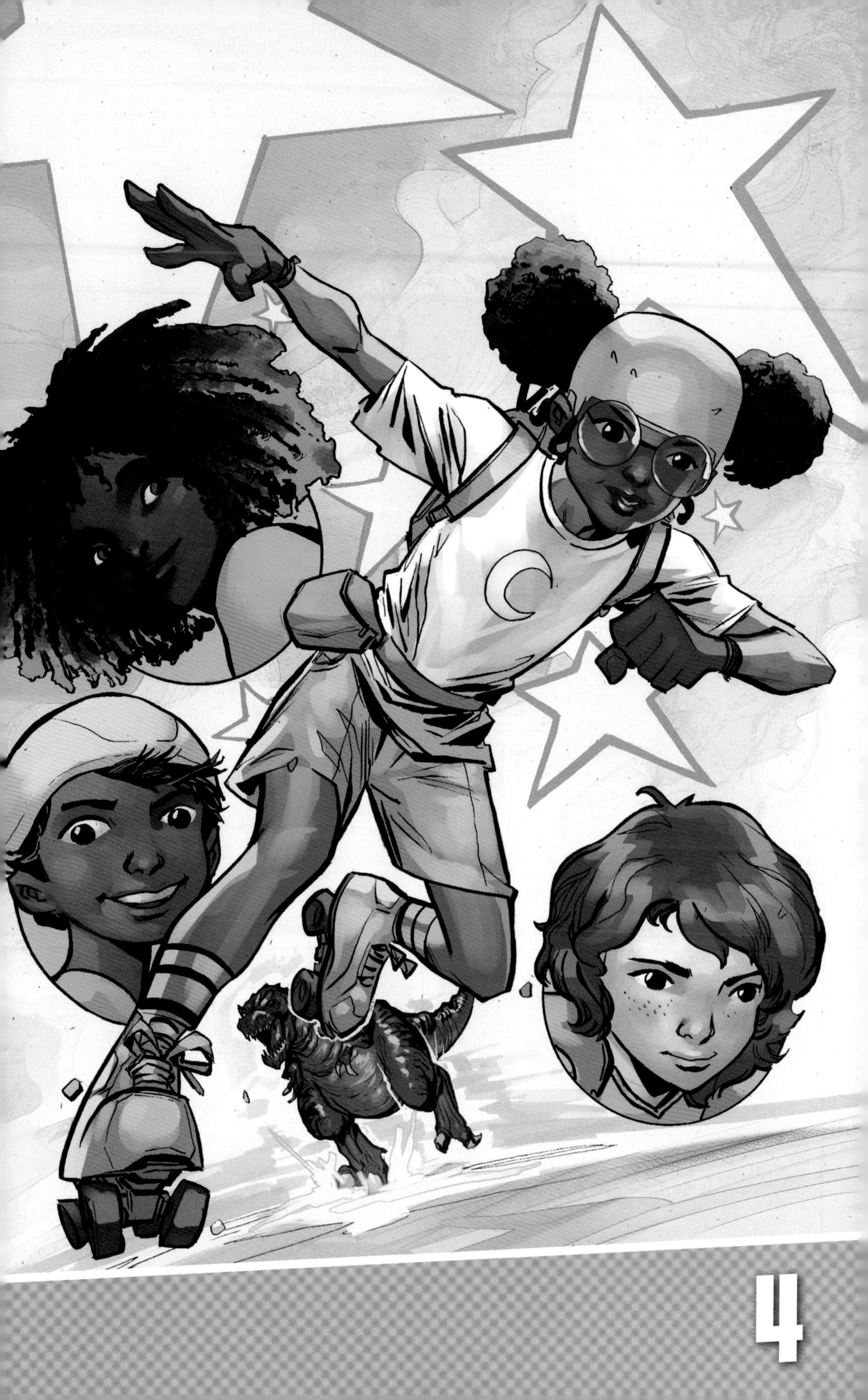

4

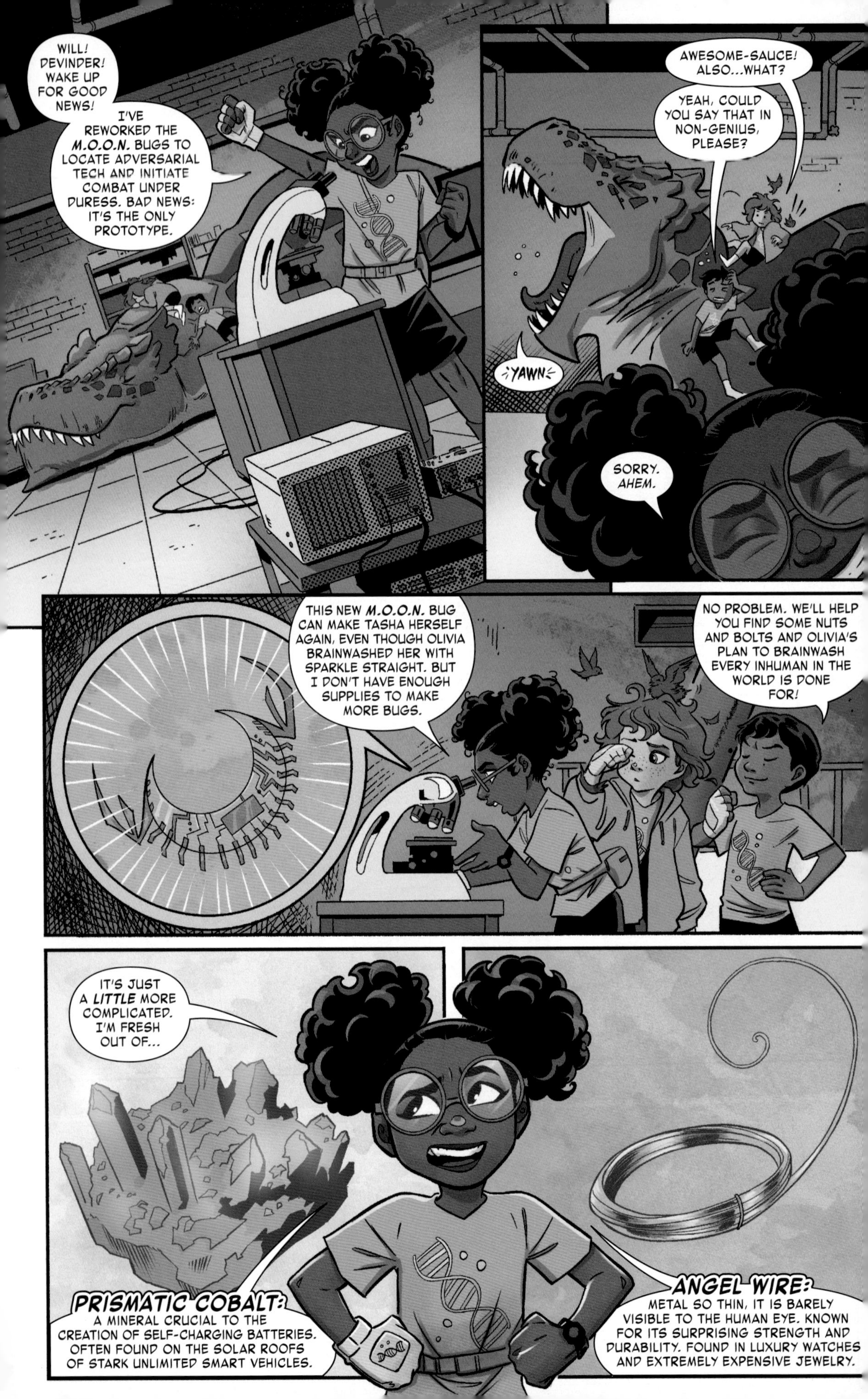
WILL! DEVINDER! WAKE UP FOR GOOD NEWS!
I'VE REWORKED THE M.O.O.N. BUGS TO LOCATE ADVERSARIAL TECH AND INITIATE COMBAT UNDER DURESS. BAD NEWS: IT'S THE ONLY PROTOTYPE.
AWESOME-SAUCE! ALSO...WHAT?
YEAH, COULD YOU SAY THAT IN NON-GENIUS, PLEASE?
YAWN
SORRY. AHEM.
THIS NEW M.O.O.N. BUG CAN MAKE TASHA HERSELF AGAIN, EVEN THOUGH OLIVIA BRAINWASHED HER WITH SPARKLE STRAIGHT. BUT I DON'T HAVE ENOUGH SUPPLIES TO MAKE MORE BUGS.
NO PROBLEM. WE'LL HELP YOU FIND SOME NUTS AND BOLTS AND OLIVIA'S PLAN TO BRAINWASH EVERY INHUMAN IN THE WORLD IS DONE FOR!
IT'S JUST A LITTLE MORE COMPLICATED. I'M FRESH OUT OF...
PRISMATIC COBALT: A MINERAL CRUCIAL TO THE CREATION OF SELF-CHARGING BATTERIES. OFTEN FOUND ON THE SOLAR ROOFS OF STARK UNLIMITED SMART VEHICLES.
ANGEL WIRE: METAL SO THIN, IT IS BARELY VISIBLE TO THE HUMAN EYE. KNOWN FOR ITS SURPRISING STRENGTH AND DURABILITY. FOUND IN LUXURY WATCHES AND EXTREMELY EXPENSIVE JEWELRY.

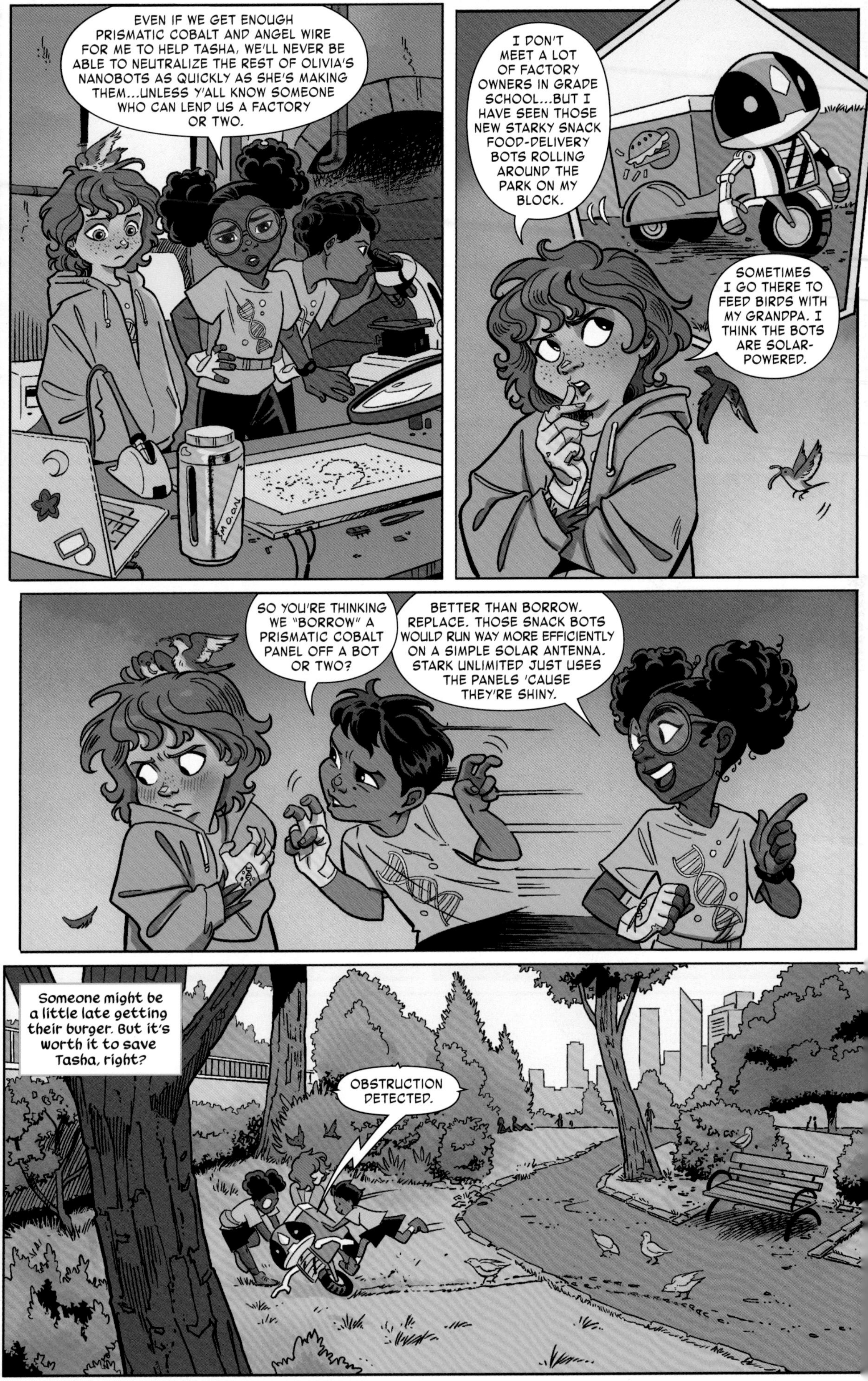
EVEN IF WE GET ENOUGH PRISMATIC COBALT AND ANGEL WIRE FOR ME TO HELP TASHA, WE'LL NEVER BE ABLE TO NEUTRALIZE THE REST OF OLIVIA'S NANOBOTS AS QUICKLY AS SHE'S MAKING THEM...UNLESS Y'ALL KNOW SOMEONE WHO CAN LEND US A FACTORY OR TWO.
I DON'T MEET A LOT OF FACTORY OWNERS IN GRADE SCHOOL...BUT I HAVE SEEN THOSE NEW STARKY SNACK FOOD-DELIVERY BOTS ROLLING AROUND THE PARK ON MY BLOCK.
SOMETIMES I GO THERE TO FEED BIRDS WITH MY GRANDPA. I THINK THE BOTS ARE SOLAR-POWERED.
SO YOU'RE THINKING WE "BORROW" A PRISMATIC COBALT PANEL OFF A BOT OR TWO?
BETTER THAN BORROW. REPLACE. THOSE SNACK BOTS WOULD RUN WAY MORE EFFICIENTLY ON A SIMPLE SOLAR ANTENNA. STARK UNLIMITED JUST USES THE PANELS 'CAUSE THEY'RE SHINY.
Someone might be a little late getting their burger. But it's worth it to save Tasha, right?
OBSTRUCTION DETECTED.

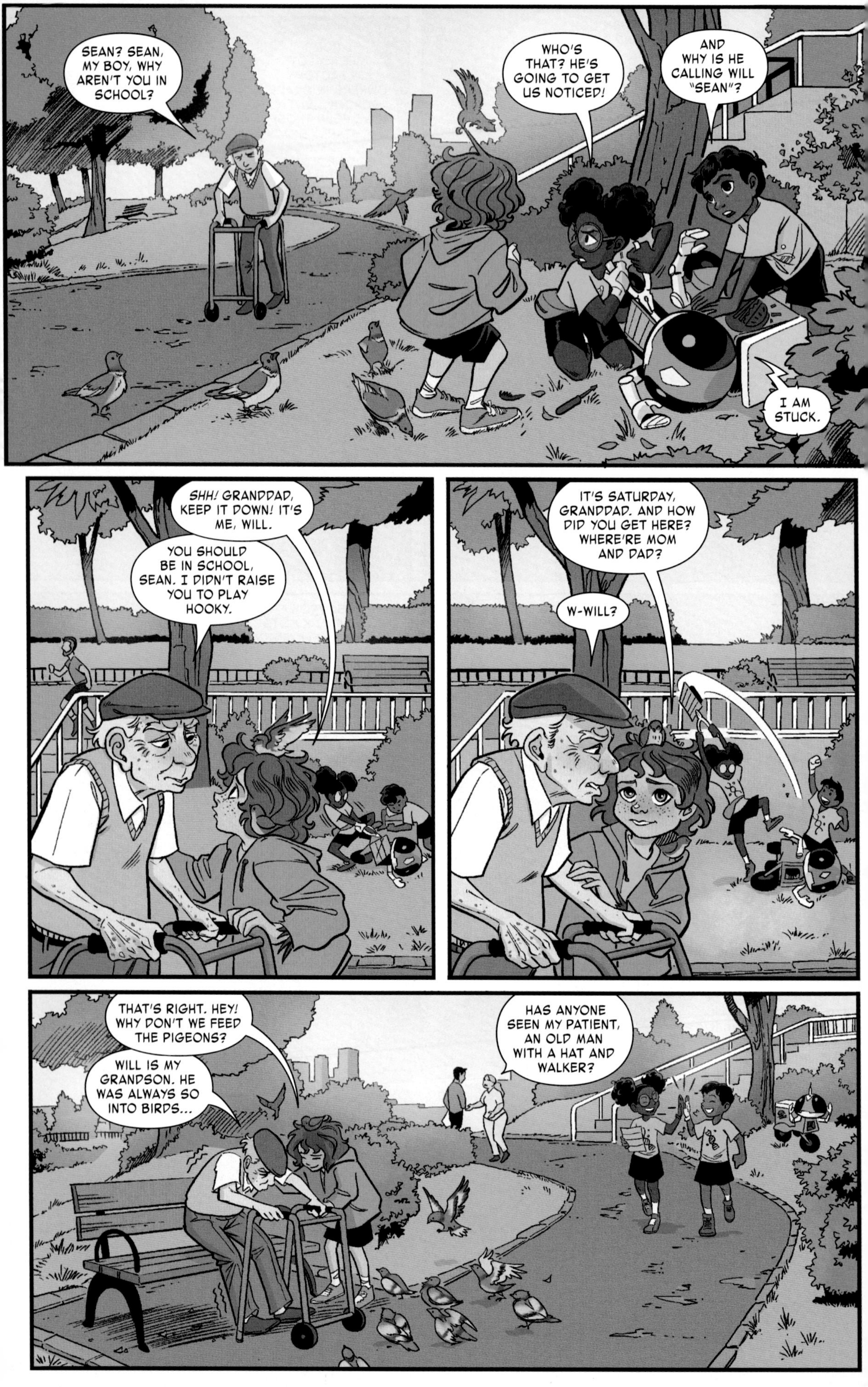
SEAN? SEAN, MY BOY, WHY AREN'T YOU IN SCHOOL?
WHO'S THAT? HE'S GOING TO GET US NOTICED!
AND WHY IS HE CALLING WILL "SEAN"?
I AM STUCK.
SHH! GRANDDAD, KEEP IT DOWN! IT'S ME, WILL.
YOU SHOULD BE IN SCHOOL, SEAN. I DIDN'T RAISE YOU TO PLAY HOOKY.
IT'S SATURDAY, GRANDDAD. AND HOW DID YOU GET HERE? WHERE'RE MOM AND DAD?
W-WILL?
THAT'S RIGHT. HEY! WHY DON'T WE FEED THE PIGEONS?
WILL IS MY GRANDSON. HE WAS ALWAYS SO INTO BIRDS...
HAS ANYONE SEEN MY PATIENT, AN OLD MAN WITH A HAT AND WALKER?

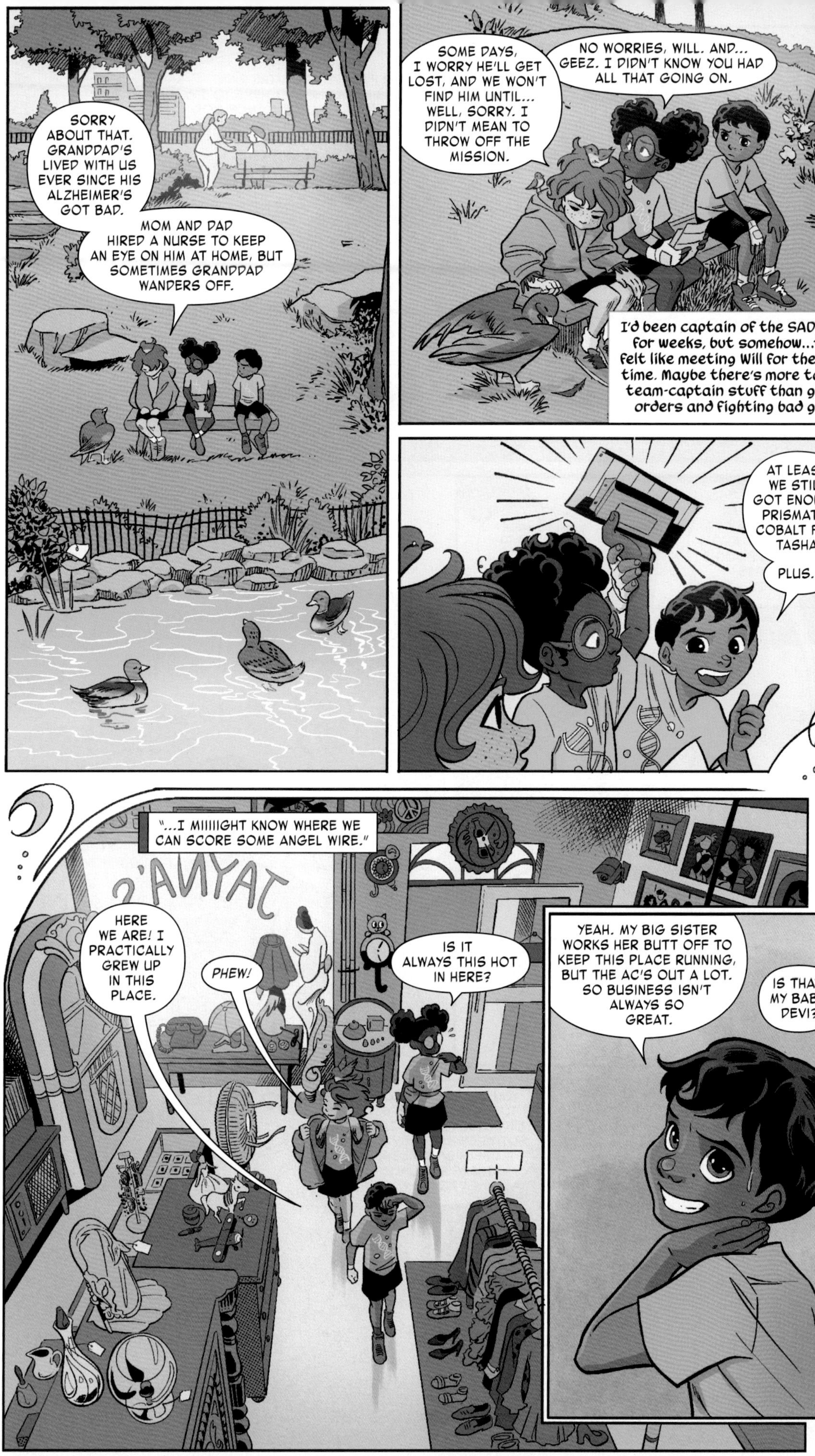
SORRY ABOUT THAT. GRANDDAD'S LIVED WITH US EVER SINCE HIS ALZHEIMER'S GOT BAD.
MOM AND DAD HIRED A NURSE TO KEEP AN EYE ON HIM AT HOME, BUT SOMETIMES GRANDDAD WANDERS OFF.
SOME DAYS, I WORRY HE'LL GET LOST, AND WE WON'T FIND HIM UNTIL... WELL, SORRY. I DIDN'T MEAN TO THROW OFF THE MISSION.
NO WORRIES, WILL. AND... GEEZ. I DIDN'T KNOW YOU HAD ALL THAT GOING ON.
I'd been captain of the SAD SAKS for weeks, but somehow...this felt like meeting Will for the first time. Maybe there's more to this team-captain stuff than giving orders and fighting bad guys.
AT LEAST WE STILL GOT ENOUGH PRISMATIC COBALT FOR TASHA!
PLUS...
"...I MIIIIGHT KNOW WHERE WE CAN SCORE SOME ANGEL WIRE."
HERE WE ARE! I PRACTICALLY GREW UP IN THIS PLACE.
PHEW!
IS IT ALWAYS THIS HOT IN HERE?
YEAH. MY BIG SISTER WORKS HER BUTT OFF TO KEEP THIS PLACE RUNNING, BUT THE AC'S OUT A LOT. SO BUSINESS ISN'T ALWAYS SO GREAT.
IS THAT MY BABY DEVI?

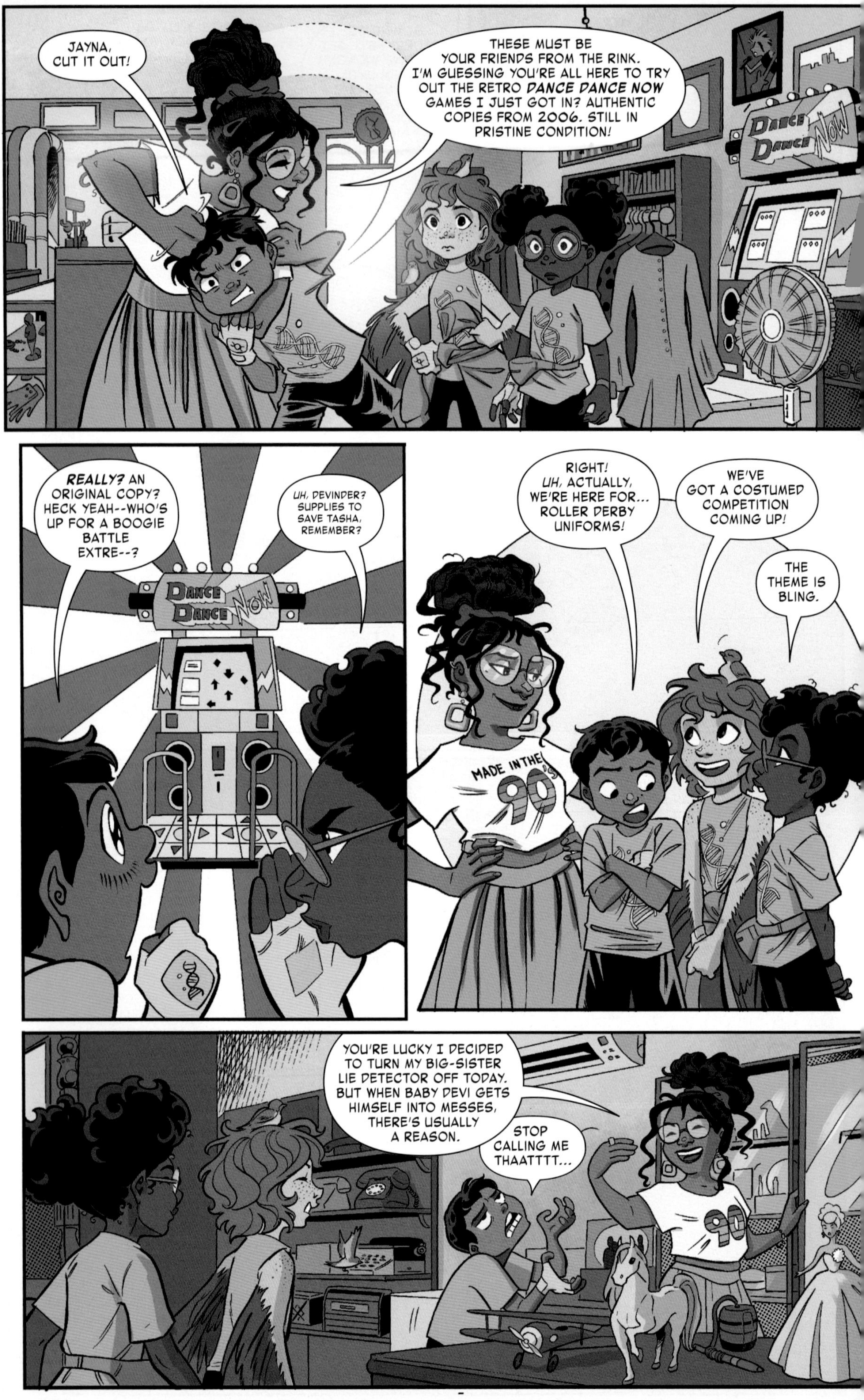
JAYNA, CUT IT OUT!
THESE MUST BE YOUR FRIENDS FROM THE RINK. I'M GUESSING YOU'RE ALL HERE TO TRY OUT THE RETRO DANCE DANCE NOW GAMES I JUST GOT IN? AUTHENTIC COPIES FROM 2006. STILL IN PRISTINE CONDITION!
DANCE DANCE NOW
REALLY? AN ORIGINAL COPY? HECK YEAH--WHO'S UP FOR A BOOGIE BATTLE EXTRE--?
UH, DEVINDER? SUPPLIES TO SAVE TASHA, REMEMBER?
DANCE DANCE NOW
RIGHT! UH, ACTUALLY, WE'RE HERE FOR... ROLLER DERBY UNIFORMS!
WE'VE GOT A COSTUMED COMPETITION COMING UP!
THE THEME IS BLING.
MADE IN THE 90'S
YOU'RE LUCKY I DECIDED TO TURN MY BIG-SISTER LIE DETECTOR OFF TODAY. BUT WHEN BABY DEVI GETS HIMSELF INTO MESSES, THERE'S USUALLY A REASON.
STOP CALLING ME THAATTTT...

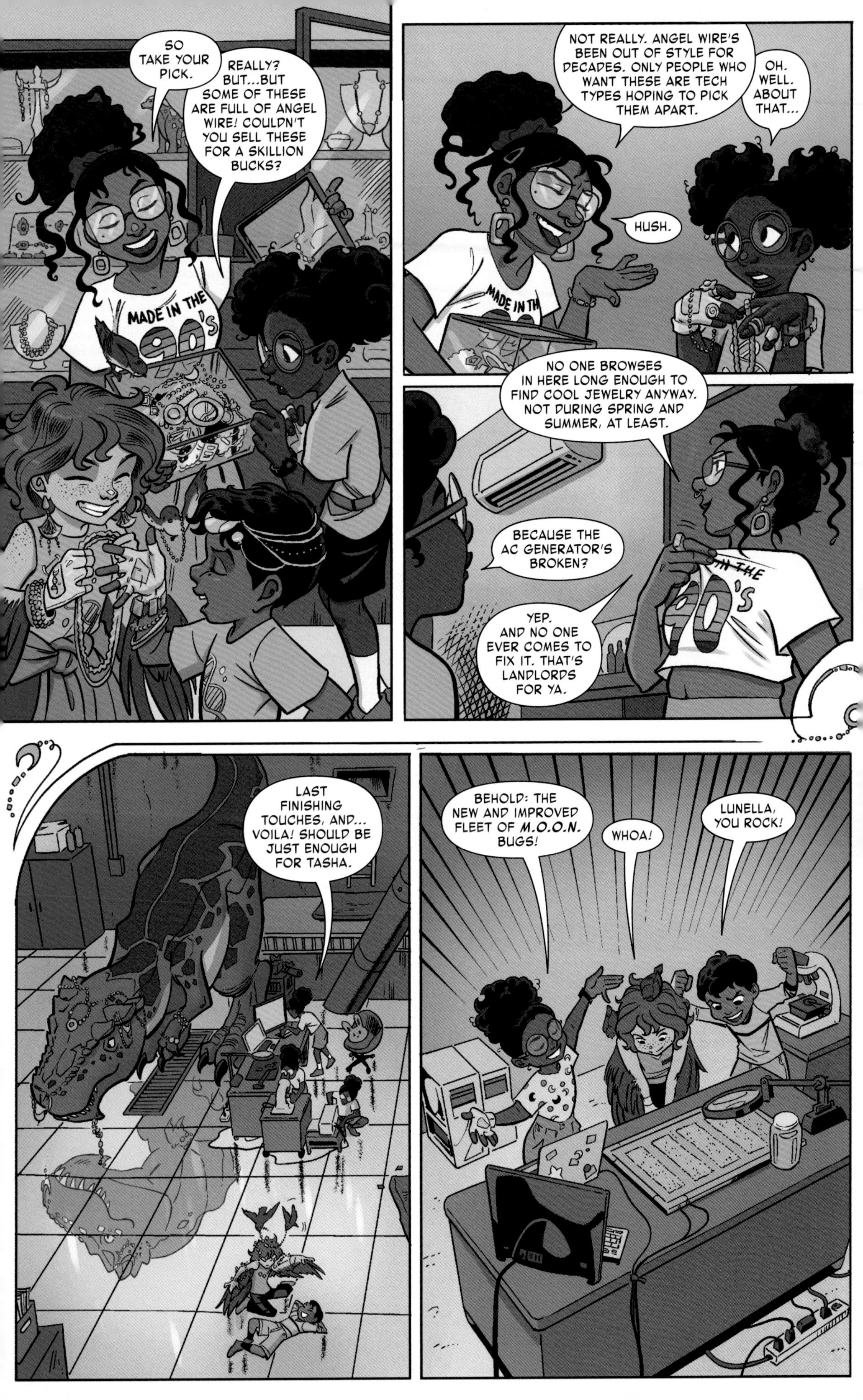
SO TAKE YOUR PICK.
REALLY? BUT...BUT SOME OF THESE ARE FULL OF ANGEL WIRE! COULDN'T YOU SELL THESE FOR A SKILLION BUCKS?
MADE IN THE 90'S
NOT REALLY. ANGEL WIRE'S BEEN OUT OF STYLE FOR DECADES. ONLY PEOPLE WHO WANT THESE ARE TECH TYPES HOPING TO PICK THEM APART.
OH. WELL. ABOUT THAT...
HUSH.
NO ONE BROWSES IN HERE LONG ENOUGH TO FIND COOL JEWELRY ANYWAY. NOT DURING SPRING AND SUMMER, AT LEAST.
BECAUSE THE AC GENERATOR'S BROKEN?
YEP. AND NO ONE EVER COMES TO FIX IT. THAT'S LANDLORDS FOR YA.
LAST FINISHING TOUCHES, AND... VOILA! SHOULD BE JUST ENOUGH FOR TASHA.
BEHOLD: THE NEW AND IMPROVED FLEET OF *M.O.O.N.* BUGS!
WHOA!
LUNELLA, YOU ROCK!

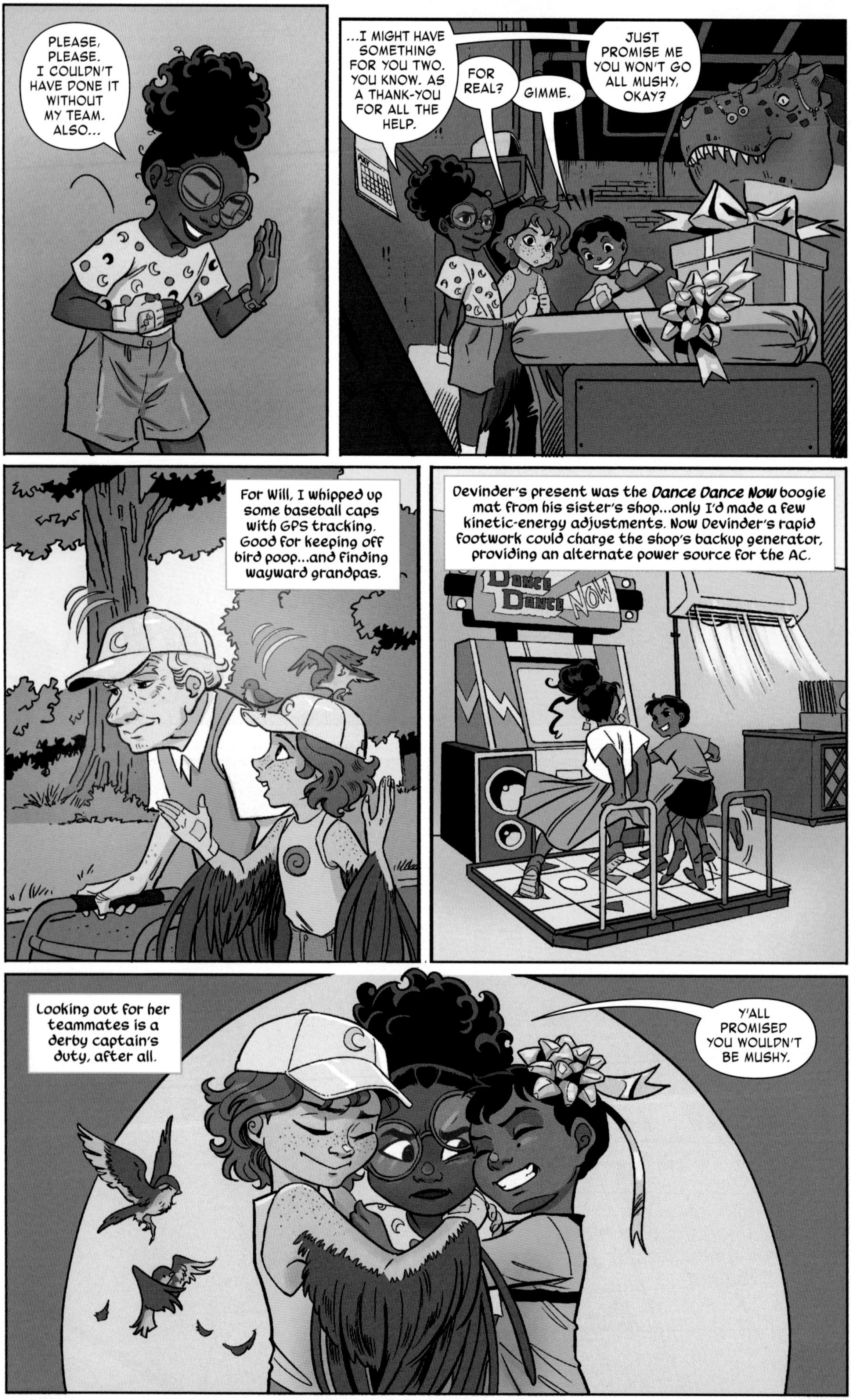
PLEASE, PLEASE. I COULDN'T HAVE DONE IT WITHOUT MY TEAM. ALSO...
...I MIGHT HAVE SOMETHING FOR YOU TWO. YOU KNOW. AS A THANK-YOU FOR ALL THE HELP.
FOR REAL?
GIMME.
JUST PROMISE ME YOU WON'T GO ALL MUSHY, OKAY?
For Will, I whipped up some baseball caps with GPS tracking. Good for keeping off bird poop...and finding wayward grandpas.
Devinder's present was the *Dance Dance Now* boogie mat from his sister's shop...only I'd made a few kinetic-energy adjustments. Now Devinder's rapid footwork could charge the shop's backup generator, providing an alternate power source for the AC.
DANCE DANCE NOW
Looking out for her teammates is a derby captain's duty, after all.
Y'ALL PROMISED YOU WOULDN'T BE MUSHY.

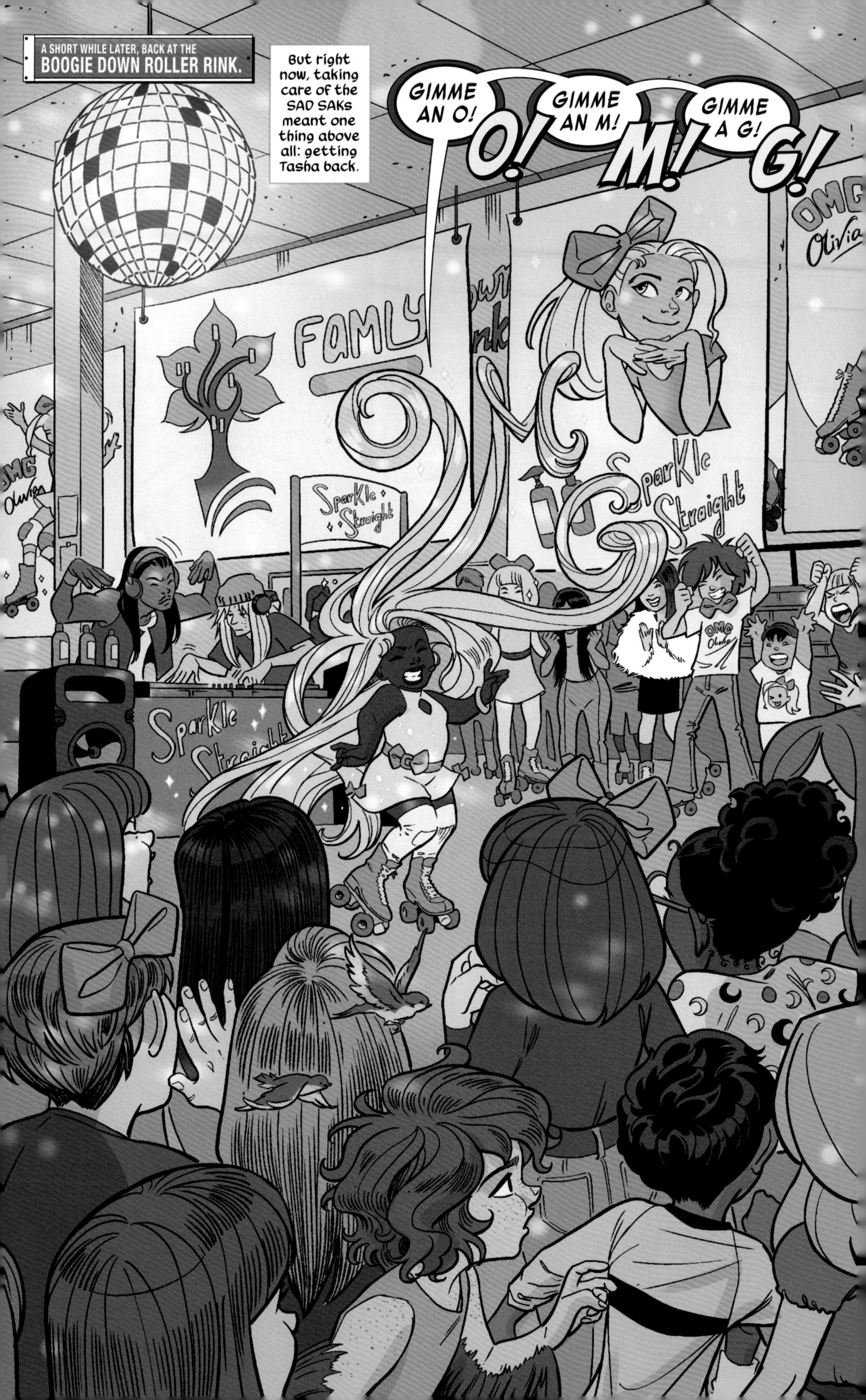
A SHORT WHILE LATER, BACK AT THE
BOOGIE DOWN ROLLER RINK.
But right now, taking care of the SAD SAKS meant one thing above all: getting Tasha back.
GIMME AN O!
O!
GIMME AN M!
M!
GIMME A G!
G!
OMG
Olivia
FAMLY
Sparkle Straight
Sparkle Straight
Sparkle Straight
Sparkle Straight
OMG
Olivia
OMG
Olivia

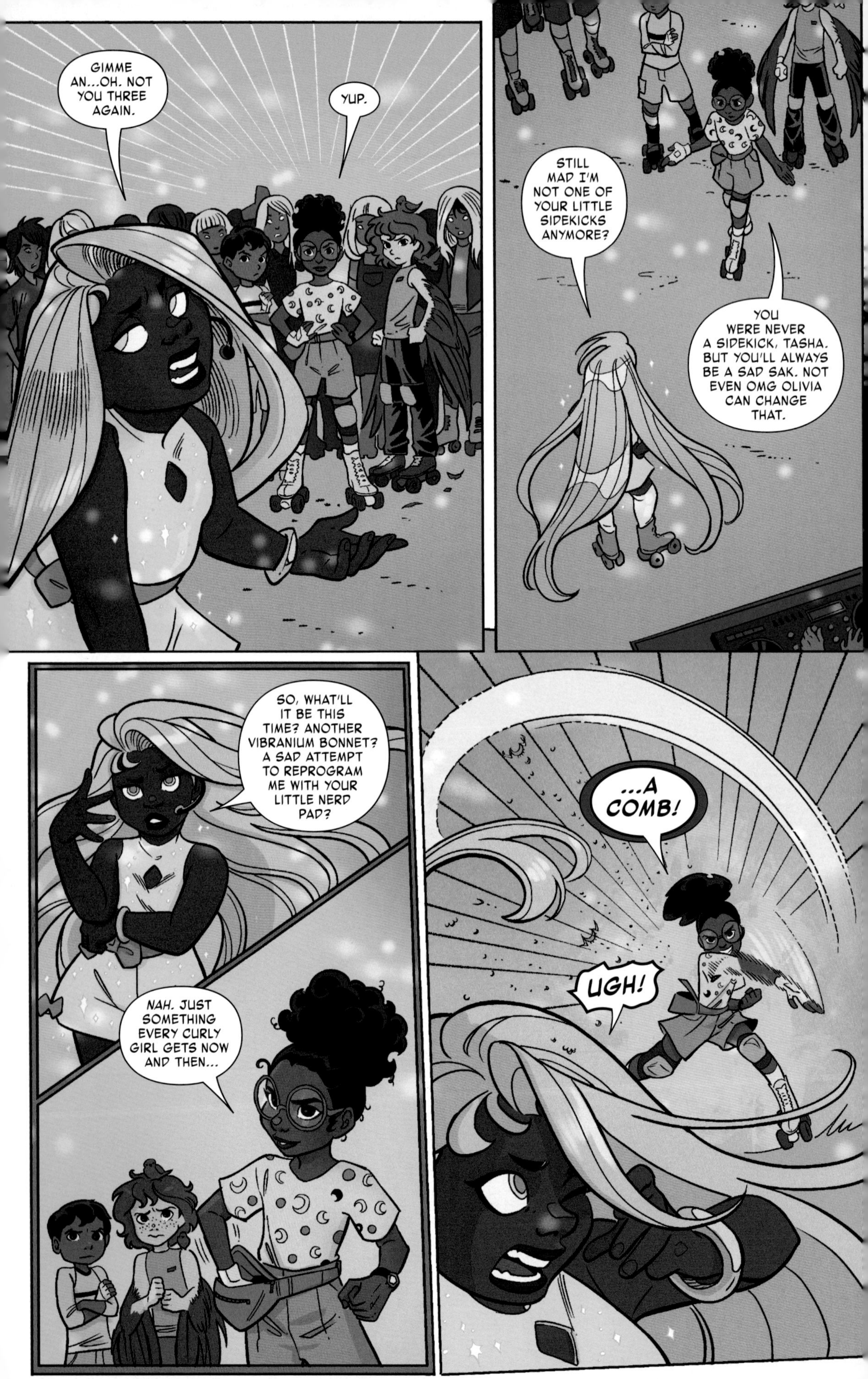
GIMME AN...OH. NOT YOU THREE AGAIN.
YUP.
STILL MAD I'M NOT ONE OF YOUR LITTLE SIDEKICKS ANYMORE?
YOU WERE NEVER A SIDEKICK, TASHA. BUT YOU'LL ALWAYS BE A SAD SAK. NOT EVEN OMG OLIVIA CAN CHANGE THAT.
SO, WHAT'LL IT BE THIS TIME? ANOTHER VIBRANIUM BONNET? A SAD ATTEMPT TO REPROGRAM ME WITH YOUR LITTLE NERD PAD?
NAH. JUST SOMETHING EVERY CURLY GIRL GETS NOW AND THEN...
...A COMB!
UGH!

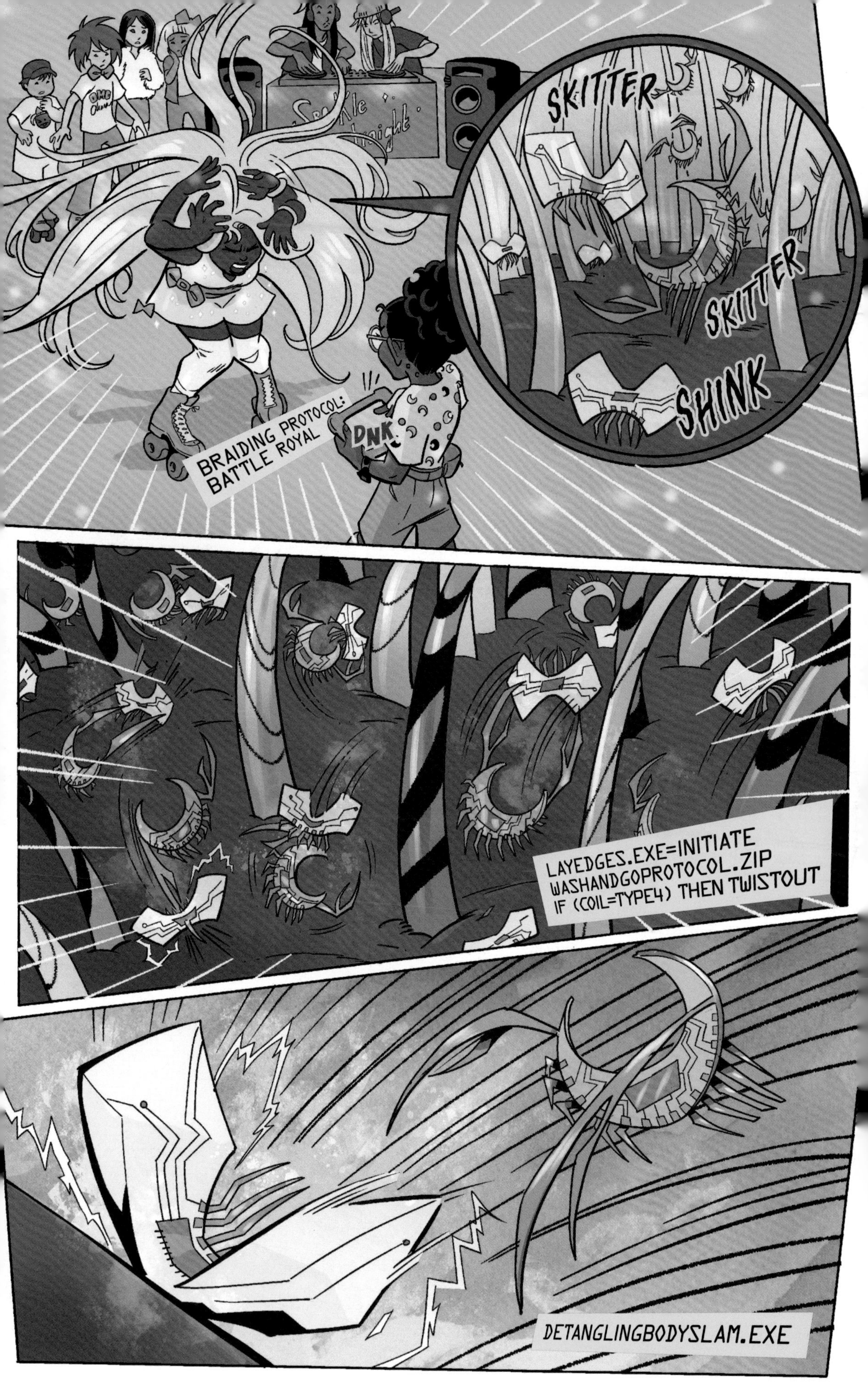
BRAIDING PROTOCOL:
BATTLE ROYAL
DNK
SKITTER
SKITTER
SHINK
LAYEDGES.EXE=INITIATE
WASHANDGOPROTOCOL.ZIP
IF (COIL=TYPE4) THEN TWISTOUT
DETANGLINGBODYSLAM.EXE

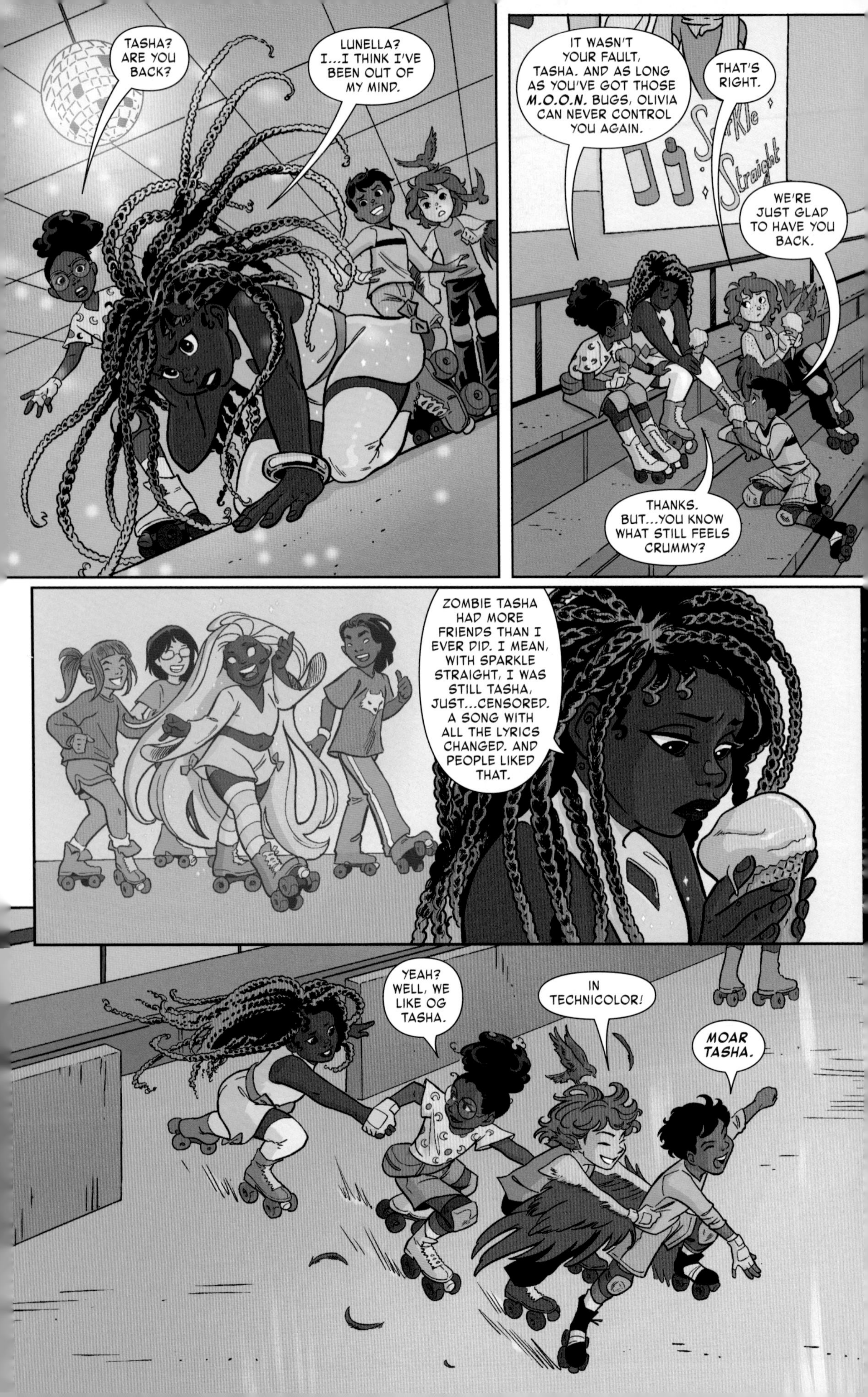
TASHA? ARE YOU BACK?
LUNELLA? I...I THINK I'VE BEEN OUT OF MY MIND.
IT WASN'T YOUR FAULT, TASHA. AND AS LONG AS YOU'VE GOT THOSE M.O.O.N. BUGS, OLIVIA CAN NEVER CONTROL YOU AGAIN.
THAT'S RIGHT.
Sparkle Straight
WE'RE JUST GLAD TO HAVE YOU BACK.
THANKS. BUT...YOU KNOW WHAT STILL FEELS CRUMMY?
ZOMBIE TASHA HAD MORE FRIENDS THAN I EVER DID. I MEAN, WITH SPARKLE STRAIGHT, I WAS STILL TASHA, JUST...CENSORED. A SONG WITH ALL THE LYRICS CHANGED. AND PEOPLE LIKED THAT.
YEAH? WELL, WE LIKE OG TASHA.
IN TECHNICOLOR!
MOAR TASHA.

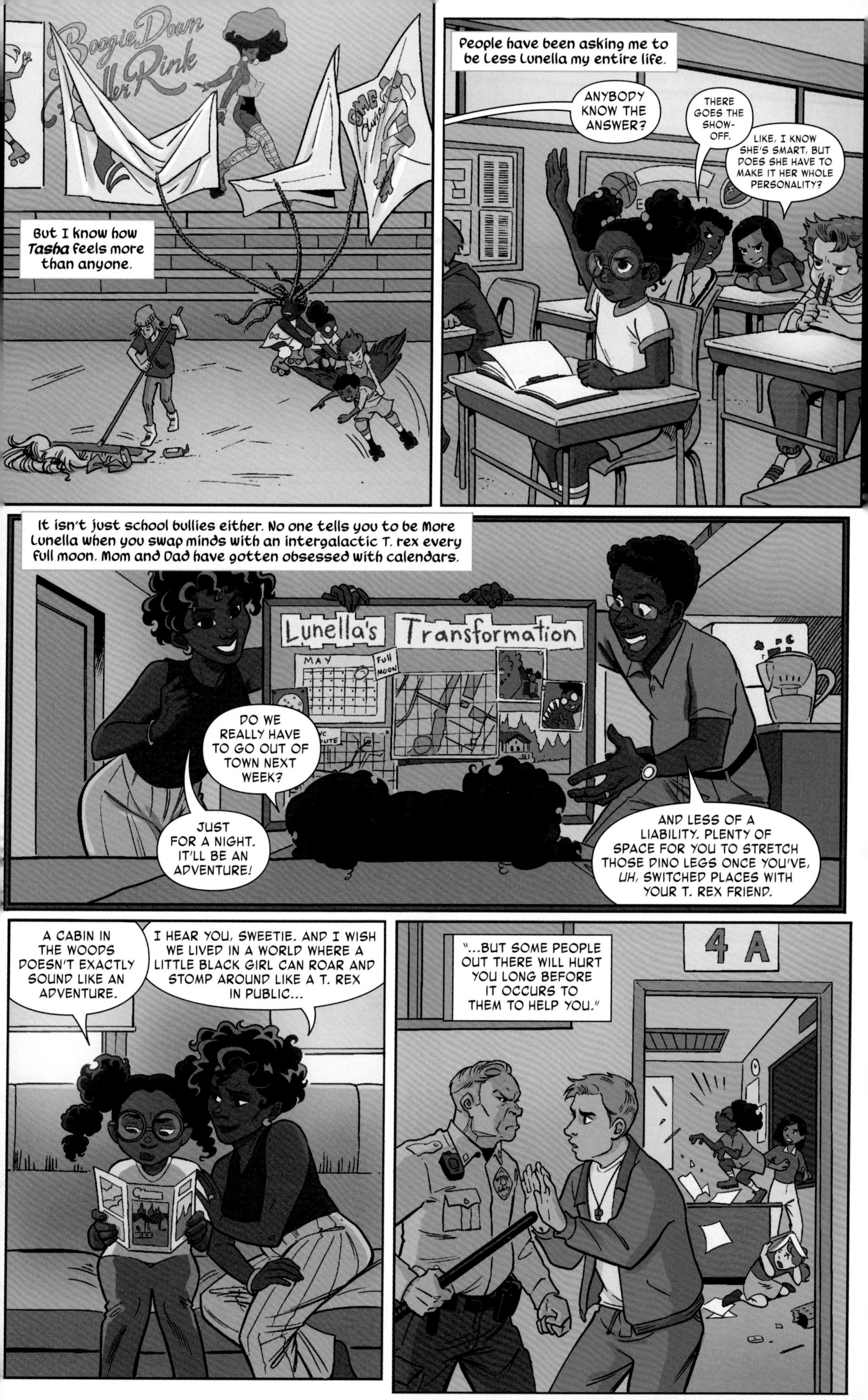
But I know how *Tasha* feels more than anyone.
People have been asking me to be less Lunella my entire life.
ANYBODY KNOW THE ANSWER?
THERE GOES THE SHOW-OFF.
LIKE, I KNOW SHE'S SMART, BUT DOES SHE HAVE TO MAKE IT HER WHOLE PERSONALITY?
It isn't just school bullies either. No one tells you to be More Lunella when you swap minds with an intergalactic T. rex every full moon. Mom and Dad have gotten obsessed with calendars.
Lunella's Transformation
MAY
FULL MOON
DO WE REALLY HAVE TO GO OUT OF TOWN NEXT WEEK?
JUST FOR A NIGHT. IT'LL BE AN ADVENTURE!
AND LESS OF A LIABILITY. PLENTY OF SPACE FOR YOU TO STRETCH THOSE DINO LEGS ONCE YOU'VE, *UH*, SWITCHED PLACES WITH YOUR T. REX FRIEND.
A CABIN IN THE WOODS DOESN'T EXACTLY SOUND LIKE AN ADVENTURE.
I HEAR YOU, SWEETIE. AND I WISH WE LIVED IN A WORLD WHERE A LITTLE BLACK GIRL CAN ROAR AND STOMP AROUND LIKE A T. REX IN PUBLIC...
"...BUT SOME PEOPLE OUT THERE WILL HURT YOU LONG BEFORE IT OCCURS TO THEM TO HELP YOU."
4 A

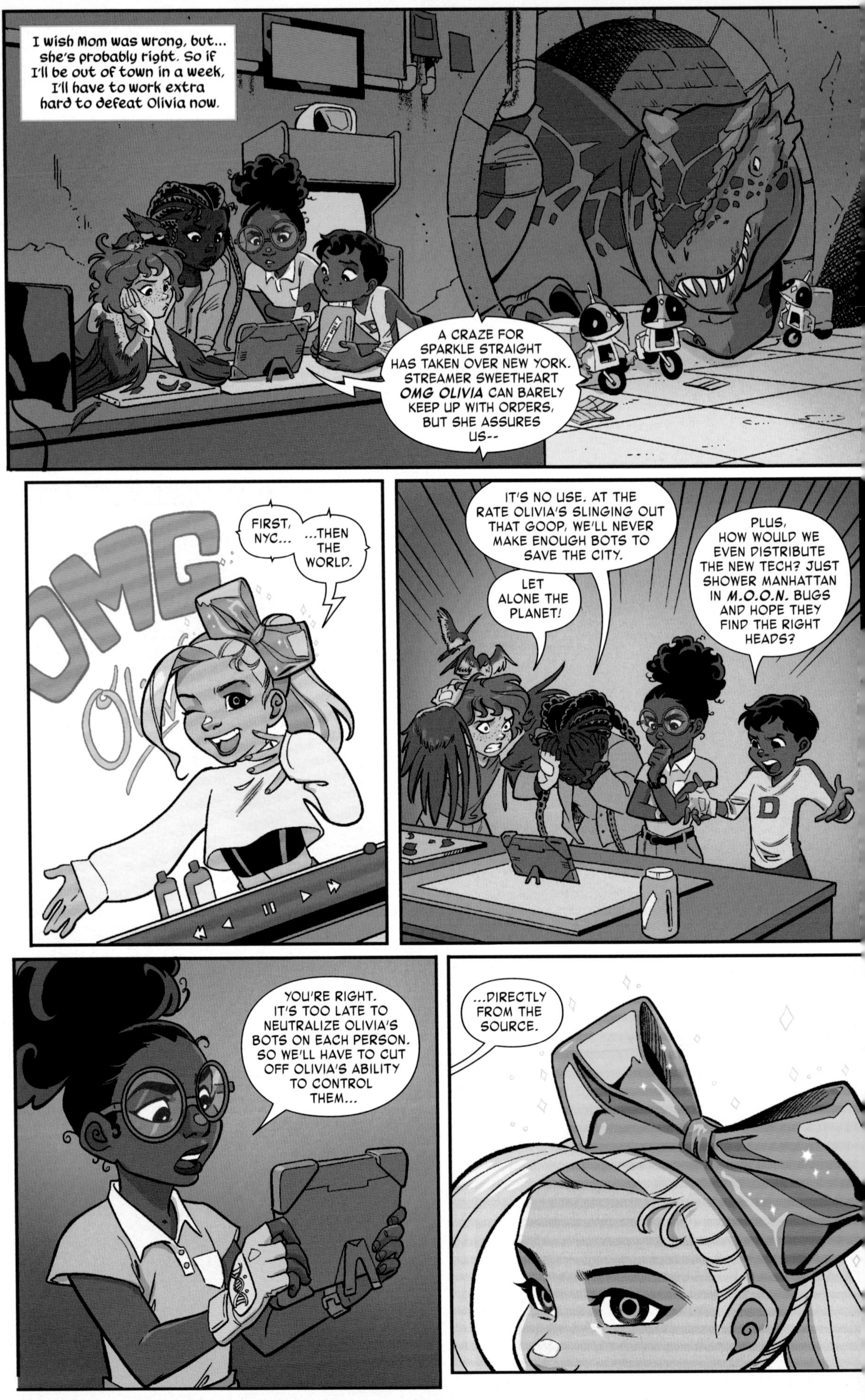
I wish Mom was wrong, but... she's probably right. So if I'll be out of town in a week, I'll have to work extra hard to defeat Olivia now.
A CRAZE FOR SPARKLE STRAIGHT HAS TAKEN OVER NEW YORK. STREAMER SWEETHEART OMG OLIVIA CAN BARELY KEEP UP WITH ORDERS, BUT SHE ASSURES US--
OMG
FIRST, NYC...
...THEN THE WORLD.
IT'S NO USE. AT THE RATE OLIVIA'S SLINGING OUT THAT GOOP, WE'LL NEVER MAKE ENOUGH BOTS TO SAVE THE CITY.
LET ALONE THE PLANET!
PLUS, HOW WOULD WE EVEN DISTRIBUTE THE NEW TECH? JUST SHOWER MANHATTAN IN M.O.O.N. BUGS AND HOPE THEY FIND THE RIGHT HEADS?
YOU'RE RIGHT. IT'S TOO LATE TO NEUTRALIZE OLIVIA'S BOTS ON EACH PERSON. SO WE'LL HAVE TO CUT OFF OLIVIA'S ABILITY TO CONTROL THEM...
...DIRECTLY FROM THE SOURCE.

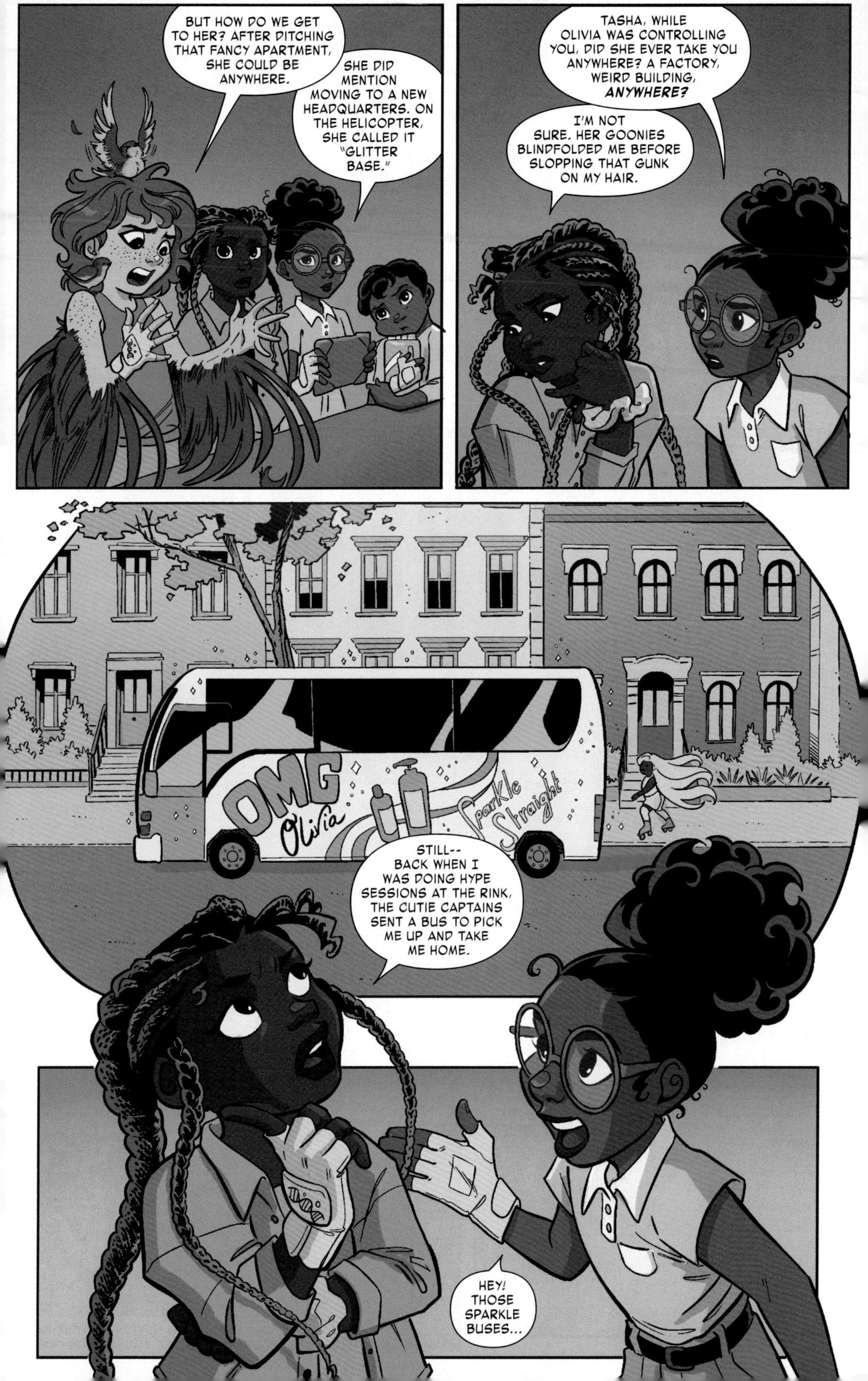

BUT HOW DO WE GET TO HER? AFTER DITCHING THAT FANCY APARTMENT, SHE COULD BE ANYWHERE.
SHE DID MENTION MOVING TO A NEW HEADQUARTERS. ON THE HELICOPTER, SHE CALLED IT "GLITTER BASE."
TASHA, WHILE OLIVIA WAS CONTROLLING YOU, DID SHE EVER TAKE YOU ANYWHERE? A FACTORY, WEIRD BUILDING, ANYWHERE?
I'M NOT SURE. HER GOONIES BLINDFOLDED ME BEFORE SLOPPING THAT GUNK ON MY HAIR.
OMG Olivia
Sparkle Straight
STILL-- BACK WHEN I WAS DOING HYPE SESSIONS AT THE RINK, THE CUTIE CAPTAINS SENT A BUS TO PICK ME UP AND TAKE ME HOME.
HEY! THOSE SPARKLE BUSES...

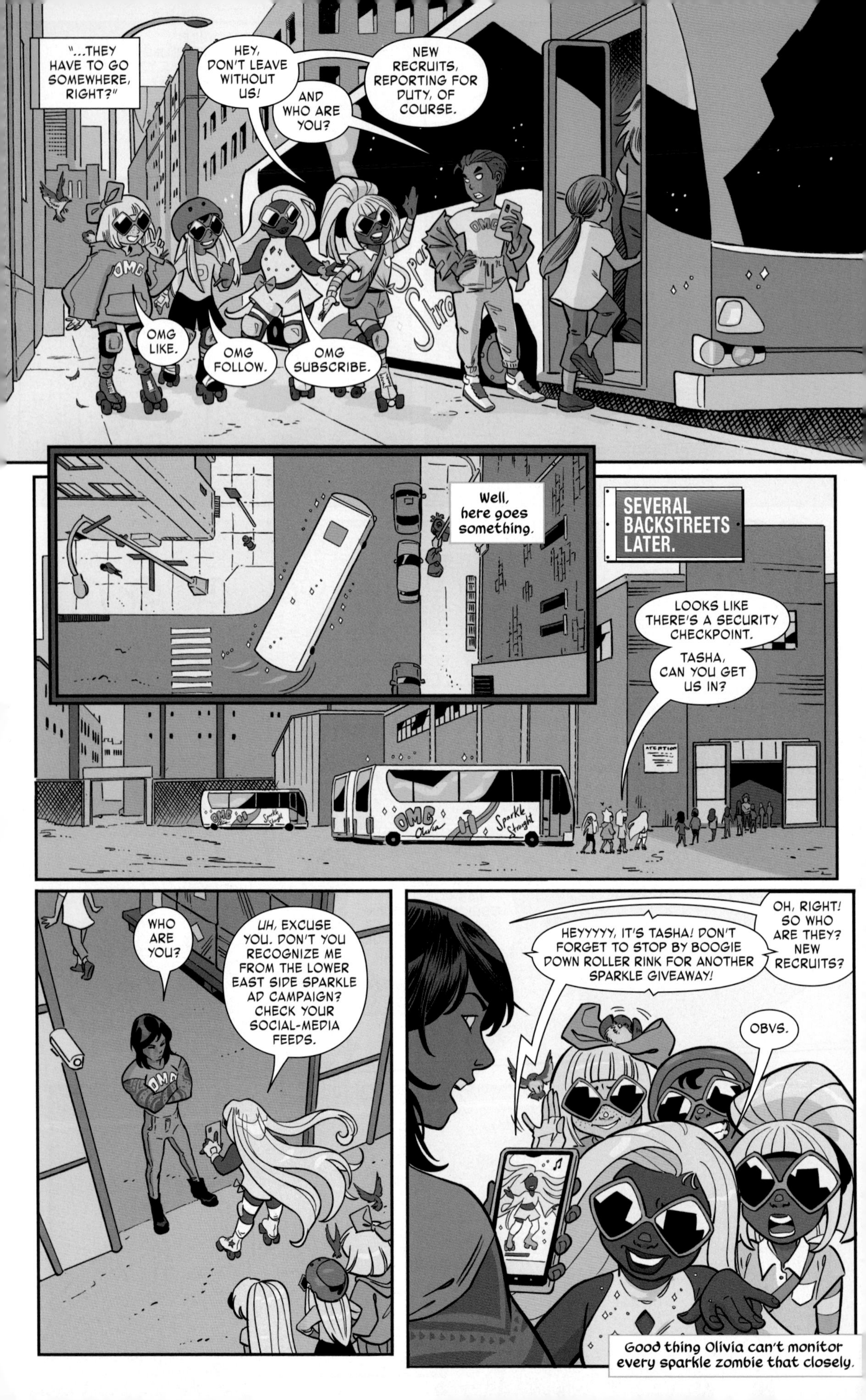
"...THEY HAVE TO GO SOMEWHERE, RIGHT?"
HEY, DON'T LEAVE WITHOUT US!
AND WHO ARE YOU?
NEW RECRUITS, REPORTING FOR DUTY, OF COURSE.
OMG LIKE.
OMG FOLLOW.
OMG SUBSCRIBE.
Well, here goes something.
SEVERAL BACKSTREETS LATER.
LOOKS LIKE THERE'S A SECURITY CHECKPOINT.
TASHA, CAN YOU GET US IN?
OMG Olivia
Sparkle Straight
WHO ARE YOU?
UH, EXCUSE YOU. DON'T YOU RECOGNIZE ME FROM THE LOWER EAST SIDE SPARKLE AD CAMPAIGN? CHECK YOUR SOCIAL-MEDIA FEEDS.
HEYYYYY, IT'S TASHA! DON'T FORGET TO STOP BY BOOGIE DOWN ROLLER RINK FOR ANOTHER SPARKLE GIVEAWAY!
OH, RIGHT! SO WHO ARE THEY? NEW RECRUITS?
OBVS.
Good thing Olivia can't monitor every sparkle zombie that closely.

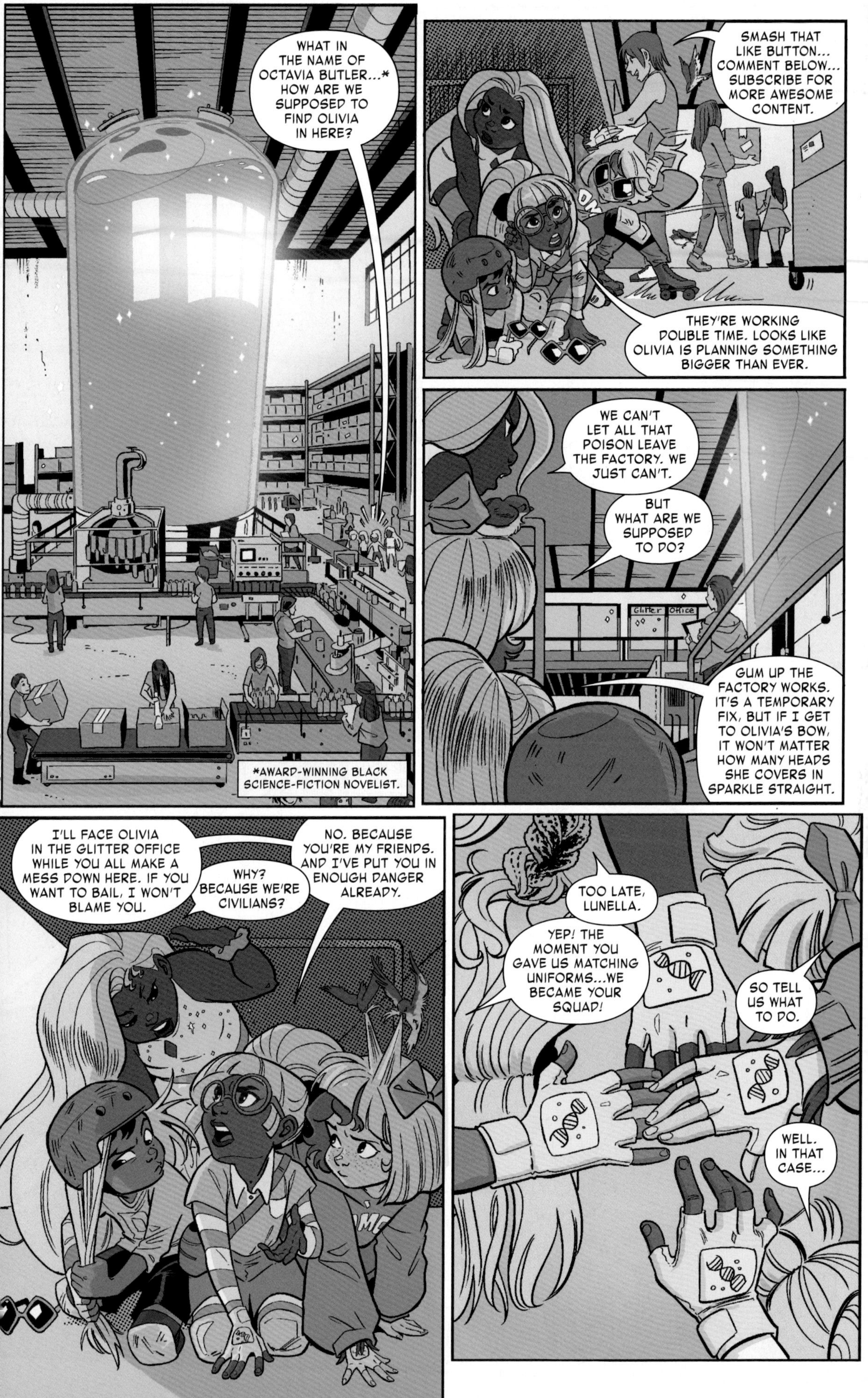
WHAT IN THE NAME OF OCTAVIA BUTLER...* HOW ARE WE SUPPOSED TO FIND OLIVIA IN HERE?
*AWARD-WINNING BLACK SCIENCE-FICTION NOVELIST.
SMASH THAT LIKE BUTTON... COMMENT BELOW... SUBSCRIBE FOR MORE AWESOME CONTENT.
THEY'RE WORKING DOUBLE TIME. LOOKS LIKE OLIVIA IS PLANNING SOMETHING BIGGER THAN EVER.
WE CAN'T LET ALL THAT POISON LEAVE THE FACTORY. WE JUST CAN'T.
BUT WHAT ARE WE SUPPOSED TO DO?
Glitter Office
GUM UP THE FACTORY WORKS. IT'S A TEMPORARY FIX, BUT IF I GET TO OLIVIA'S BOW, IT WON'T MATTER HOW MANY HEADS SHE COVERS IN SPARKLE STRAIGHT.
I'LL FACE OLIVIA IN THE GLITTER OFFICE WHILE YOU ALL MAKE A MESS DOWN HERE. IF YOU WANT TO BAIL, I WON'T BLAME YOU.
WHY? BECAUSE WE'RE CIVILIANS?
NO. BECAUSE YOU'RE MY FRIENDS. AND I'VE PUT YOU IN ENOUGH DANGER ALREADY.
TOO LATE, LUNELLA.
YEP! THE MOMENT YOU GAVE US MATCHING UNIFORMS...WE BECAME YOUR SQUAD!
SO TELL US WHAT TO DO.
WELL. IN THAT CASE...

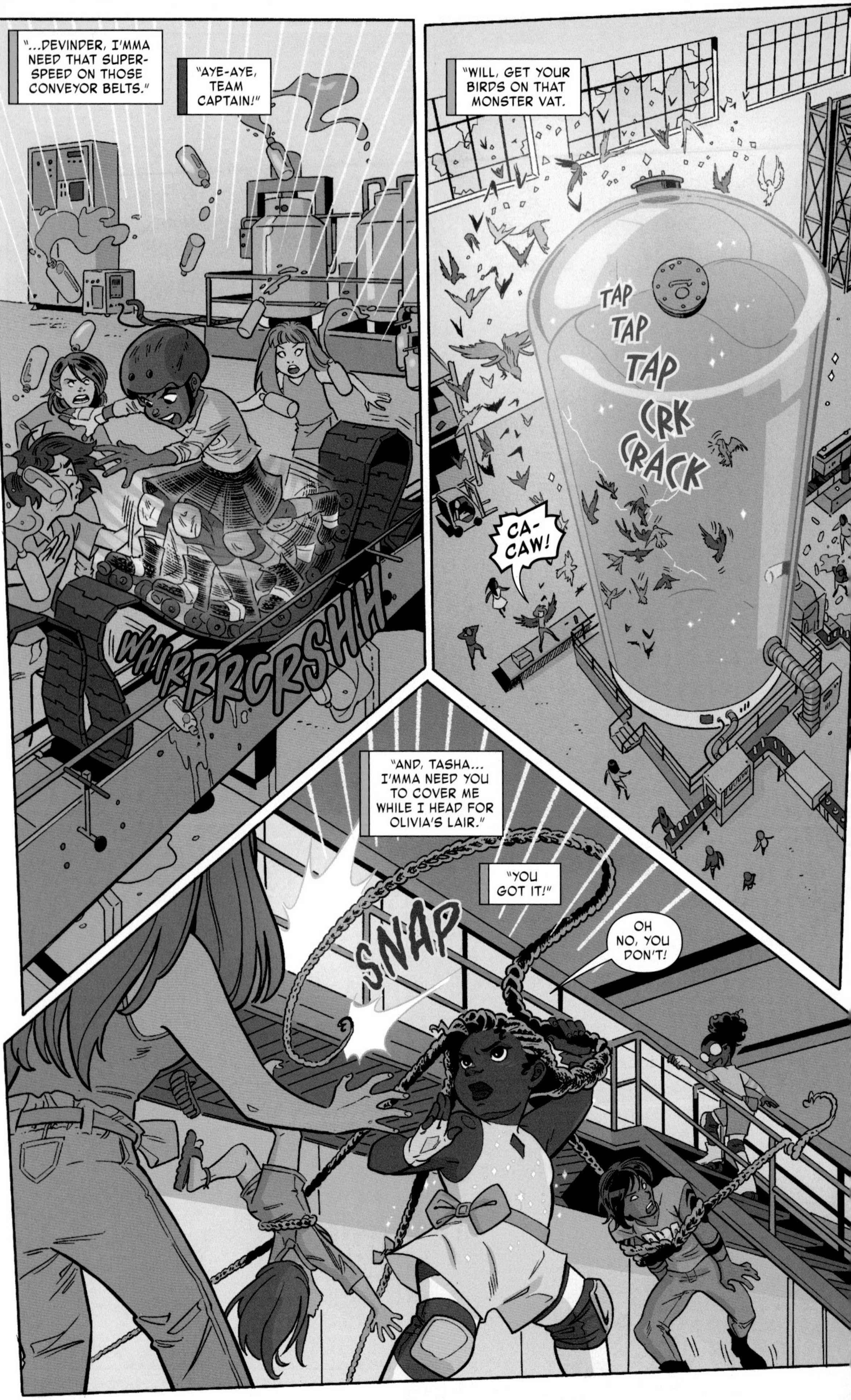
"...DEVINDER, I'MMA NEED THAT SUPER-SPEED ON THOSE CONVEYOR BELTS."
"AYE-AYE, TEAM CAPTAIN!"
WHIRRRCRSHH
"WILL, GET YOUR BIRDS ON THAT MONSTER VAT.
TAP TAP TAP CRK CRACK
CA-CAW!
"AND, TASHA... I'MMA NEED YOU TO COVER ME WHILE I HEAD FOR OLIVIA'S LAIR."
"YOU GOT IT!"
SNAP
OH NO, YOU DON'T!

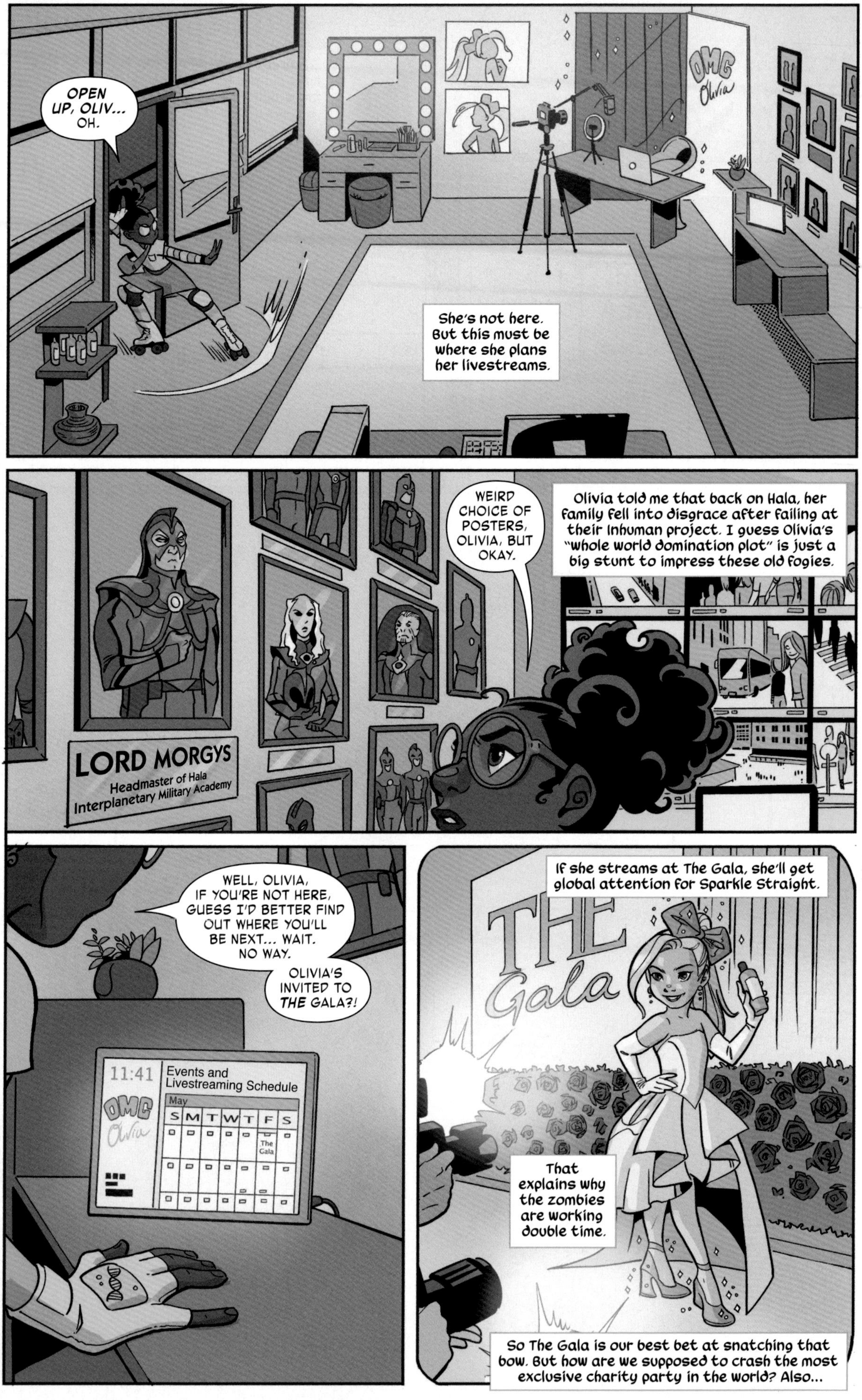
OPEN UP, OLIV... OH.
She's not here. But this must be where she plans her livestreams.
OMG Olivia
WEIRD CHOICE OF POSTERS, OLIVIA, BUT OKAY.
Olivia told me that back on Hala, her family fell into disgrace after failing at their Inhuman project. I guess Olivia's "whole world domination plot" is just a big stunt to impress these old fogies.
LORD MORGYS
Headmaster of Hala Interplanetary Military Academy
WELL, OLIVIA, IF YOU'RE NOT HERE, GUESS I'D BETTER FIND OUT WHERE YOU'LL BE NEXT... WAIT. NO WAY.
OLIVIA'S INVITED TO THE GALA?!
11:41
Events and Livestreaming Schedule
OMG Olivia
May
S M T W T F S
The Gala
If she streams at The Gala, she'll get global attention for Sparkle Straight.
THE Gala
That explains why the zombies are working double time.
So The Gala is our best bet at snatching that bow. But how are we supposed to crash the most exclusive charity party in the world? Also...

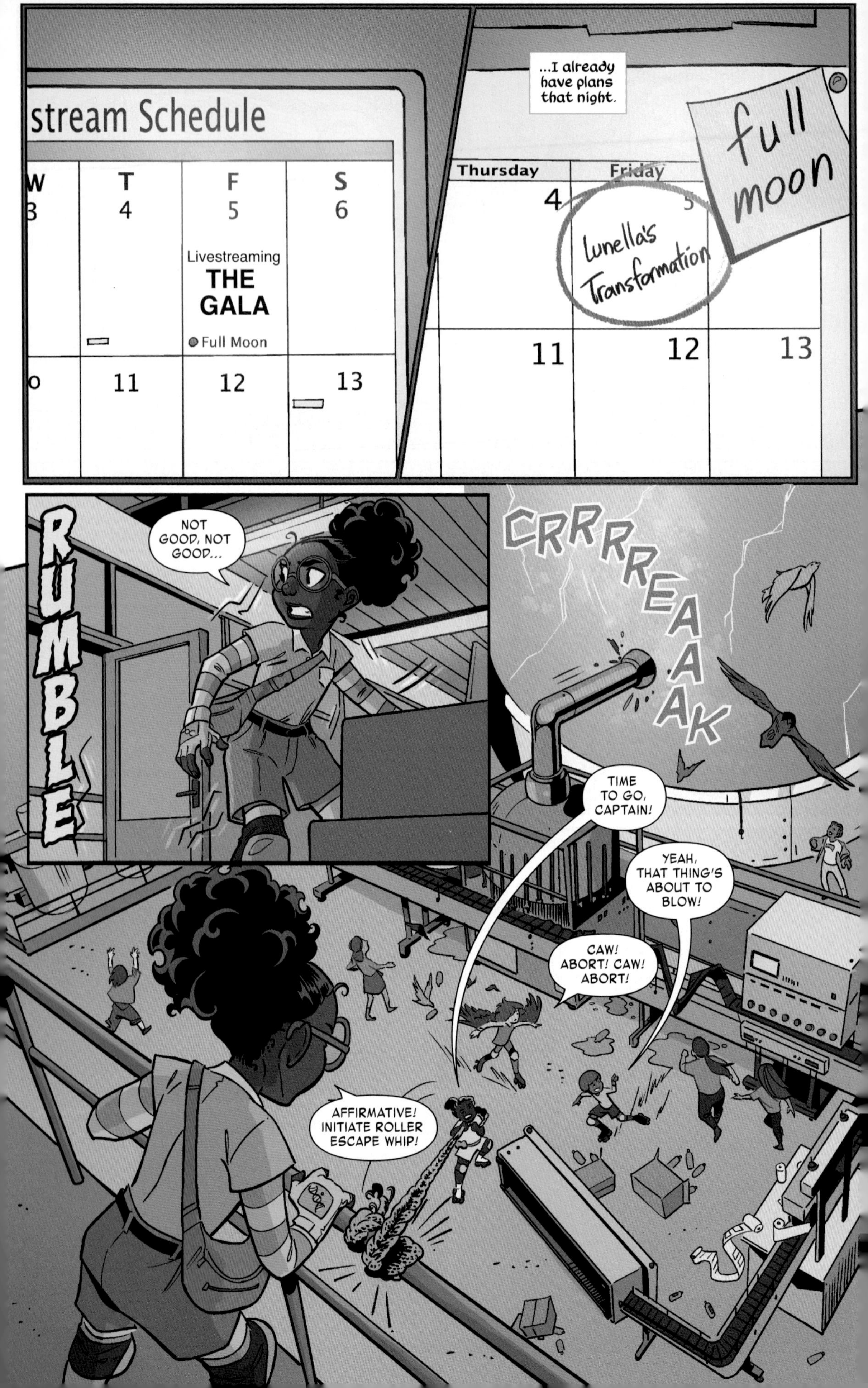
stream Schedule
W T F S
3 4 5 6
Livestreaming THE GALA
Full Moon
0 11 12 13
...I already have plans that night.
full moon
Thursday Friday
4 5
Lunella's Transformation
11 12 13
RUMBLE
NOT GOOD, NOT GOOD...
CRRRREAAAAK
TIME TO GO, CAPTAIN!
YEAH, THAT THING'S ABOUT TO BLOW!
CAW! ABORT! CAW! ABORT!
AFFIRMATIVE! INITIATE ROLLER ESCAPE WHIP!

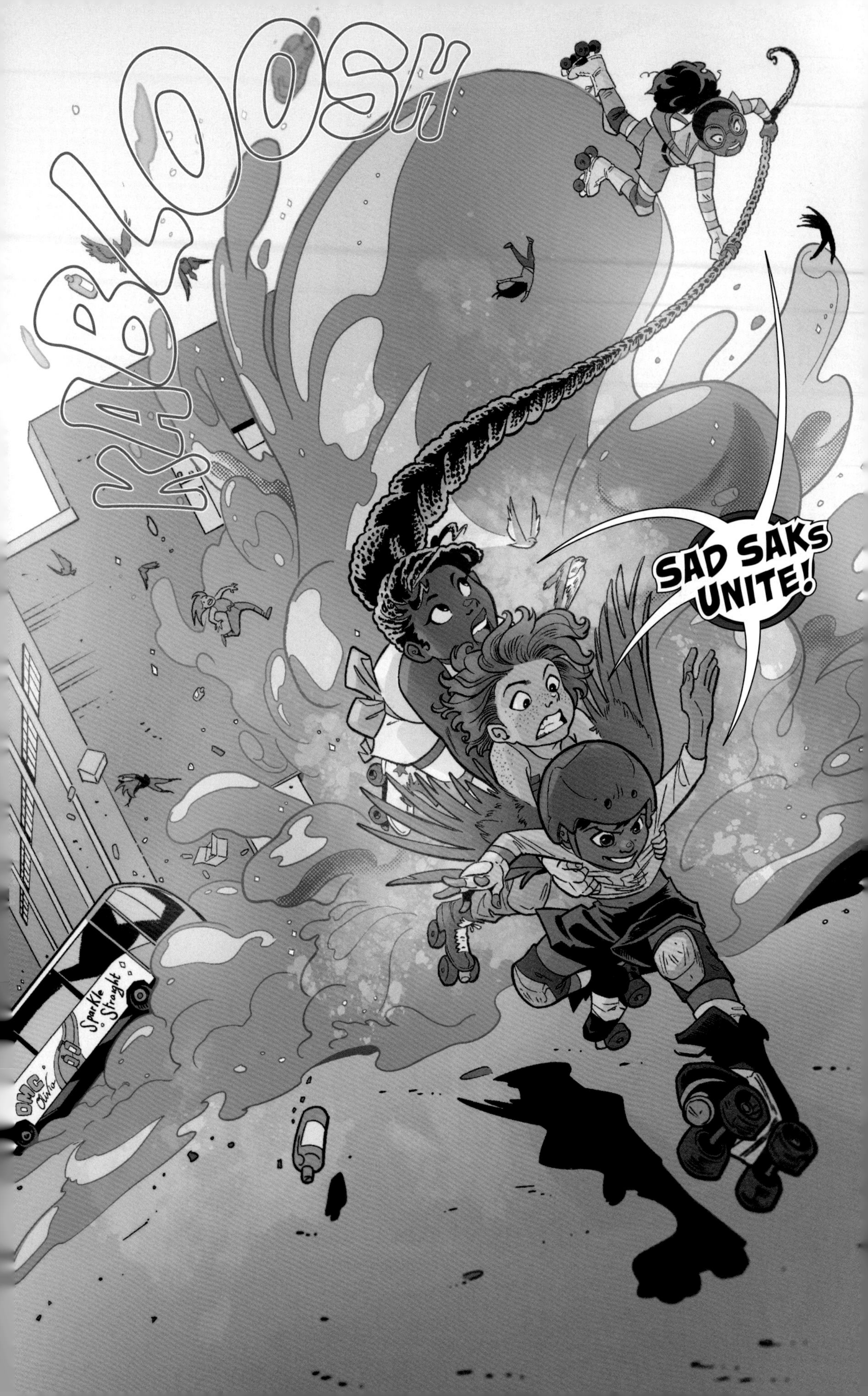
KABLOOSH
SAD SAKS UNITE!
Sparkle Straight
OMG

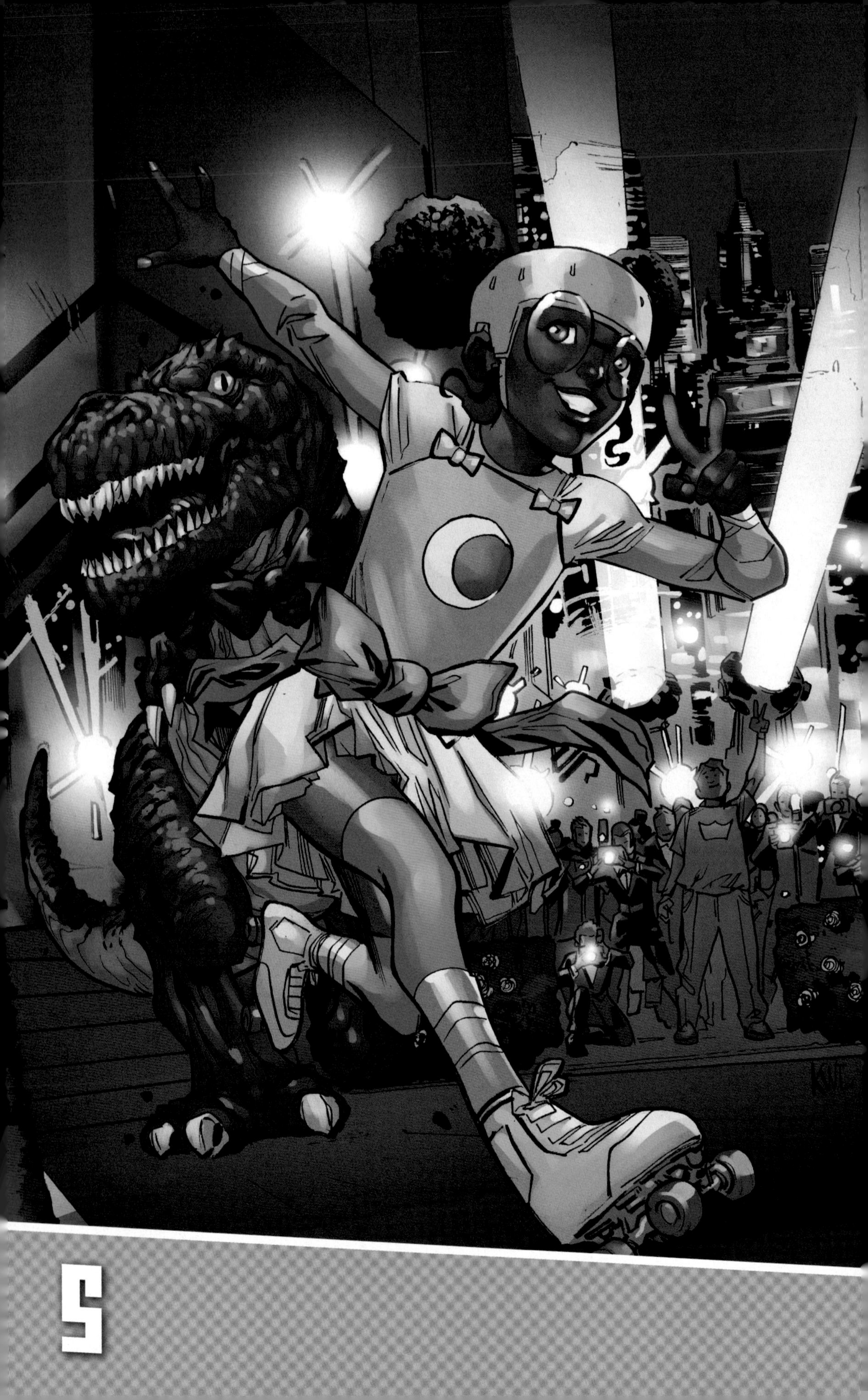

5

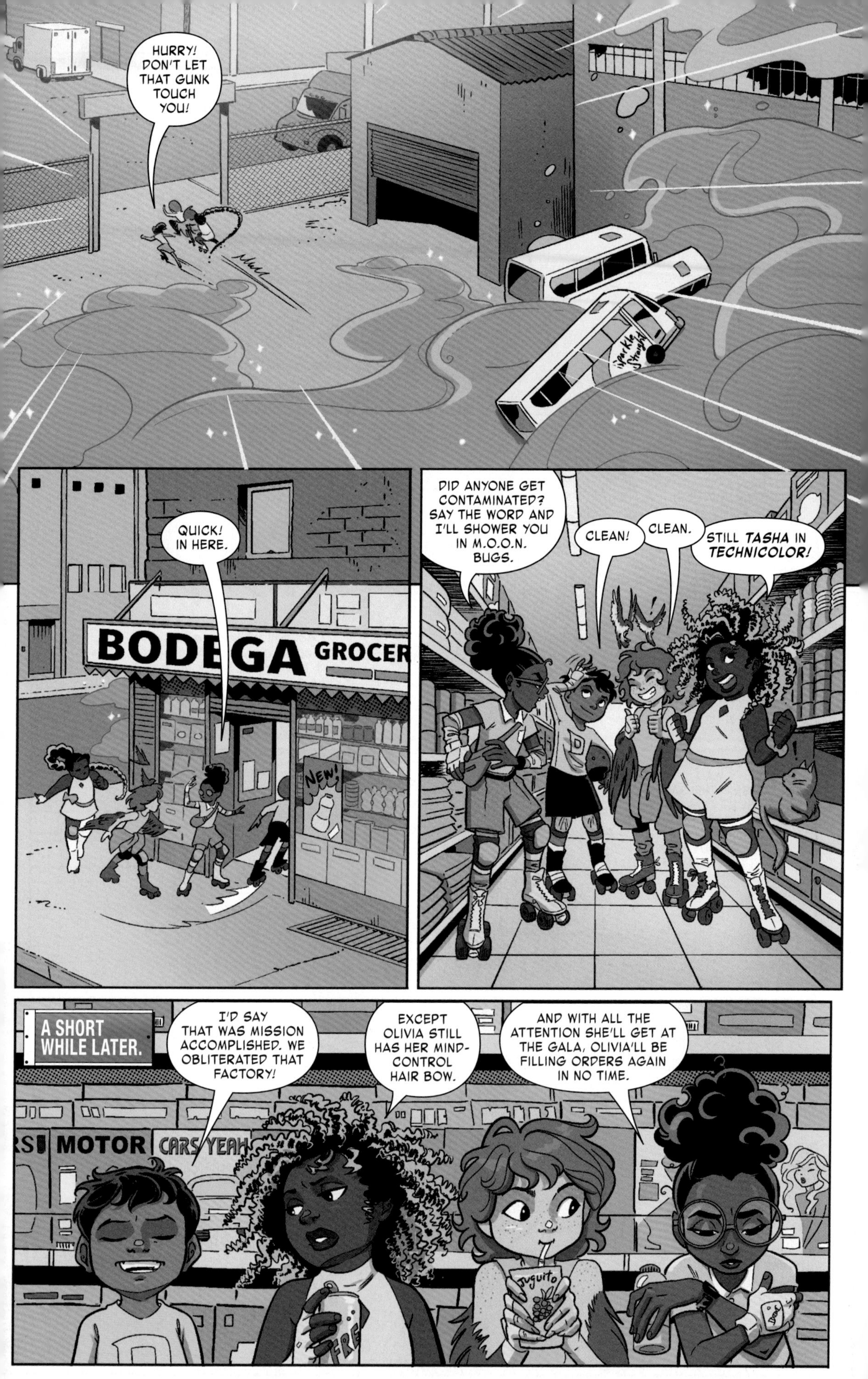
HURRY! DON'T LET THAT GUNK TOUCH YOU!
QUICK! IN HERE.
BODEGA GROCER
NEW!
DID ANYONE GET CONTAMINATED? SAY THE WORD AND I'LL SHOWER YOU IN M.O.O.N. BUGS.
CLEAN!
CLEAN.
STILL *TASHA* IN *TECHNICOLOR!*
A SHORT WHILE LATER.
I'D SAY THAT WAS MISSION ACCOMPLISHED. WE OBLITERATED THAT FACTORY!
EXCEPT OLIVIA STILL HAS HER MIND-CONTROL HAIR BOW.
AND WITH ALL THE ATTENTION SHE'LL GET AT THE GALA, OLIVIA'LL BE FILLING ORDERS AGAIN IN NO TIME.
MOTOR
CARS YEAH
Juguito

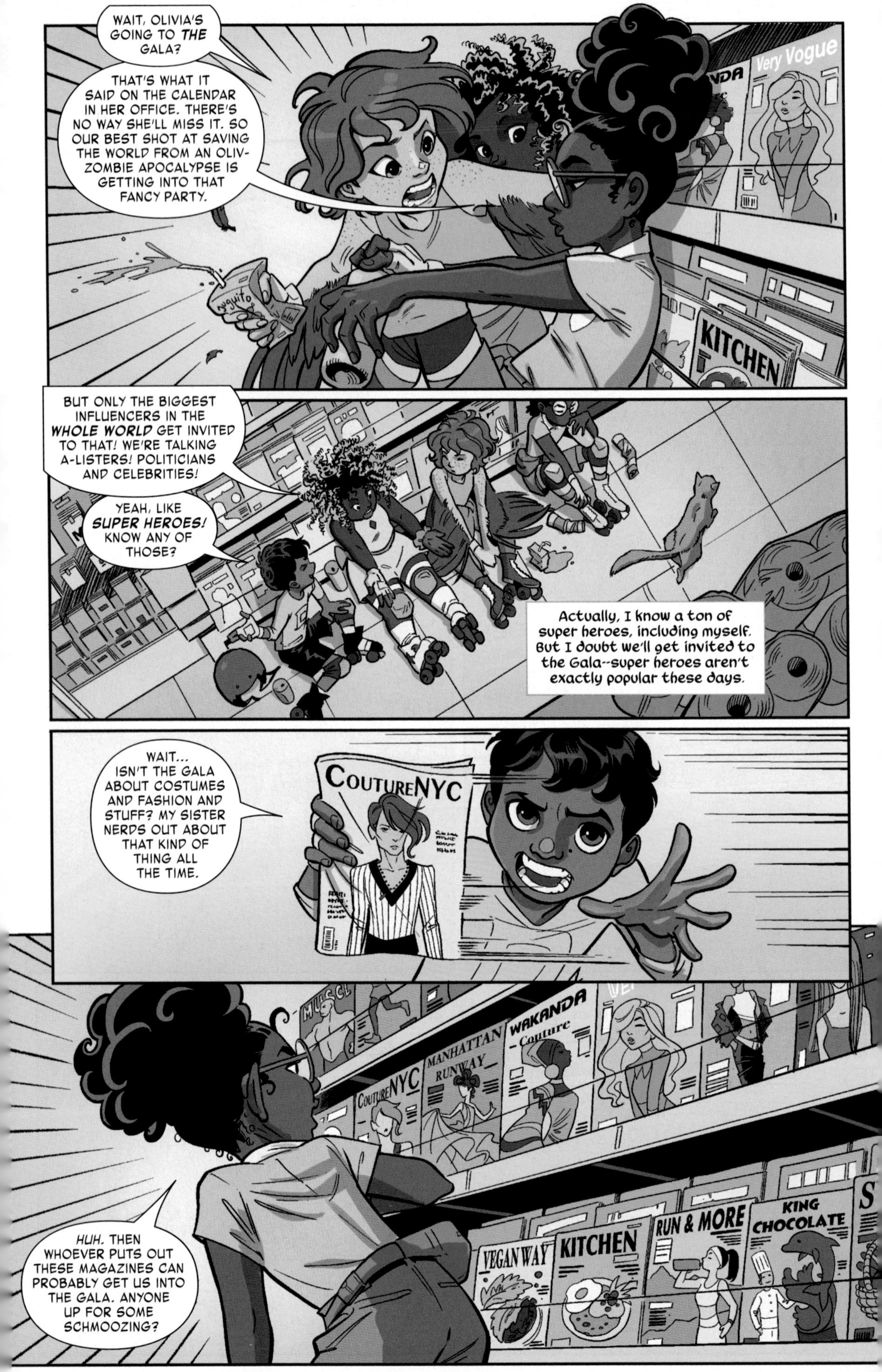
WAIT, OLIVIA'S GOING TO *THE* GALA?
THAT'S WHAT IT SAID ON THE CALENDAR IN HER OFFICE. THERE'S NO WAY SHE'LL MISS IT. SO OUR BEST SHOT AT SAVING THE WORLD FROM AN OLIV-ZOMBIE APOCALYPSE IS GETTING INTO THAT FANCY PARTY.
Very Vogue
KITCHEN
BUT ONLY THE BIGGEST INFLUENCERS IN THE *WHOLE WORLD* GET INVITED TO THAT! WE'RE TALKING A-LISTERS! POLITICIANS AND CELEBRITIES!
YEAH, LIKE *SUPER HEROES!* KNOW ANY OF THOSE?
Actually, I know a ton of super heroes, including myself. But I doubt we'll get invited to the Gala--super heroes aren't exactly popular these days.
WAIT... ISN'T THE GALA ABOUT COSTUMES AND FASHION AND STUFF? MY SISTER NERDS OUT ABOUT THAT KIND OF THING ALL THE TIME.
CoutureNYC
WAKANDA Couture
MANHATTAN RUNWAY
CoutureNYC
VEGAN WAY
KITCHEN
RUN & MORE
KING CHOCOLATE
HUH. THEN WHOEVER PUTS OUT THESE MAGAZINES CAN PROBABLY GET US INTO THE GALA. ANYONE UP FOR SOME SCHMOOZING?

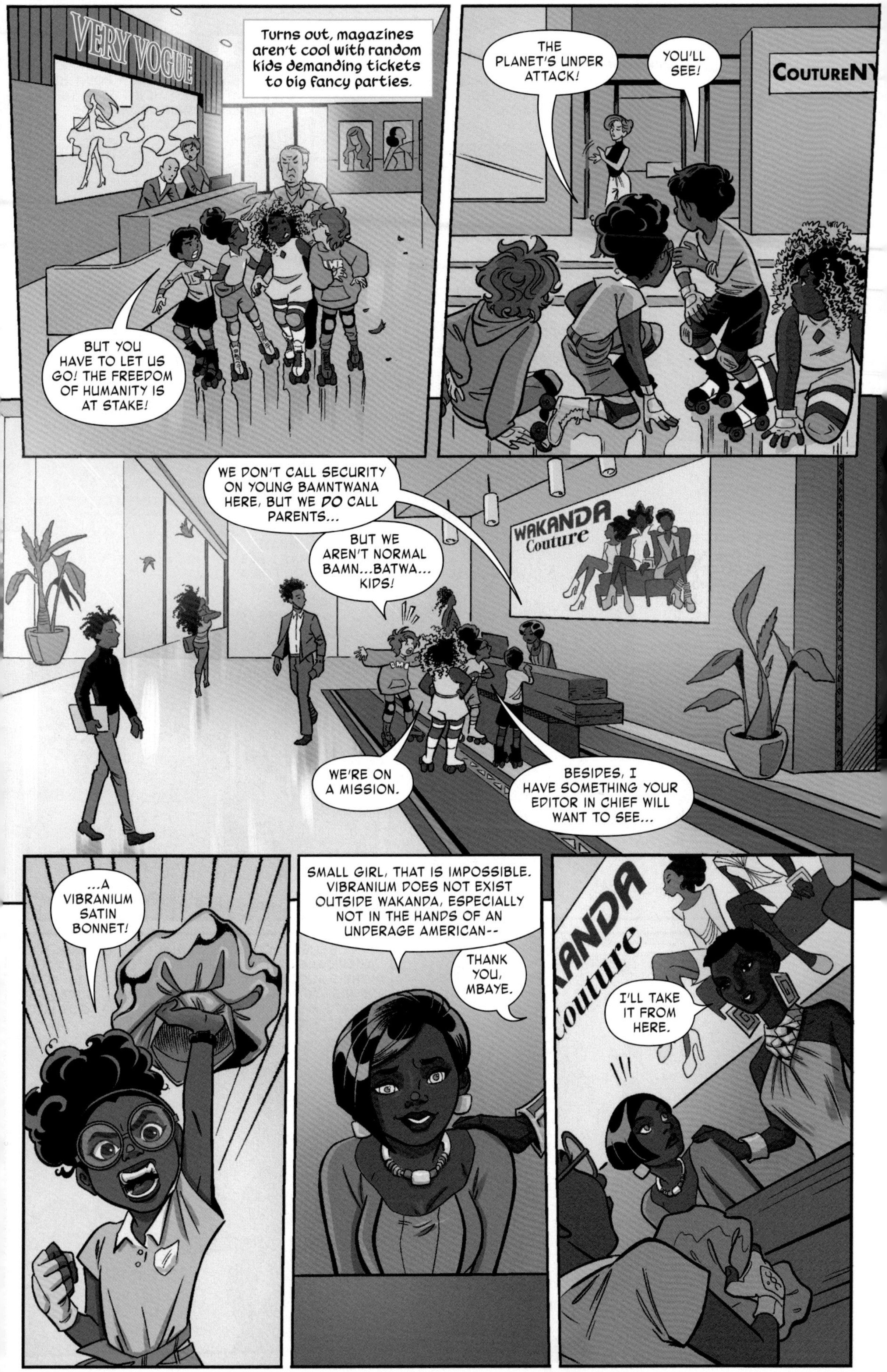
VERY VOGUE
Turns out, magazines aren't cool with random kids demanding tickets to big fancy parties.
BUT YOU HAVE TO LET US GO! THE FREEDOM OF HUMANITY IS AT STAKE!
THE PLANET'S UNDER ATTACK!
YOU'LL SEE!
COUTURENY
WE DON'T CALL SECURITY ON YOUNG BAMNTWANA HERE, BUT WE DO CALL PARENTS...
BUT WE AREN'T NORMAL BAMN...BATWA... KIDS!
WAKANDA Couture
WE'RE ON A MISSION.
BESIDES, I HAVE SOMETHING YOUR EDITOR IN CHIEF WILL WANT TO SEE...
...A VIBRANIUM SATIN BONNET!
SMALL GIRL, THAT IS IMPOSSIBLE. VIBRANIUM DOES NOT EXIST OUTSIDE WAKANDA, ESPECIALLY NOT IN THE HANDS OF AN UNDERAGE AMERICAN--
THANK YOU, MBAYE.
I'LL TAKE IT FROM HERE.

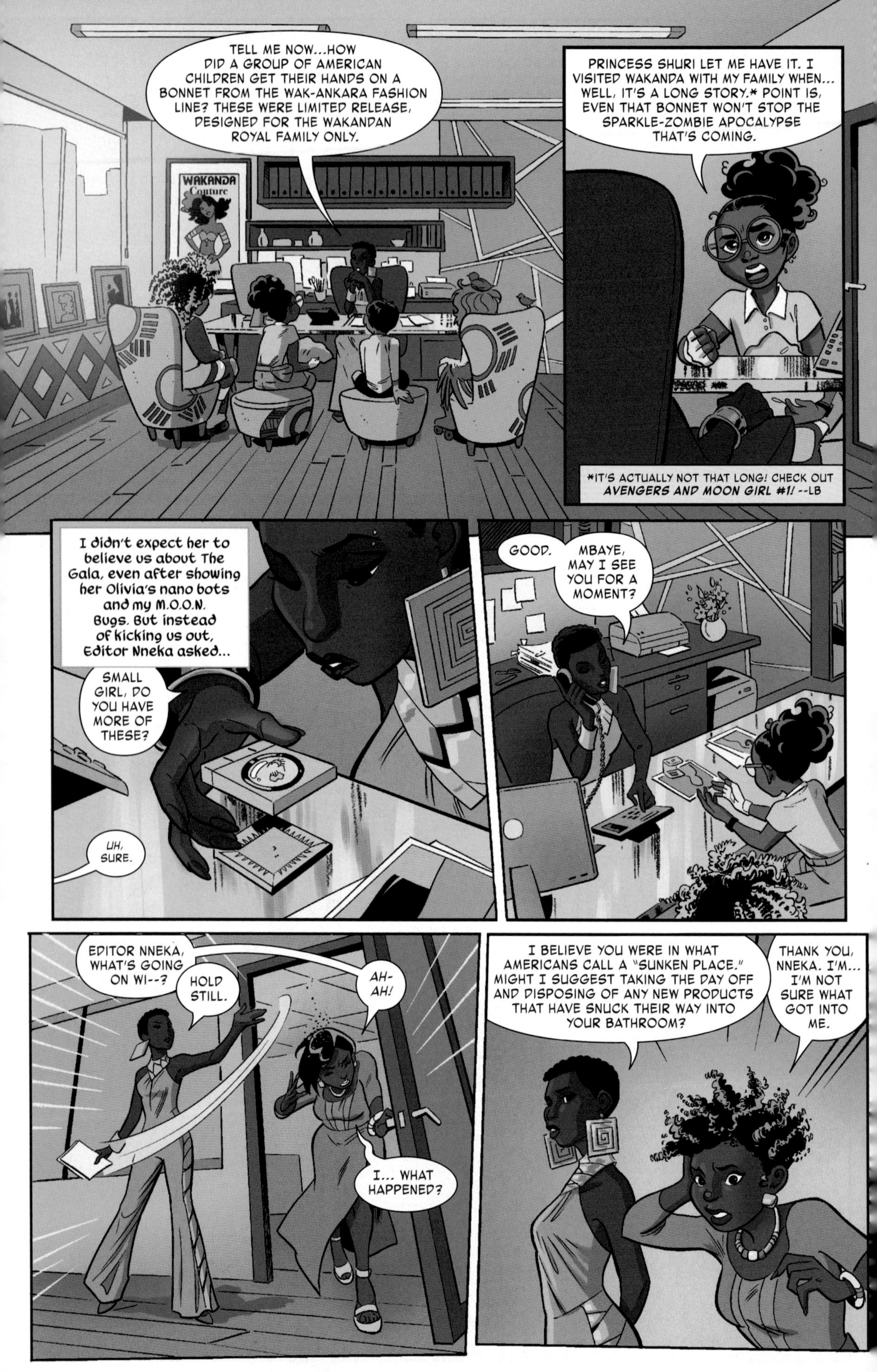
TELL ME NOW...HOW DID A GROUP OF AMERICAN CHILDREN GET THEIR HANDS ON A BONNET FROM THE WAK-ANKARA FASHION LINE? THESE WERE LIMITED RELEASE, DESIGNED FOR THE WAKANDAN ROYAL FAMILY ONLY.
WAKANDA Couture
PRINCESS SHURI LET ME HAVE IT. I VISITED WAKANDA WITH MY FAMILY WHEN... WELL, IT'S A LONG STORY.* POINT IS, EVEN THAT BONNET WON'T STOP THE SPARKLE-ZOMBIE APOCALYPSE THAT'S COMING.
*IT'S ACTUALLY NOT THAT LONG! CHECK OUT AVENGERS AND MOON GIRL #1! --LB
I didn't expect her to believe us about The Gala, even after showing her Olivia's nano bots and my M.O.O.N. Bugs. But instead of kicking us out, Editor Nneka asked...
SMALL GIRL, DO YOU HAVE MORE OF THESE?
UH, SURE.
GOOD.
MBAYE, MAY I SEE YOU FOR A MOMENT?
EDITOR NNEKA, WHAT'S GOING ON WI--?
HOLD STILL.
AH-AH!
I... WHAT HAPPENED?
I BELIEVE YOU WERE IN WHAT AMERICANS CALL A "SUNKEN PLACE." MIGHT I SUGGEST TAKING THE DAY OFF AND DISPOSING OF ANY NEW PRODUCTS THAT HAVE SNUCK THEIR WAY INTO YOUR BATHROOM?
THANK YOU, NNEKA. I'M... I'M NOT SURE WHAT GOT INTO ME.

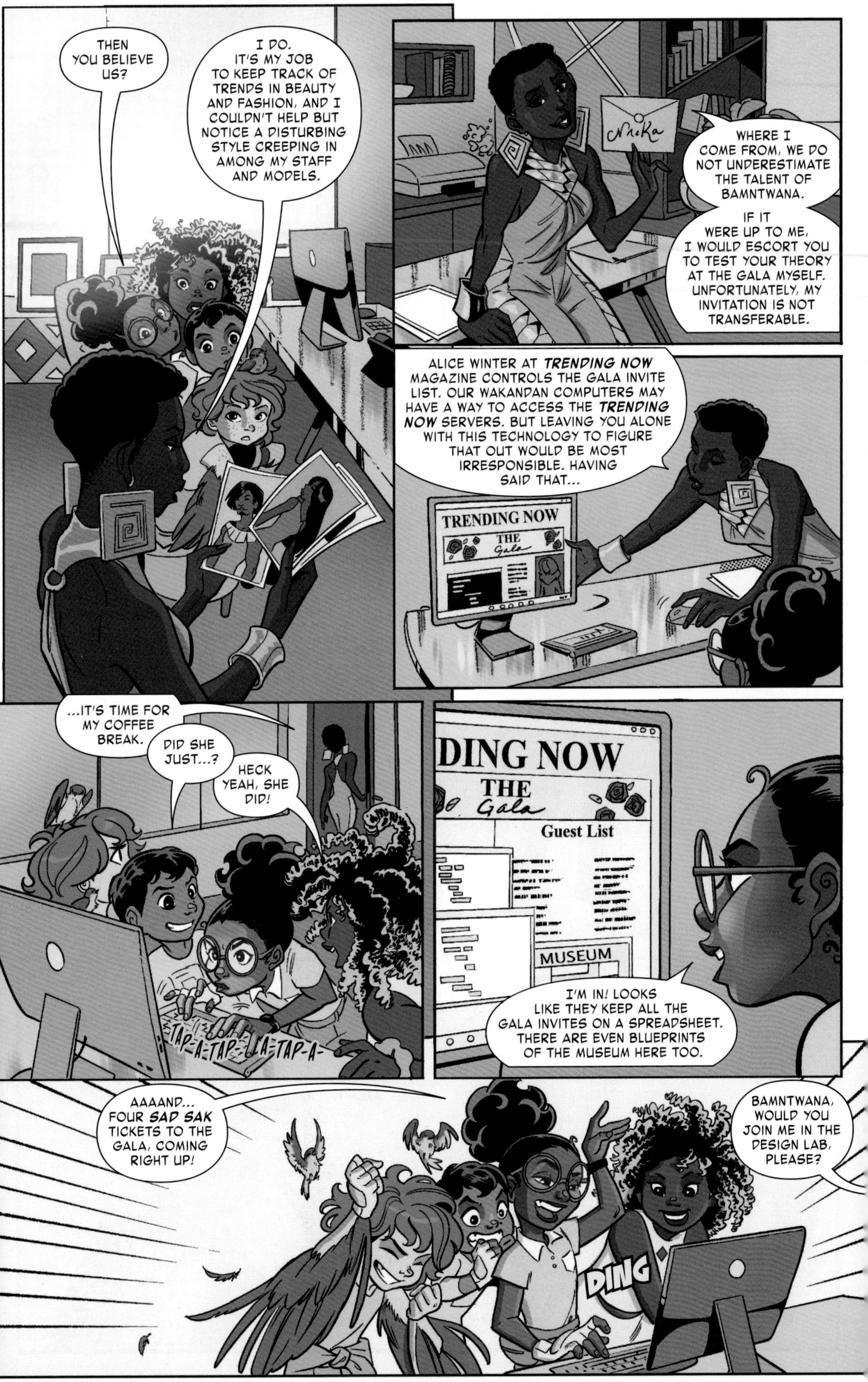
THEN YOU BELIEVE US?
I DO. IT'S MY JOB TO KEEP TRACK OF TRENDS IN BEAUTY AND FASHION, AND I COULDN'T HELP BUT NOTICE A DISTURBING STYLE CREEPING IN AMONG MY STAFF AND MODELS.
WHERE I COME FROM, WE DO NOT UNDERESTIMATE THE TALENT OF BAMNTWANA.
IF IT WERE UP TO ME, I WOULD ESCORT YOU TO TEST YOUR THEORY AT THE GALA MYSELF. UNFORTUNATELY, MY INVITATION IS NOT TRANSFERABLE.
ALICE WINTER AT *TRENDING NOW* MAGAZINE CONTROLS THE GALA INVITE LIST. OUR WAKANDAN COMPUTERS MAY HAVE A WAY TO ACCESS THE *TRENDING NOW* SERVERS. BUT LEAVING YOU ALONE WITH THIS TECHNOLOGY TO FIGURE THAT OUT WOULD BE MOST IRRESPONSIBLE. HAVING SAID THAT...
TRENDING NOW
THE Gala
...IT'S TIME FOR MY COFFEE BREAK.
DID SHE JUST...?
HECK YEAH, SHE DID!
TAP-A-TAP-A-TAP-A-
DING NOW
THE Gala
Guest List
MUSEUM
I'M IN! LOOKS LIKE THEY KEEP ALL THE GALA INVITES ON A SPREADSHEET. THERE ARE EVEN BLUEPRINTS OF THE MUSEUM HERE TOO.
AAAAND... FOUR ***SAD SAK*** TICKETS TO THE GALA, COMING RIGHT UP!
BAMNTWANA, WOULD YOU JOIN ME IN THE DESIGN LAB, PLEASE?
DING

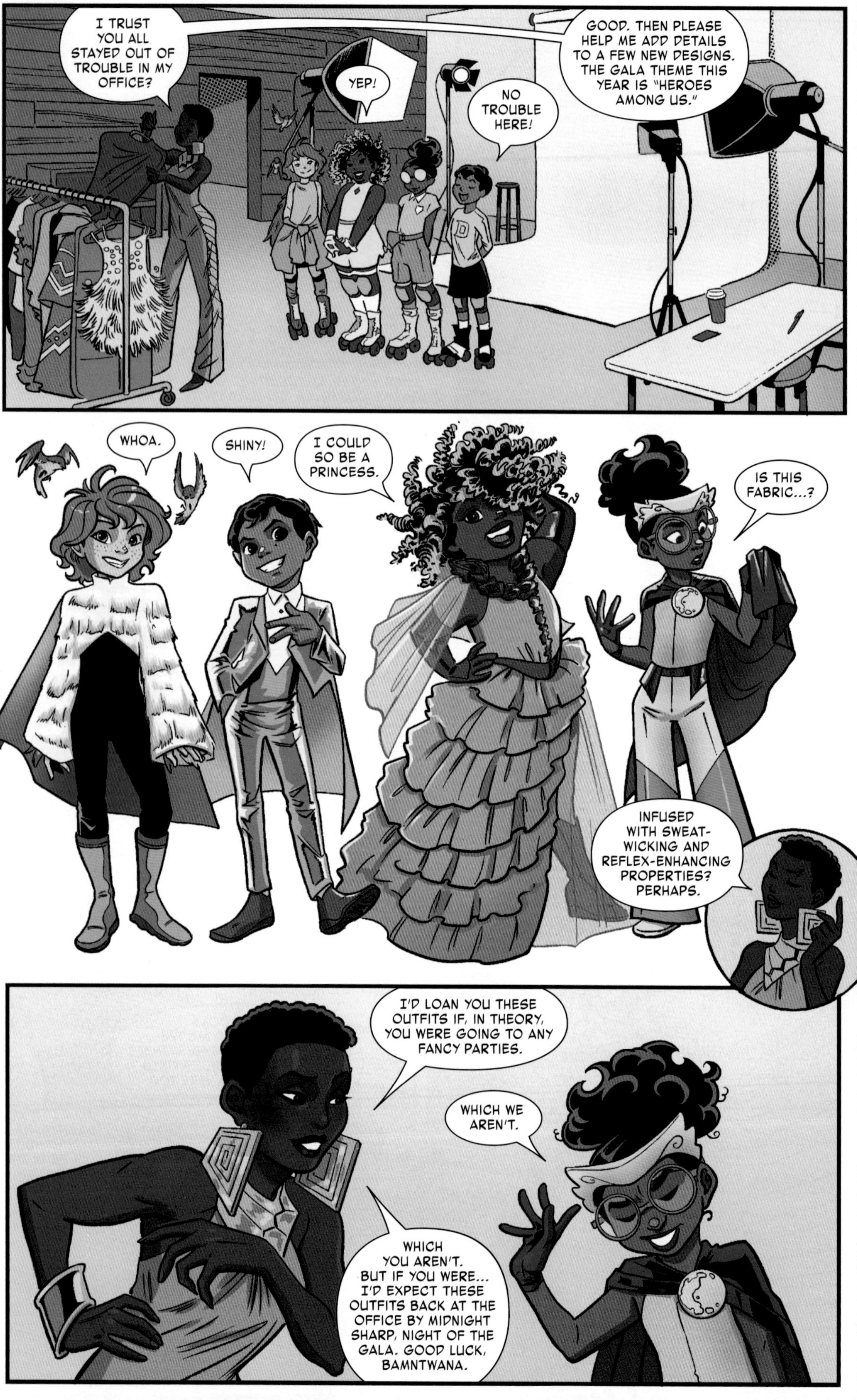
I TRUST YOU ALL STAYED OUT OF TROUBLE IN MY OFFICE?
YEP!
NO TROUBLE HERE!
GOOD. THEN PLEASE HELP ME ADD DETAILS TO A FEW NEW DESIGNS. THE GALA THEME THIS YEAR IS "HEROES AMONG US."
WHOA.
SHINY!
I COULD SO BE A PRINCESS.
IS THIS FABRIC...?
INFUSED WITH SWEAT-WICKING AND REFLEX-ENHANCING PROPERTIES? PERHAPS.
I'D LOAN YOU THESE OUTFITS IF, IN THEORY, YOU WERE GOING TO ANY FANCY PARTIES.
WHICH WE AREN'T.
WHICH YOU AREN'T. BUT IF YOU WERE... I'D EXPECT THESE OUTFITS BACK AT THE OFFICE BY MIDNIGHT SHARP, NIGHT OF THE GALA. GOOD LUCK, BAMNTWANA.

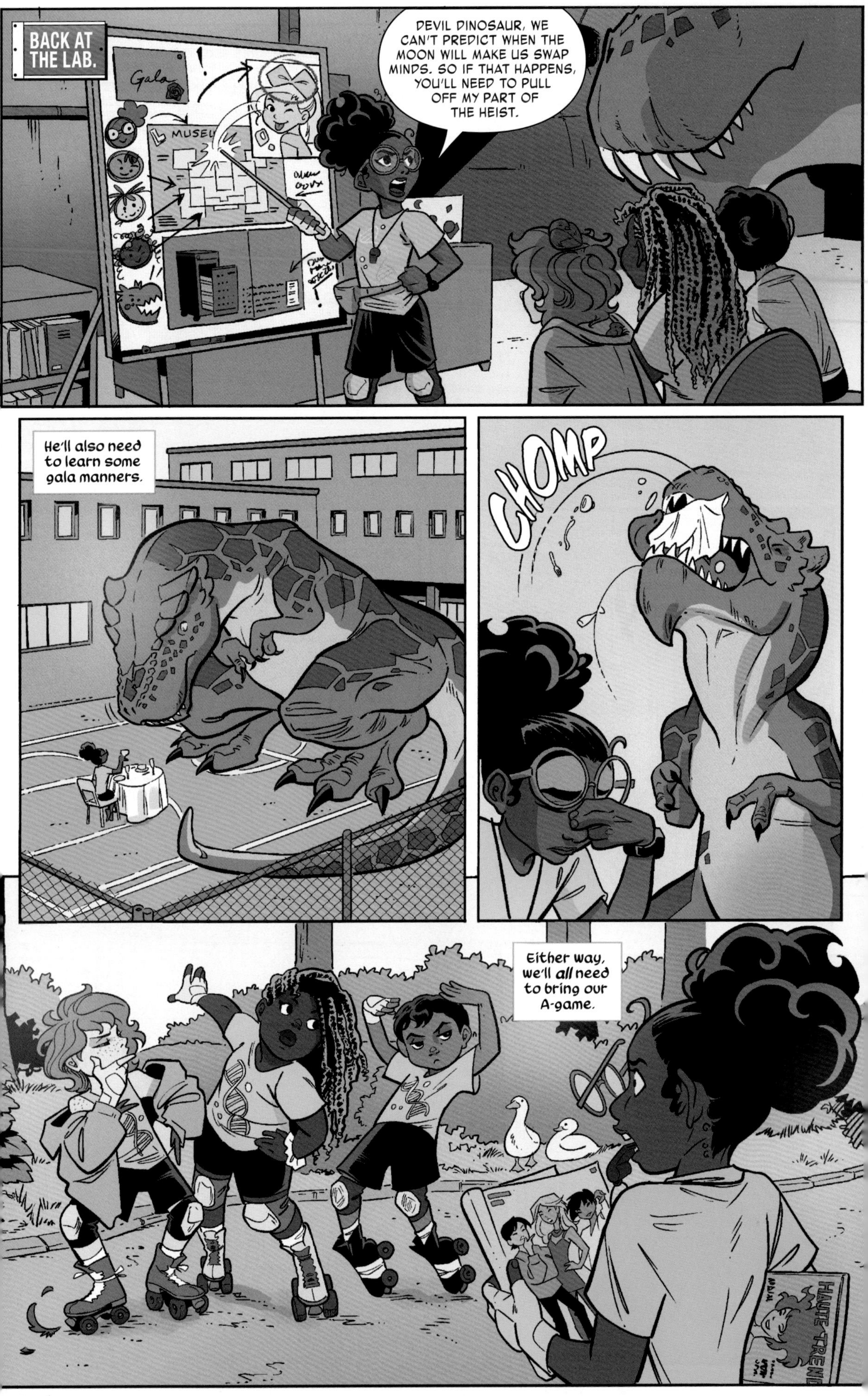
BACK AT THE LAB.
DEVIL DINOSAUR, WE CAN'T PREDICT WHEN THE MOON WILL MAKE US SWAP MINDS. SO IF THAT HAPPENS, YOU'LL NEED TO PULL OFF MY PART OF THE HEIST.
He'll also need to learn some gala manners.
CHOMP
Either way, we'll *all* need to bring our A-game.

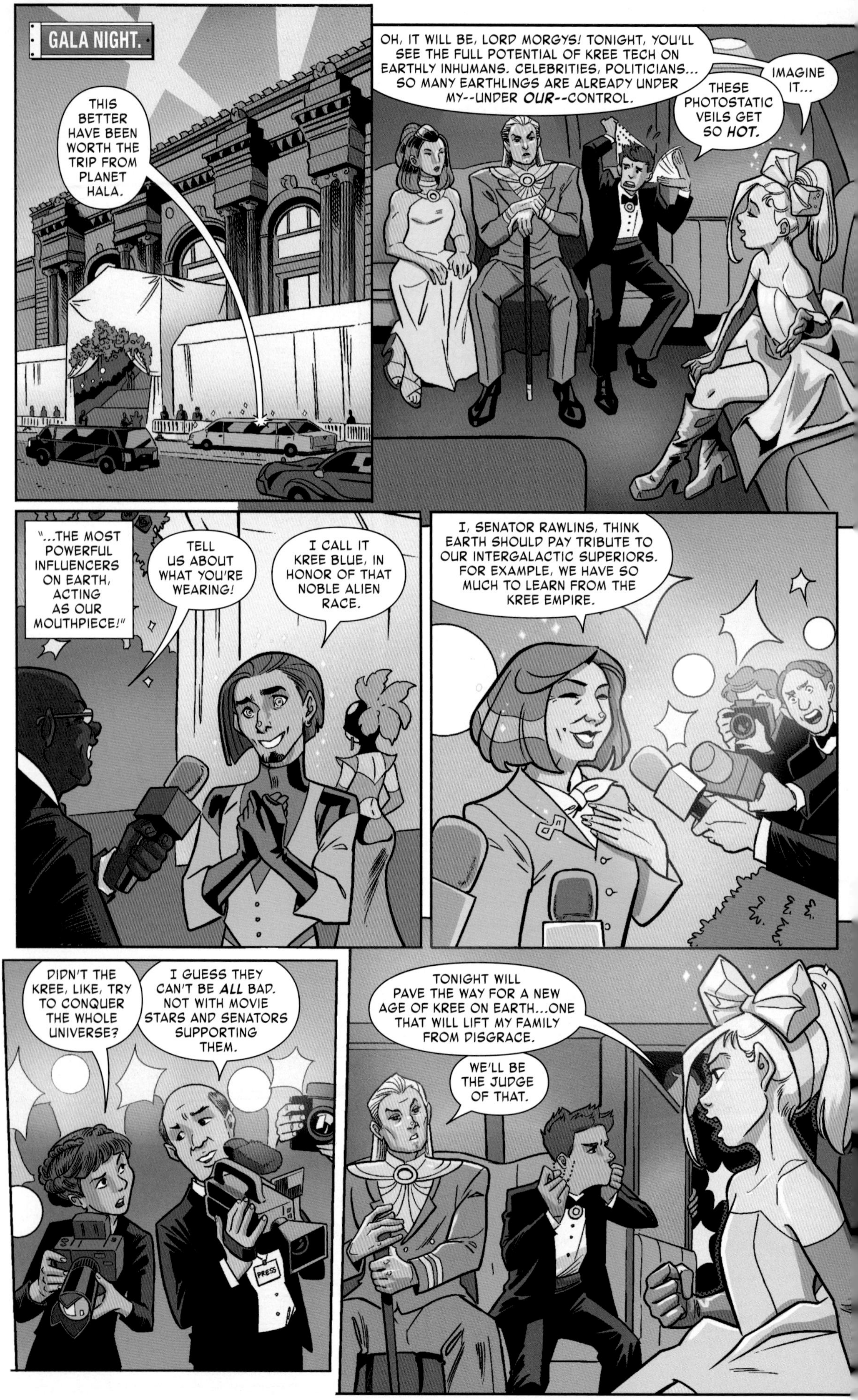
GALA NIGHT.
THIS BETTER HAVE BEEN WORTH THE TRIP FROM PLANET HALA.
OH, IT WILL BE, LORD MORGYS! TONIGHT, YOU'LL SEE THE FULL POTENTIAL OF KREE TECH ON EARTHLY INHUMANS. CELEBRITIES, POLITICIANS... SO MANY EARTHLINGS ARE ALREADY UNDER MY--UNDER OUR--CONTROL.
IMAGINE IT...
THESE PHOTOSTATIC VEILS GET SO HOT.
"...THE MOST POWERFUL INFLUENCERS ON EARTH, ACTING AS OUR MOUTHPIECE!"
TELL US ABOUT WHAT YOU'RE WEARING!
I CALL IT KREE BLUE, IN HONOR OF THAT NOBLE ALIEN RACE.
I, SENATOR RAWLINS, THINK EARTH SHOULD PAY TRIBUTE TO OUR INTERGALACTIC SUPERIORS. FOR EXAMPLE, WE HAVE SO MUCH TO LEARN FROM THE KREE EMPIRE.
DIDN'T THE KREE, LIKE, TRY TO CONQUER THE WHOLE UNIVERSE?
I GUESS THEY CAN'T BE ALL BAD. NOT WITH MOVIE STARS AND SENATORS SUPPORTING THEM.
PRESS
TONIGHT WILL PAVE THE WAY FOR A NEW AGE OF KREE ON EARTH...ONE THAT WILL LIFT MY FAMILY FROM DISGRACE.
WE'LL BE THE JUDGE OF THAT.

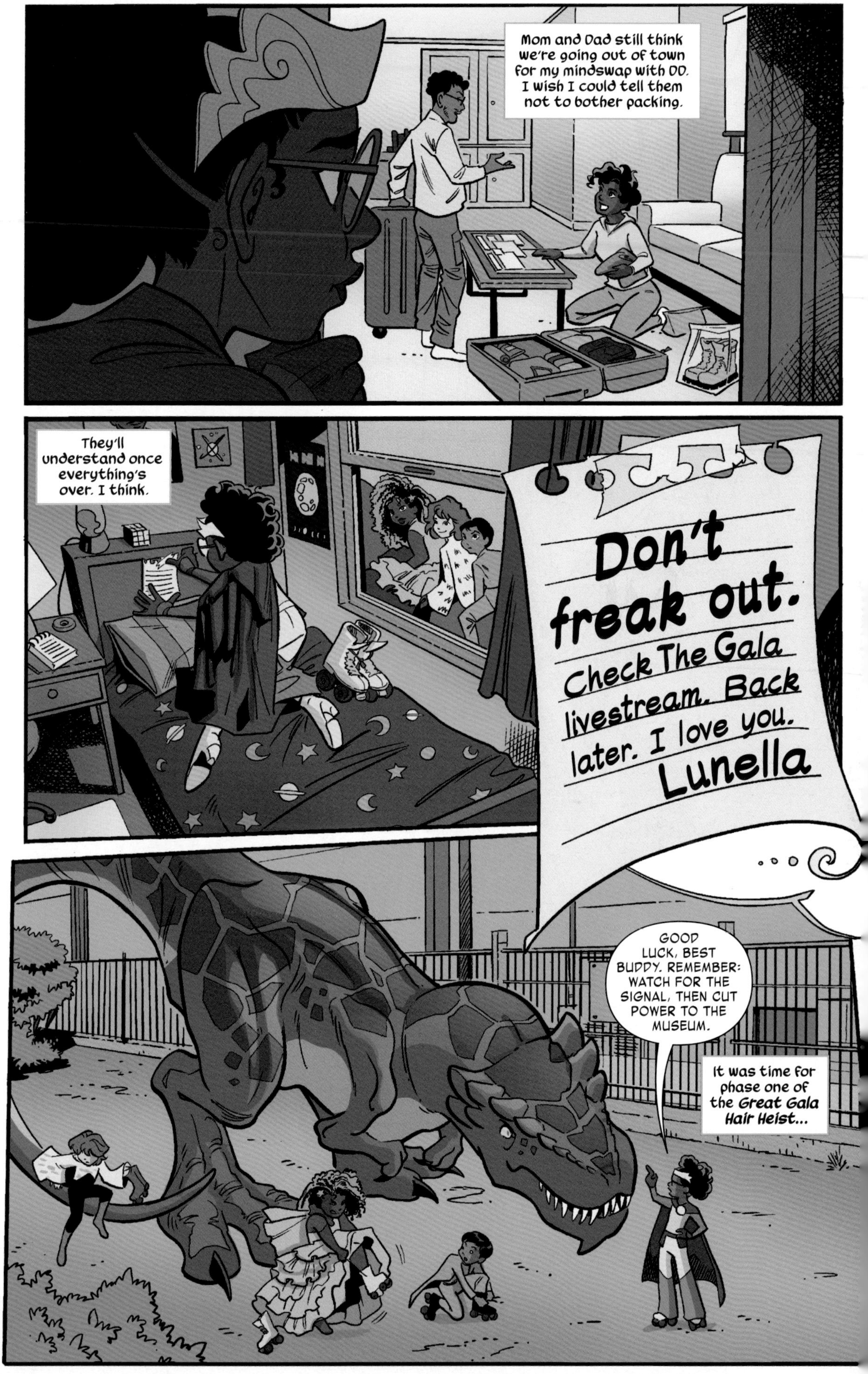
Mom and Dad still think we're going out of town for my mindswap with DD. I wish I could tell them not to bother packing.
They'll understand once everything's over. I think.
Don't freak out. Check The Gala livestream. Back later. I love you. Lunella
GOOD LUCK, BEST BUDDY. REMEMBER: WATCH FOR THE SIGNAL, THEN CUT POWER TO THE MUSEUM.
It was time for phase one of the Great Gala Hair Heist...

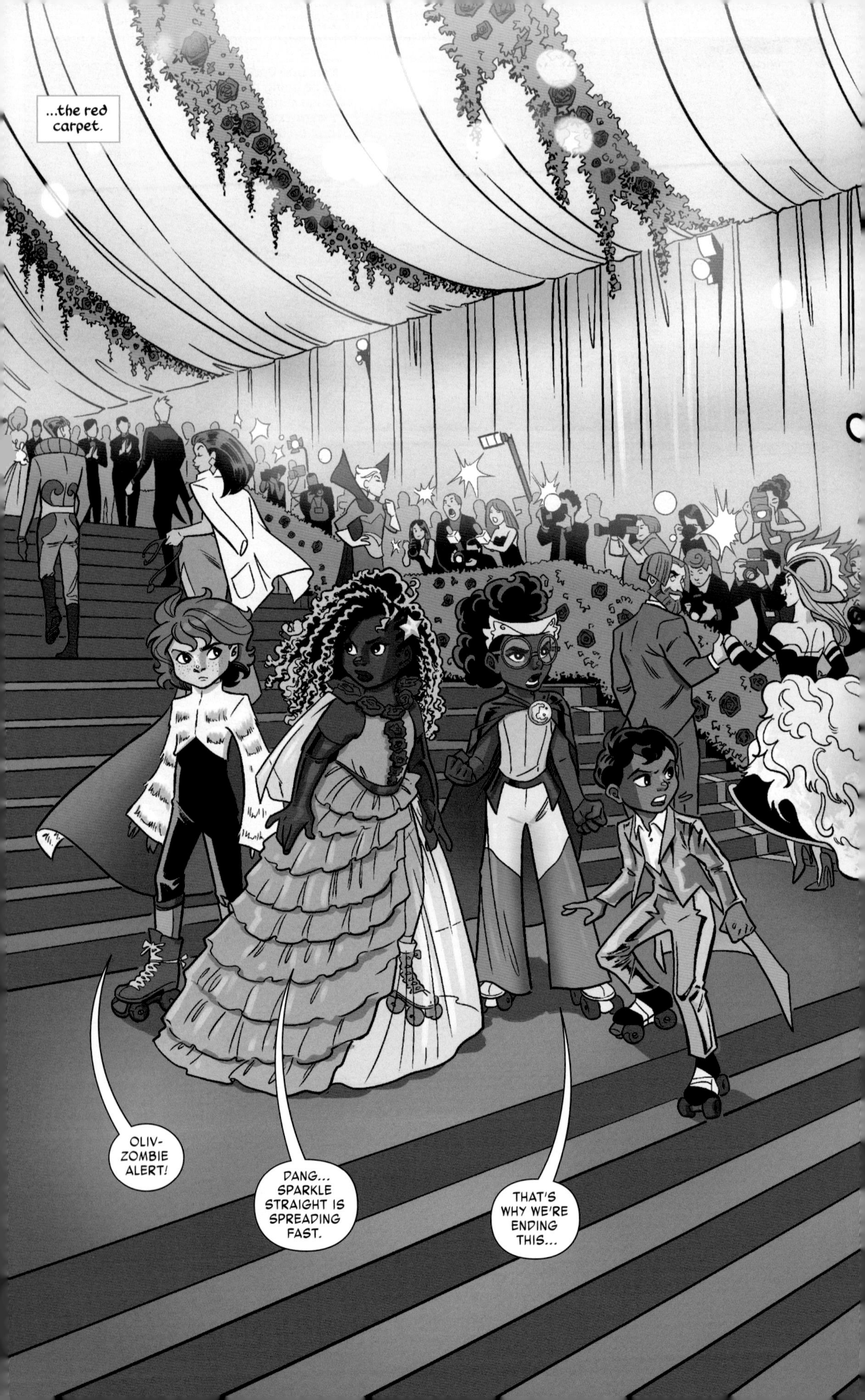
...the red carpet.
OLIV-ZOMBIE ALERT!
DANG... SPARKLE STRAIGHT IS SPREADING FAST.
THAT'S WHY WE'RE ENDING THIS...

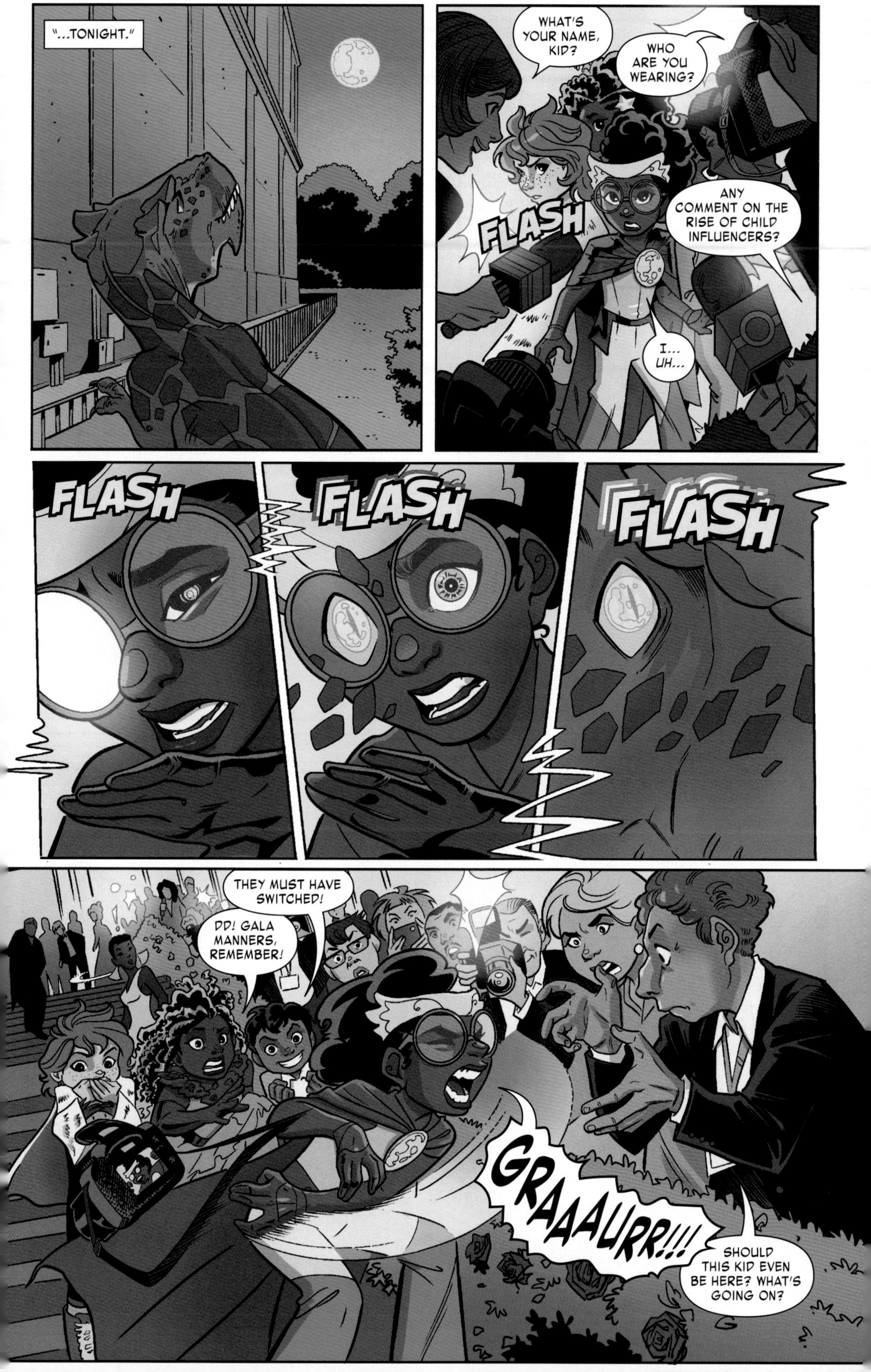
"...TONIGHT."
WHAT'S YOUR NAME, KID?
WHO ARE YOU WEARING?
FLASH
ANY COMMENT ON THE RISE OF CHILD INFLUENCERS?
I... UH...
FLASH
FLASH
FLASH
THEY MUST HAVE SWITCHED!
DD! GALA MANNERS, REMEMBER!
GRAAAURR!!!
SHOULD THIS KID EVEN BE HERE? WHAT'S GOING ON?

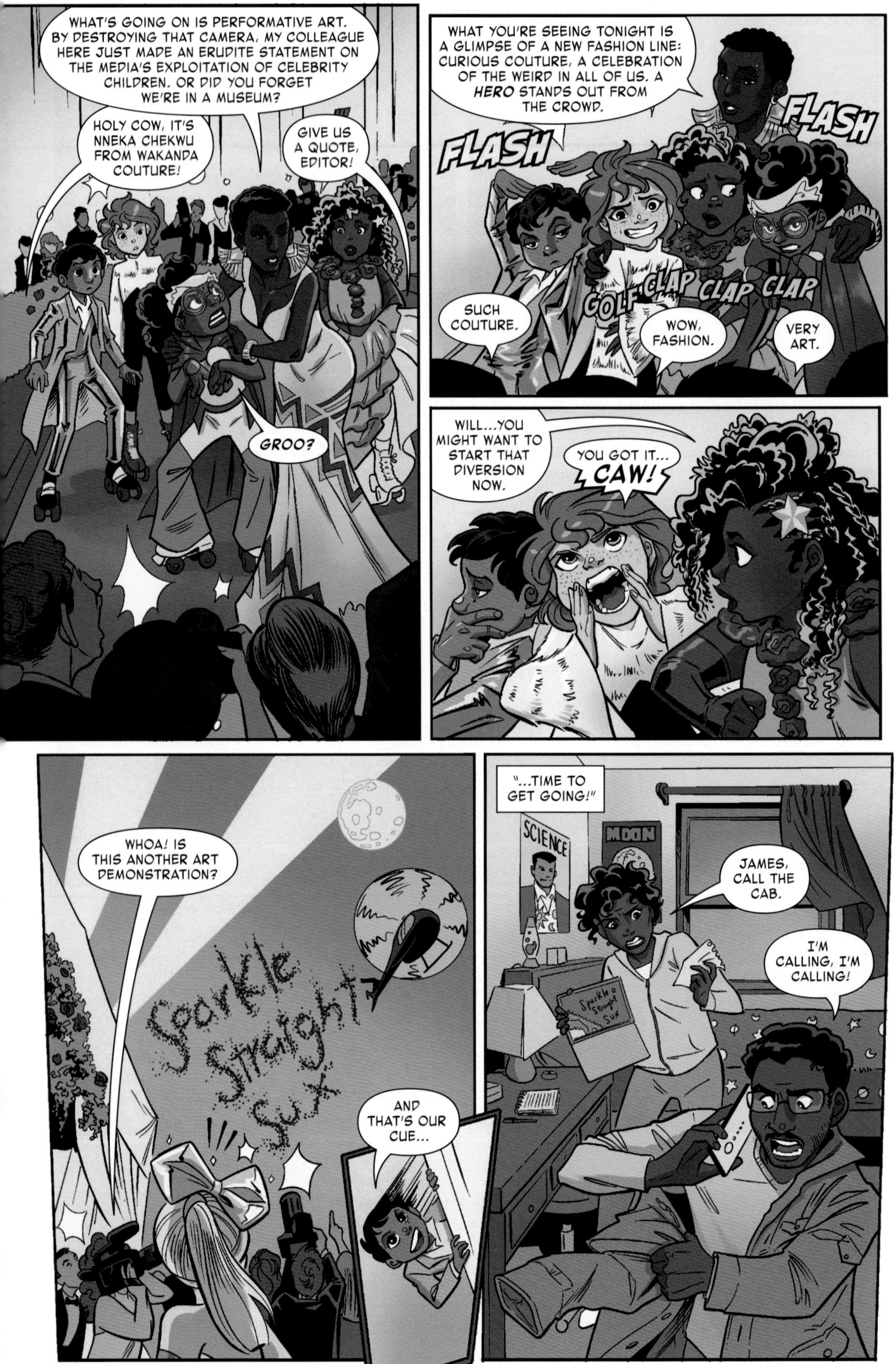
WHAT'S GOING ON IS PERFORMATIVE ART. BY DESTROYING THAT CAMERA, MY COLLEAGUE HERE JUST MADE AN ERUDITE STATEMENT ON THE MEDIA'S EXPLOITATION OF CELEBRITY CHILDREN. OR DID YOU FORGET WE'RE IN A MUSEUM?
HOLY COW, IT'S NNEKA CHEKWU FROM WAKANDA COUTURE!
GIVE US A QUOTE, EDITOR!
GROO?
WHAT YOU'RE SEEING TONIGHT IS A GLIMPSE OF A NEW FASHION LINE: CURIOUS COUTURE, A CELEBRATION OF THE WEIRD IN ALL OF US. A *HERO* STANDS OUT FROM THE CROWD.
FLASH
FLASH
GOLF CLAP CLAP CLAP CLAP
SUCH COUTURE.
WOW, FASHION.
VERY ART.
WILL...YOU MIGHT WANT TO START THAT DIVERSION NOW.
YOU GOT IT... **CAW!**
WHOA! IS THIS ANOTHER ART DEMONSTRATION?
Sparkle Straight Sux
AND THAT'S OUR CUE...
"...TIME TO GET GOING!"
SCIENCE
MOON
JAMES, CALL THE CAB.
I'M CALLING, I'M CALLING!

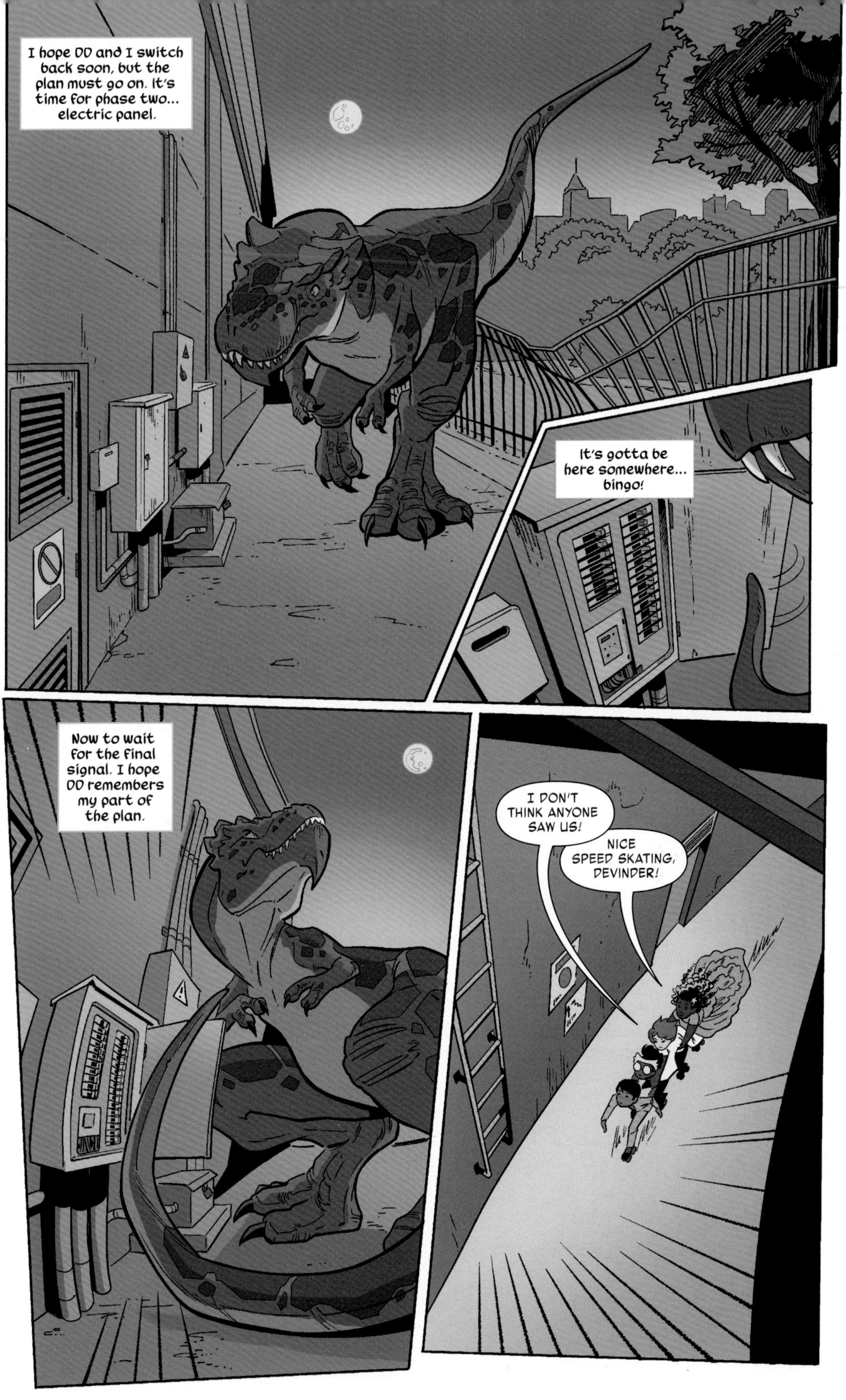
I hope DD and I switch back soon, but the plan must go on. It's time for phase two... electric panel.
It's gotta be here somewhere... bingo!
Now to wait for the final signal. I hope DD remembers my part of the plan.
I DON'T THINK ANYONE SAW US!
NICE SPEED SKATING, DEVINDER!

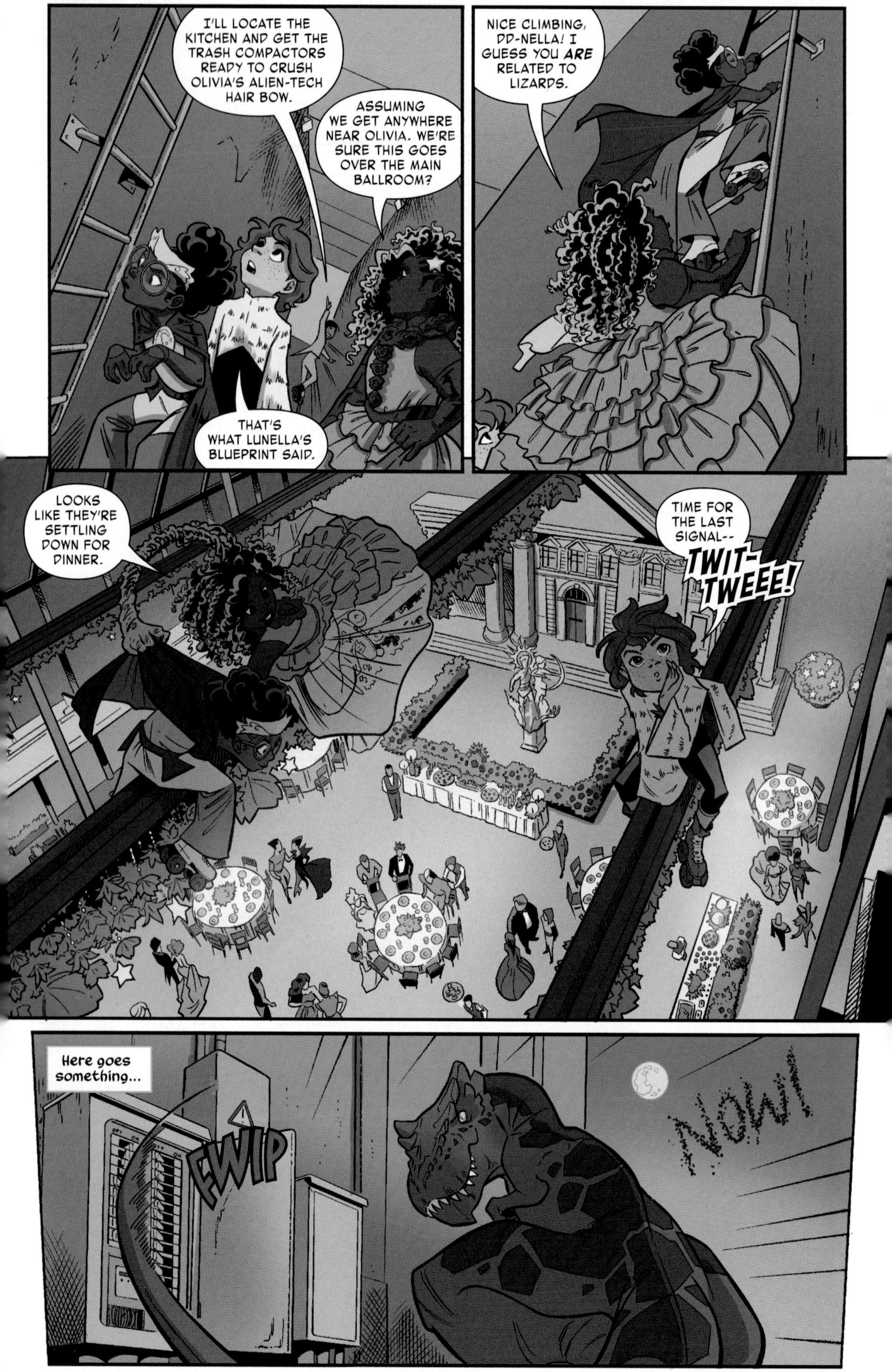
I'LL LOCATE THE KITCHEN AND GET THE TRASH COMPACTORS READY TO CRUSH OLIVIA'S ALIEN-TECH HAIR BOW.
ASSUMING WE GET ANYWHERE NEAR OLIVIA. WE'RE SURE THIS GOES OVER THE MAIN BALLROOM?
THAT'S WHAT LUNELLA'S BLUEPRINT SAID.
NICE CLIMBING, DD-NELLA! I GUESS YOU ARE RELATED TO LIZARDS.
LOOKS LIKE THEY'RE SETTLING DOWN FOR DINNER.
TIME FOR THE LAST SIGNAL--
TWIT-TWEEE!
Here goes something...
FWIP
NOW!

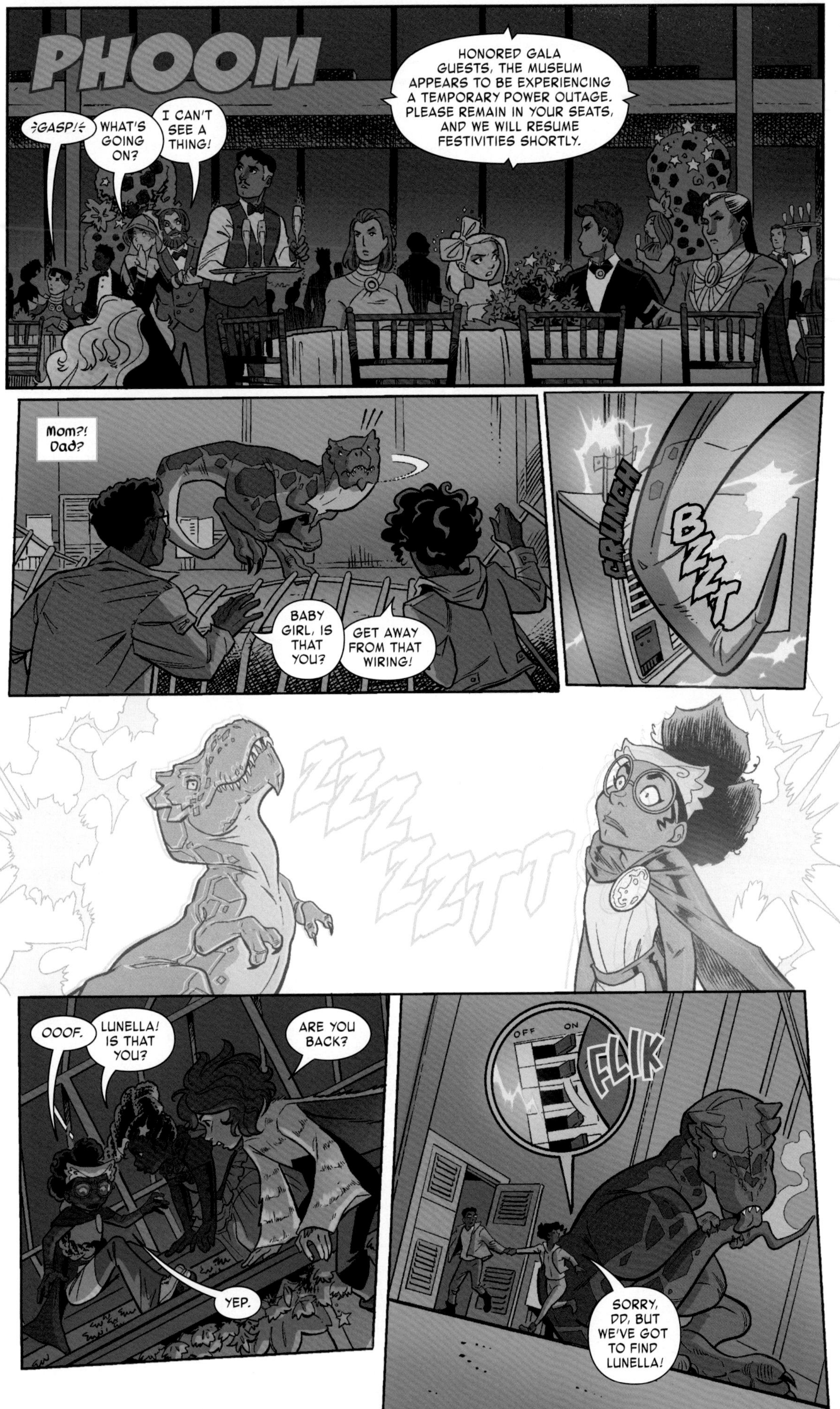
PHOOM
≠GASP!≠
WHAT'S GOING ON?
I CAN'T SEE A THING!
HONORED GALA GUESTS, THE MUSEUM APPEARS TO BE EXPERIENCING A TEMPORARY POWER OUTAGE. PLEASE REMAIN IN YOUR SEATS, AND WE WILL RESUME FESTIVITIES SHORTLY.
Mom?! Dad?
BABY GIRL, IS THAT YOU?
GET AWAY FROM THAT WIRING!
CRUNCH
BZZT
ZZZZZTT
OOOF.
LUNELLA! IS THAT YOU?
ARE YOU BACK?
YEP.
OFF ON
FLIK
SORRY, DD, BUT WE'VE GOT TO FIND LUNELLA!

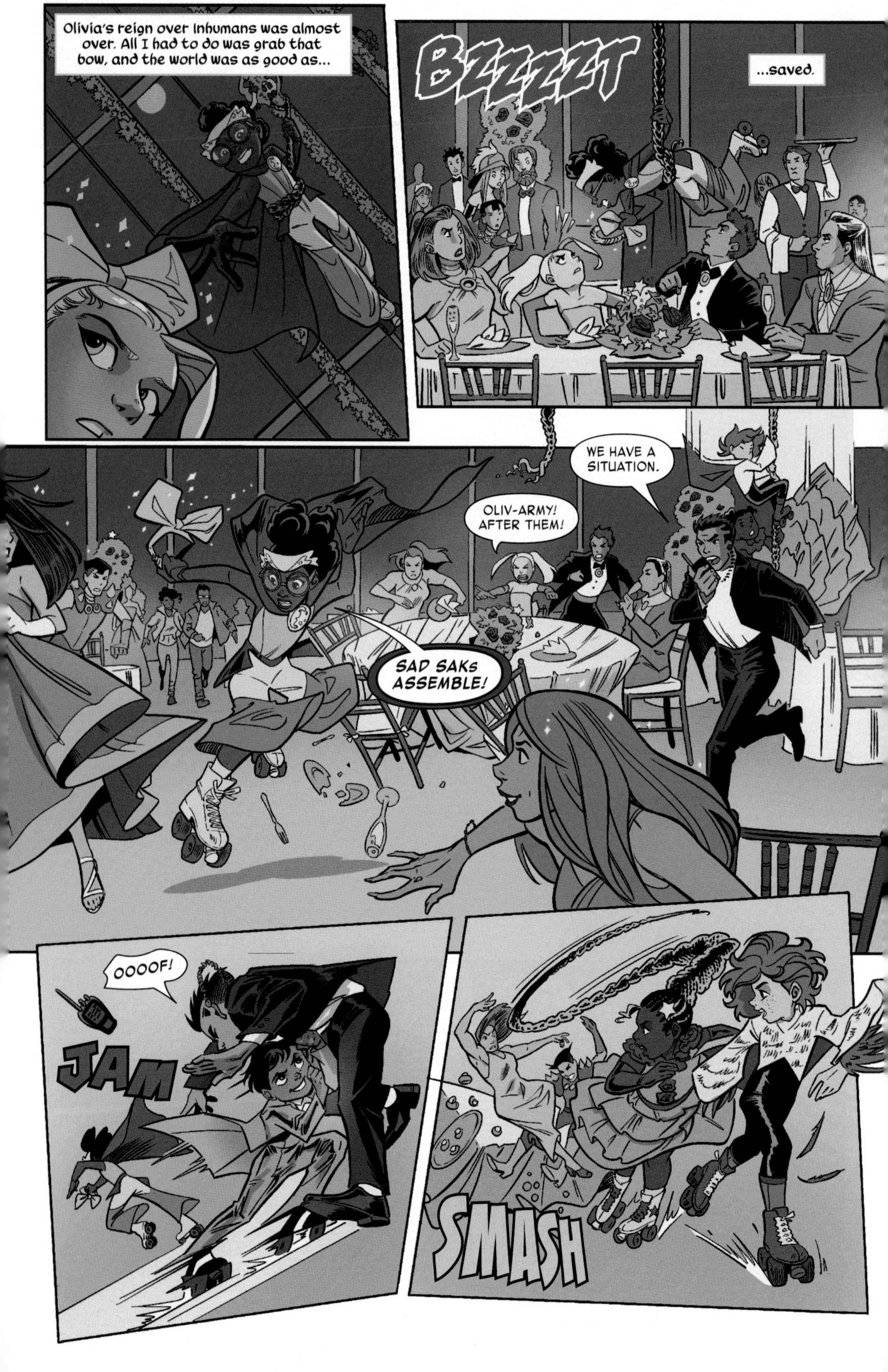

Olivia's reign over Inhumans was almost over. All I had to do was grab that bow, and the world was as good as...
BZZZZT
...saved.
SAD SAKs ASSEMBLE!
OLIV-ARMY! AFTER THEM!
WE HAVE A SITUATION.
OOOOF!
JAM
SMASH

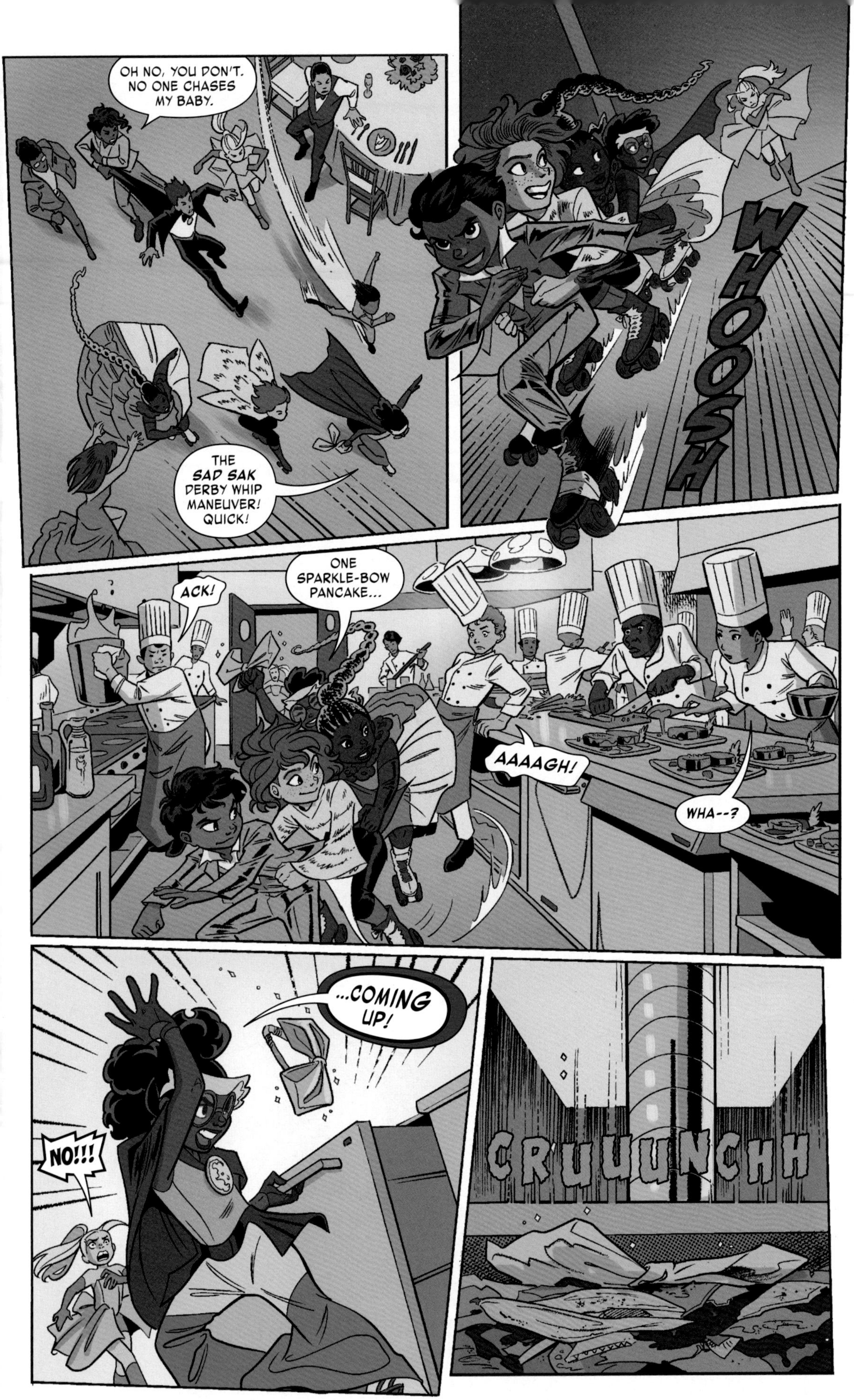
OH NO, YOU DON'T. NO ONE CHASES MY BABY.
THE SAD SAK DERBY WHIP MANEUVER! QUICK!
WHOOOOSH
ACK!
ONE SPARKLE-BOW PANCAKE...
AAAAGH!
WHA--?
...COMING UP!
NO!!!
CRUUUNCHH

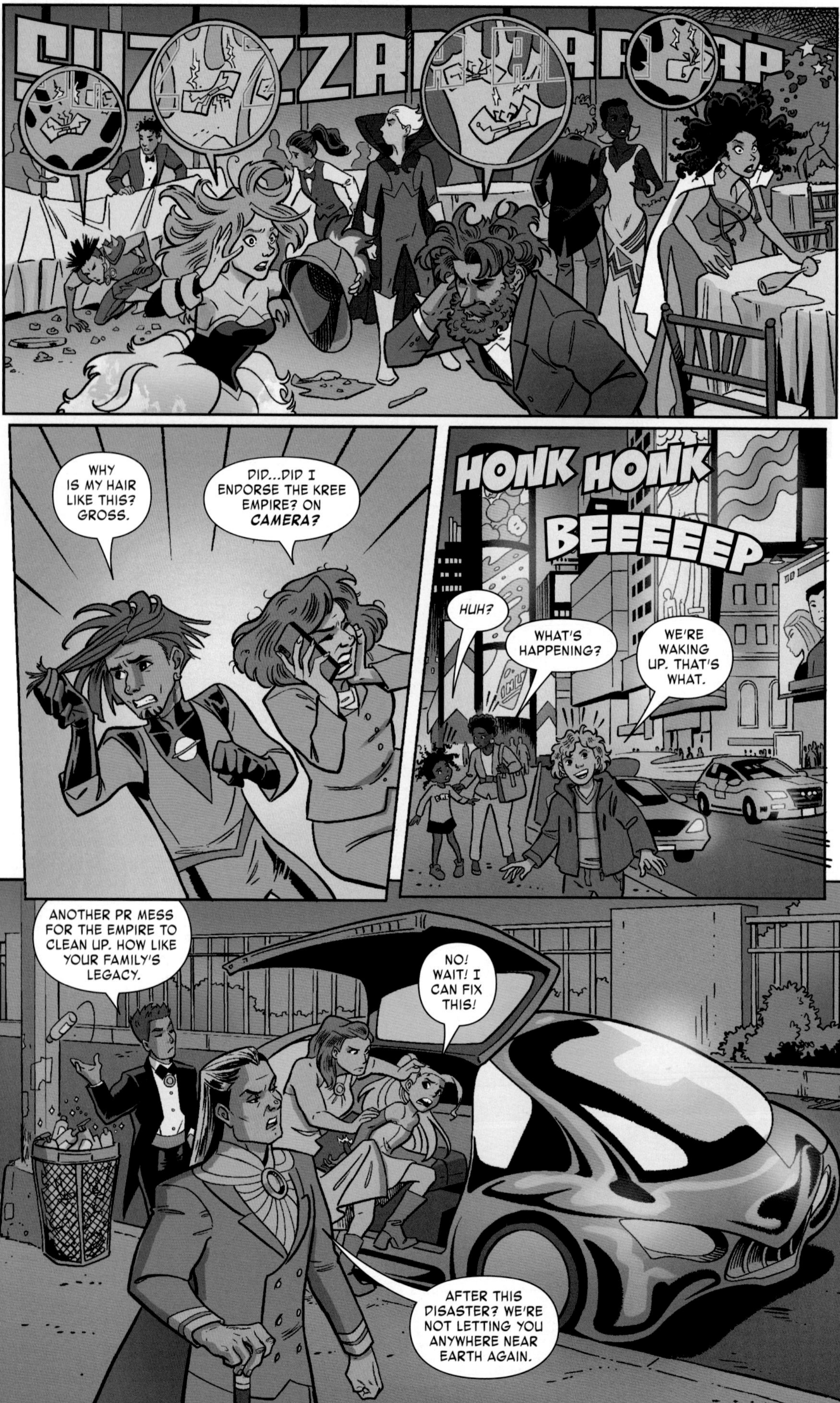
WHY IS MY HAIR LIKE THIS? GROSS.
DID...DID I ENDORSE THE KREE EMPIRE? ON CAMERA?
HONK HONK
BEEEEEP
HUH?
WHAT'S HAPPENING?
WE'RE WAKING UP. THAT'S WHAT.
ANOTHER PR MESS FOR THE EMPIRE TO CLEAN UP. HOW LIKE YOUR FAMILY'S LEGACY.
NO! WAIT! I CAN FIX THIS!
AFTER THIS DISASTER? WE'RE NOT LETTING YOU ANYWHERE NEAR EARTH AGAIN.

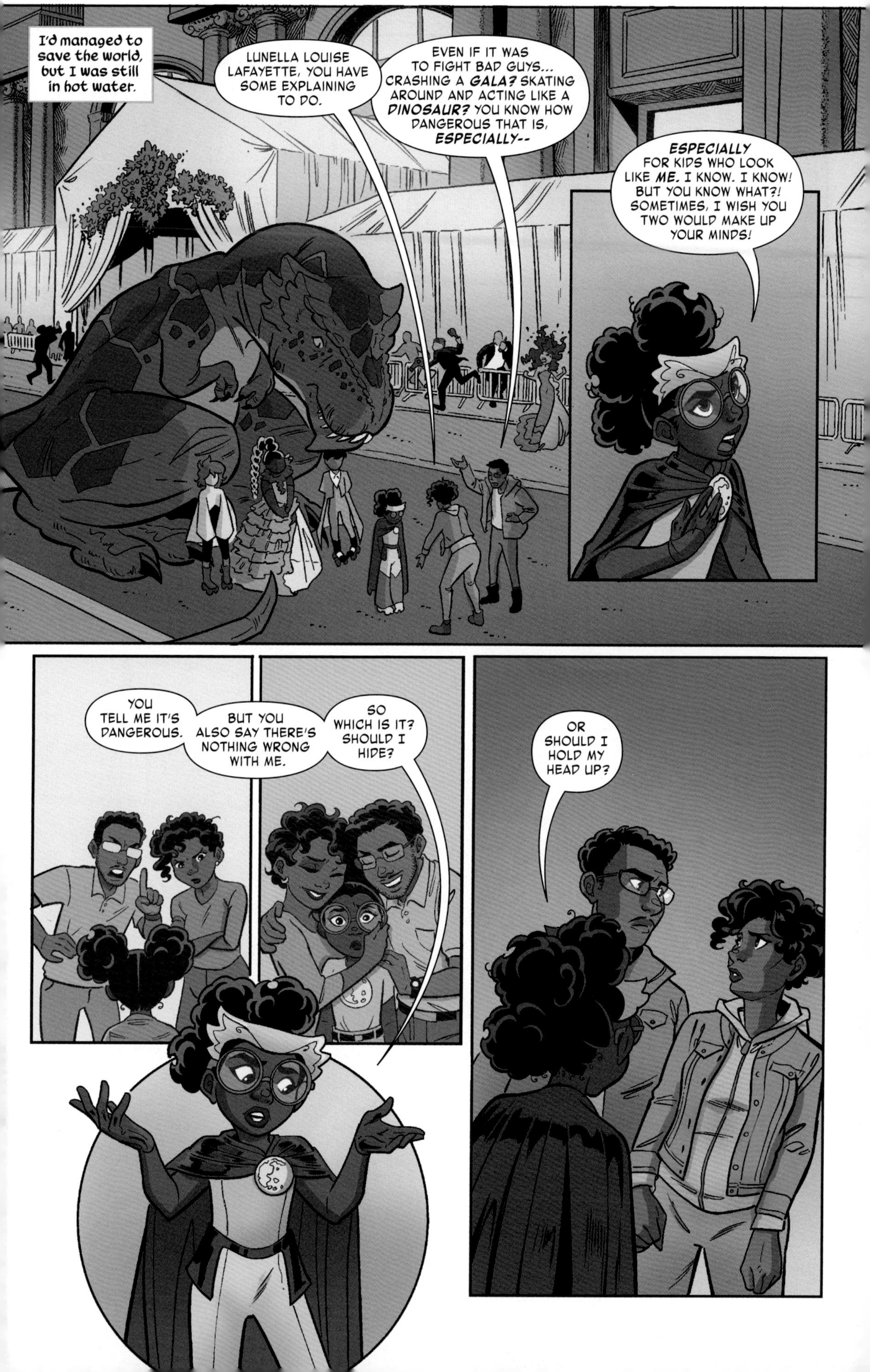
I'd managed to save the world, but I was still in hot water.
LUNELLA LOUISE LAFAYETTE, YOU HAVE SOME EXPLAINING TO DO.
EVEN IF IT WAS TO FIGHT BAD GUYS... CRASHING A GALA? SKATING AROUND AND ACTING LIKE A DINOSAUR? YOU KNOW HOW DANGEROUS THAT IS, ESPECIALLY--
ESPECIALLY FOR KIDS WHO LOOK LIKE ME. I KNOW. I KNOW! BUT YOU KNOW WHAT?! SOMETIMES, I WISH YOU TWO WOULD MAKE UP YOUR MINDS!
YOU TELL ME IT'S DANGEROUS.
BUT YOU ALSO SAY THERE'S NOTHING WRONG WITH ME.
SO WHICH IS IT? SHOULD I HIDE?
OR SHOULD I HOLD MY HEAD UP?

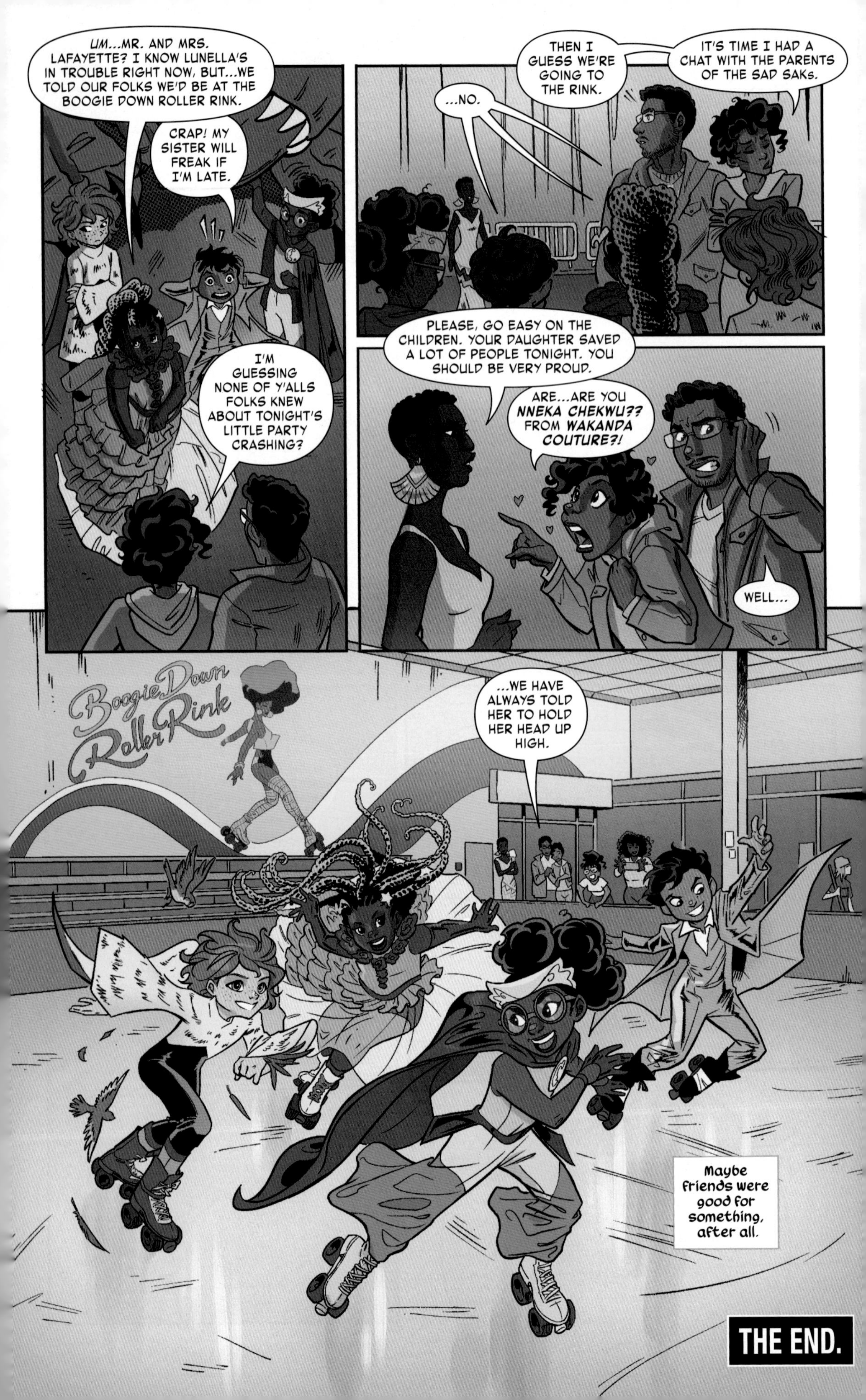
UM...MR. AND MRS. LAFAYETTE? I KNOW LUNELLA'S IN TROUBLE RIGHT NOW, BUT...WE TOLD OUR FOLKS WE'D BE AT THE BOOGIE DOWN ROLLER RINK.
CRAP! MY SISTER WILL FREAK IF I'M LATE.
I'M GUESSING NONE OF Y'ALLS FOLKS KNEW ABOUT TONIGHT'S LITTLE PARTY CRASHING?
...NO.
THEN I GUESS WE'RE GOING TO THE RINK.
IT'S TIME I HAD A CHAT WITH THE PARENTS OF THE SAD SAKs.
PLEASE, GO EASY ON THE CHILDREN. YOUR DAUGHTER SAVED A LOT OF PEOPLE TONIGHT. YOU SHOULD BE VERY PROUD.
ARE...ARE YOU NNEKA CHEKWU?? FROM WAKANDA COUTURE?!
WELL...
Boogie Down Roller Rink
...WE HAVE ALWAYS TOLD HER TO HOLD HER HEAD UP HIGH.
Maybe friends were good for something, after all.
THE END.

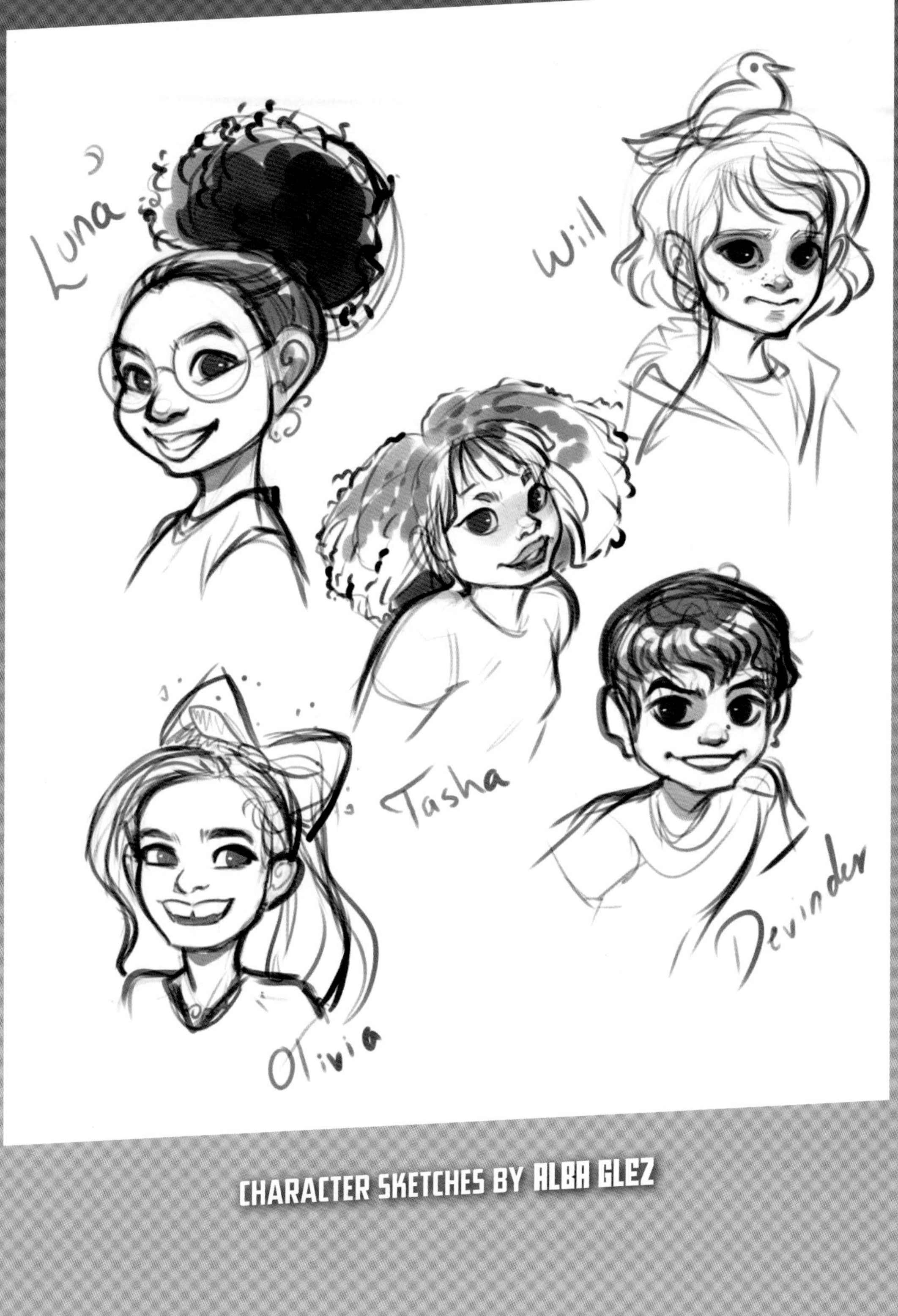
Luna
Will
Tasha
Devinder
Olivia

CHARACTER SKETCHES BY ALBA GLEZ

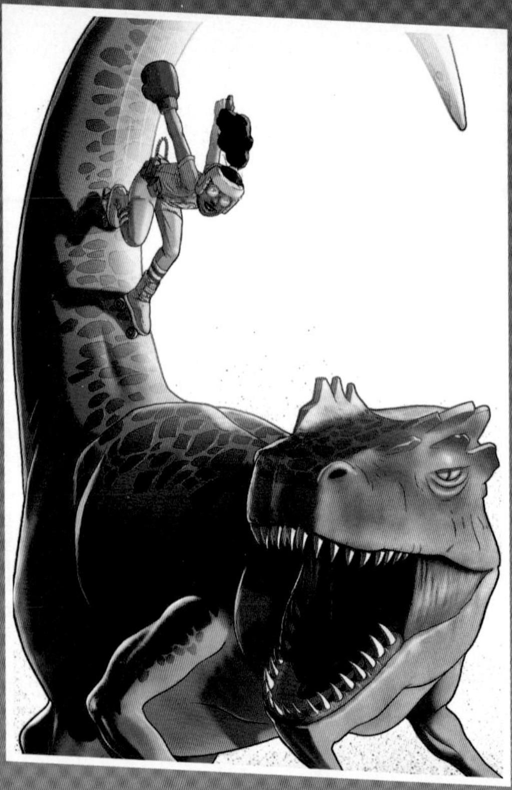

#1 VARIANT BY DOTUN AKANDE

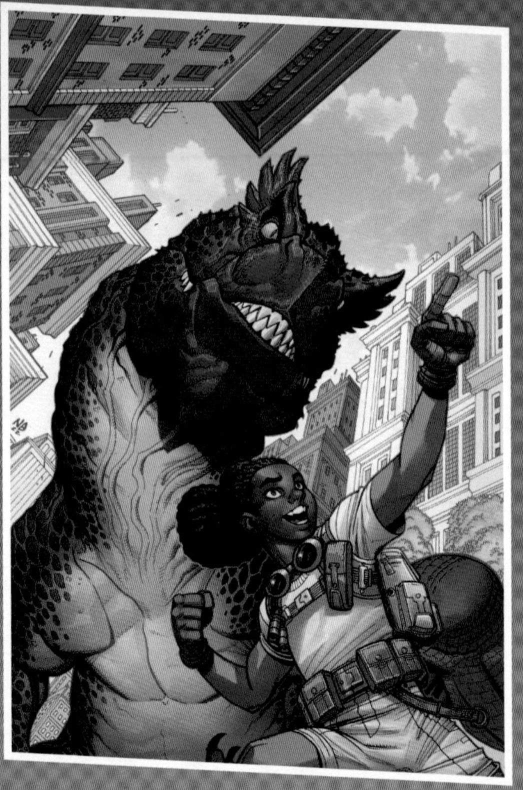

#1 VARIANT BY
NICK BRADSHAW & ROMULO FAJARDO JR.

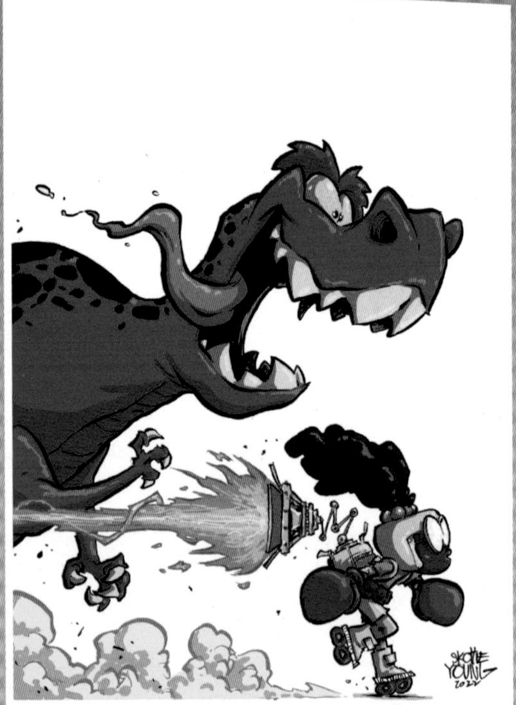
SKOTTIE YOUNG 2022

#1 VARIANT BY SKOTTIE YOUNG

#1 MARVEL UNIVERSE VARIANT BY PEACH MOMOKO

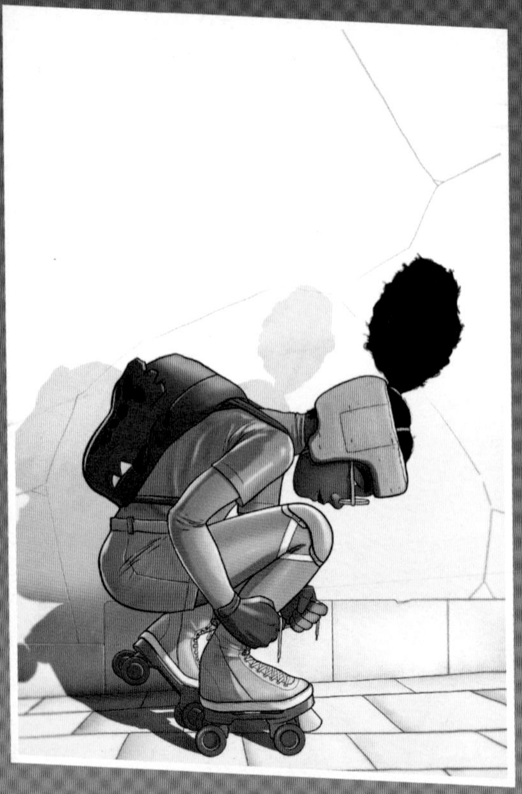

#2 VARIANT BY DOTUN AKANDE

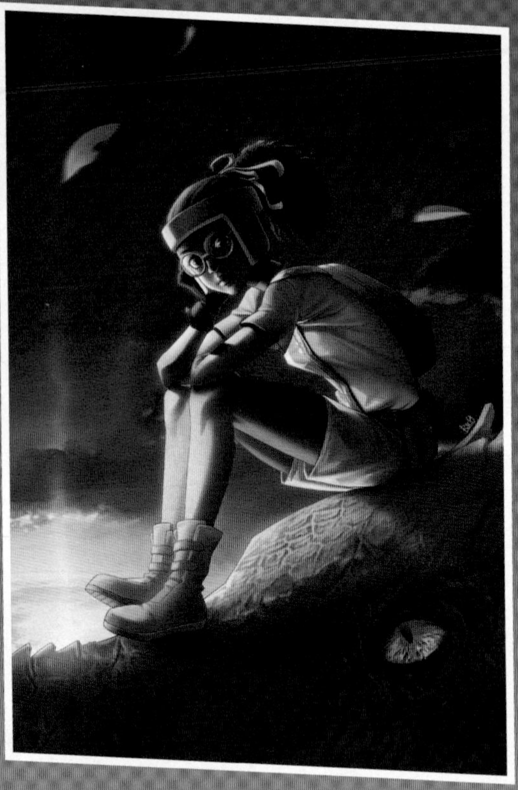

#2 VARIANT BY R1C0

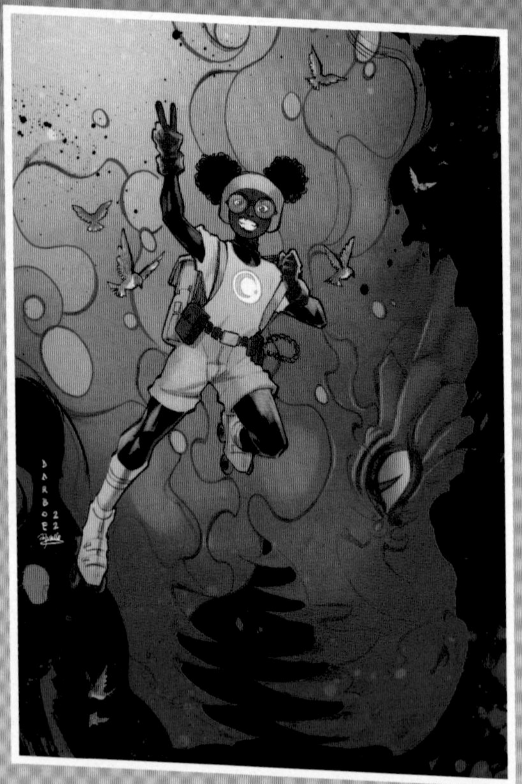

#3 VARIANT BY
KAREN S. DARBOE & RACHELLE ROSENBERG

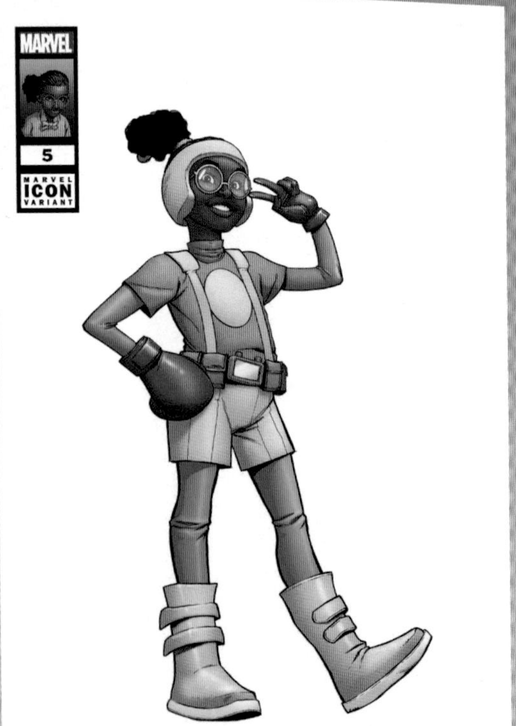
MARVEL
5
MARVEL ICON VARIANT

#5 MARVEL ICON VARIANT BY
STEFANO CASELLI & EDGAR DELGADO